The Modernisation of the Rules Implementing Art 81 and Art 82 ECT and its Implications for Italy

European University Studies

Europäische Hochschulschriften
Publications Universitaires Européennes

Series II
Law

Reihe II Série II
Rechtswissenschaft
Droit

Vol./Bd. 4052

PETER LANG
Frankfurt am Main · Berlin · Bern · Bruxelles · New York · Oxford · Wien

Georg Miribung

The Modernisation of the Rules Implementing Art 81 and Art 82 ECT and its Implications for Italy

PETER LANG
Europäischer Verlag der Wissenschaften

Bibliographic Information published by Die Deutsche Bibliothek
Die Deutsche Bibliothek lists this publication in the Deutsche Nationalbibliografie; detailed bibliographic data is available in the internet at <http://dnb.ddb.de>.

Zugl.: Innsbruck, Univ., Diss., 2004

ISSN 0531-7312
ISBN 3-631-53086-2
US-ISBN 0-8204-7368-5

www.peterlang.de

Acknowledgments

This dissertation was submitted at the law-department of the University of Innsbruck to be awarded the academic title of Doctor of Laws in autumn 2003. Its completion was very exciting, but also demanding to try to get everything right and to have the manuscript delivered in time.

I am grateful to Prof Peter Hilpold for his advice and for reading, correcting and approving the dissertation.
I am very much indebted to my family and especially to my mother, who taught me, by many ways, to insist and believe in my capacities and me.
Further appreciation goes to my friends, for all the incomparable and cheerful moments.

Lastly, I want to express deep gratitude to my girlfriend Sabine, for her patience, support, tenderness and the love she gives me.

Content

1 Introduction

This dissertation deals with European Competition law. More precisely, it concentrates on the amendment of the procedural rules that implement Art 81 and Art 82 of the European Community Treaty (ECT). These latter contain rules on competition. The starting point of the discussion considers a system that is based on centralised application of the Community's competition rules by the Commission. The system has been amended in order that the enforcement of the law is shared with the competition authorities and courts of the Member States. Such decentralisation will be combined with a new approach in the enforcement of the law. In fact, whereas initially enforcement was done according to an *ex-ante* control, the new regime shifts to an *ex-post* control of the EC competition rules (so-called legal exemption system).

As Mario Monti, the Commissioner responsible for competition policy affirms,

> "this reform [will] not only enable enforcement to, in many instances, be carried out closer to the companies and consumers affected by competition problems, but [will] furthermore enable the Commission to concentrate its efforts on the most serious instances of anti-competitive behaviour, on investigating major cross-border mergers, as well as on progressing the liberalisation of new sectors and policing state aid. The reforms should result in enhanced enforcement by effectively increasing the number of potential prosecutors, and by facilitating private enforcement."[1]

Even though tendencies of decentralisation had been noted during the last decade,[2] the reform-process, which was rather unexpectedly initiated in 1999 with the publication of the Commission's White Paper, found its second stage in the publication of a draft-regulation,[3] the purpose of which was to amend the existing procedural rules[4] and was concluded – or maybe not – with the adoption of Reg 1/2003.[5] Reasons for the modernisation were mainly the overload of work due to the monopoly of the Commission in enforcing Art 81 par 3 ECT. This hampers the Commission in fulfilling its task of protecting competition.

---

1 See *Monti*, A European Competition policy for today and tomorrow, Journal of World Competition 2000, 1 (2).

2 See chapter 3.2.

3 Proposal for a Council Regulation on the implementation of the rules on competition laid down in Art 81 and Art 82 of the Treaty and amending Regulations 1017/68, 2988/74, 4056/86 and 3975/87; hereinafter referred to as 'Proposal'.

4 As contained in Council Reg 17/62 implementing Art 85 and Art 86 of the Treaty; hereinafter referred to as 'Reg 17'.

5 Council Reg 1/2003 of 16 December 2002 on the implementation laid down in Art 81 and Art 82 of the Treaty; hereinafter referred to as 'Reg 1'.

Roughly, the centre-piece of this paper is on the one hand dedicated to the consequences the legal exemption system brings with it, and on the other hand to the consequences for national authorities and courts as new players on the stage. Of course, such an analysis also requests granting particular attention to the compatibility of the European law with the national laws governing the powers of domestic courts and national competition authorities. This will be further considered in a case study dedicated to the impact of the reform on Italian courts, its competition authority and the relevant laws in this field.
As a result, it has proved to be useful to divide the dissertation into three parts.
The first part (chapter 2) provides the general background necessary to better understand the whole theme. It begins by clarifying the most important concepts of competition theory and afterwards describes the importance of competition policy for the European Union, also from a historical point of view. Especially the link between this theme and economic concepts and the consequent interdisciplinary approach of this paper, have made this dissertation particularly interesting for me.
Then, as the procedural law cannot be fully comprehended without indicating the substantial rules, which eventually have to be applied by the law-enforcing bodies by means of the procedural rules, particular concern will be given to Art 81 and Art 82 ECT. As will be seen, the application-sphere of these articles is rather wide. Hence, in order to better grasp the scope of Art 81 and Art 82 ECT and especially, to provide some indications of the limit of their application, it is also necessary to briefly consider specific competition rules applying to certain branches of the economy, which have been exempted from the application of Art 81 and Art 82 ECT. A concluding remark will be devoted to some Commission notices, which were issued to clarify doubts in respect of the just application of these articles.
The second part (chapter 3) of my dissertation concentrates on the process of modernisation by first explaining the reasons that led to reform. The starting point is the first regulation implementing Art 81 and Art 82 ECT (Reg 17) and the path that led to its adoption in 1962. Herewith, it will be clarified why the then adopted approach made quite a lot of sense, whereas nowadays it might be considered to be outdated. These observations, and the description of the norms contained in Reg 17, will then be followed by outlining the objectives and reasons for the process of modernisation. Then I will depict how the legal exemption system shall work.
Next, I will comment on the various issues that arose during the modernisation process, some of which, in my opinion, still seem to have not yet been sufficiently resolved. Corollary of the analysis will obviously always be a comparison between Reg 17 and Reg 1.

To begin with, I will concentrate on the essential question of whether the new regime is compatible with the Treaty of Rome or whether the treaty has to be amended in order that the new enforcement system can be embedded within its framework. Then I will focus on some remarks regarding the transparency of both the old and the new regime. A point in question in this context is furthermore, how information about competition-distorting behaviour can be provided under the new system. Next, I will concentrate on the new relationship between EC competition law and national competition law.

Afterwards, the analysis will draw its attention to specific issues regarding decentralisation to national authorities on the one hand and decentralisation to national courts on the other. Particular points in question in this context are the coherent and consistent application of the law, what cannot be taken for granted in a system where different bodies, which are subjected to different national procedural rules, enforce the new rules. As will be seen, the reform introduces a new mechanism whereby coherence and consistency shall be guaranteed.

Then I will look at the flipside of the coin and I will consider the situation of undertakings, which are ultimately the main-addressees of the new regime. It will be investigated whether the new system is able to assure legal certainty, which is essential for undertakings to pursue their businesses. Moreover, the reform also has indirect effects on the duties of the European Court of Justice and on the Court of First Instance. Next, the occurrence of the Eastern Enlargement of the European Union and accordingly the accession to the Union of states whose experience with concepts of competition policy is not deeply rooted, bears the question of the right *modus* to evolve competition mechanisms in these countries. Hence, it will be considered whether the new approach might be helpful in order to attain this goal. The next subchapter will be devoted to the enhancement of the investigative powers of the Commission.

As explained, the main reason for decentralisation is the work-overload, which the Commission has to bear. Accordingly, I will briefly look at the question of whether alternative regimes, which may also simply consist in the amendment of the old system, could possibly achieve this aim as well.

The last part of my dissertation (chapter 4) examines the possible consequences for Italian courts and the Antitrust Authority and especially for the rules that govern the functioning of these bodies. This makes it necessary to illustrate the laws that govern the functioning of the Italian bodies in this context. Accordingly, I will outline the legal foundations for the application of EC competition law by the Authority and national courts.

Then, I will comment upon the issues, which regard the national procedural rules and its compatibility with the new reality and also those, which complete the remarks and criticisms mentioned in the second part of my dissertation: they shall be understood as illustrative examples to fully comprehend the reform. Accordingly, I will question which difficulties might arise in respect of decentralisation for the Italian Competition Authority and highlight necessary amendments in respect of national competition law. Then, I will consider the Italian judiciary in the context of the pursued decentralised application of Art 81 and Art 82 ECT. More specifically, I will consider their ability and whether they are experienced to handle this task, problems regarding co-operation with the Commission and other national competition authorities and lastly, I will criticise some further discrepancies between existing national procedural law and the new Regulation.

In the concluding remarks, I will sum up the most important issues of my dissertation.

2 Introduction to EC Competition law

2.1 Interpolation: basics of competition theory

This chapter can only briefly attempt to draw a picture of this highly complex issue. In short, I will elucidate competition theory and clarify the most important concepts necessary to comprehend the whole debate to which my dissertation is dedicated.

According to Schmidt/Schmidt,[6] competition as understood in the context of EC competition law, has to be understood as a workable competition-process, in which the actors in pursuing their own interest attempt to gain a preferential position in the dynamic competition process. This shall be achieved through the adoption of parameters (price, quality, discount, conditions, service, quantity and marketing) but may last only temporarily as advantages will decline once competing actors imitate the successful action.[7]

---

6 See *Schmidt/Schmidt*, Europäische Wettbewerbspolitik - Eine Einführung (1997) 13-14.

7 Economists use four economic models to illustrate the rational behaviour of sellers under two extreme sets of conditions: these two extremes are perfect monopoly and perfect competition. However, they are hard to find in the real world. In a perfect monopoly, a provider of goods has 100 per cent control of the market and there are no close or even similar products or services to which buyers can turn. Such a situation is normally only possible through state intervention (ie nationalised body such as a post office). The other extreme is pure (or atomistic) competition. In such case, the number of competitors must be so big that their own market share is tiny. Hence, none alone has sufficient influence to alter price levels of the balance of supply and demand (as an example, one can think about many agricultural producers of the same crop).

The other two models are situated between these two extreme positions and are defined as oligopoly and workable competition. An oligopoly is built by a market with some degree of competition, in other words, where only a handful of competitive undertakings (2-8) compete. The last model (workable competition) is characterised by the fact that there are fewer rivals in the market then needed to have perfect competition. Workable competition is characterised by a much sharper degree and different tempo of mutual reaction than in an oligopoly. The borderline between these two models is vague though, and most of the markets within the Community fall within one of these last two categories.

Defining workable competition is not an easy task. It may be quite easy in case the products sold on the market are identical or differences are marginal (ie differences between various brands of petrol or oil placed on the market by competing oil companies): in such circumstances competition takes place primarily on the price and to a lesser extent in terms of the level of service or conditions of sale.

But generally products have more distinct characteristics. Consequently, the customer must weigh up which of rather heterogeneous products do better match its own personal needs. Here it is possible to have competition on different fronts: price cuts,

More precisely,

> "competition is the relationship between any number of undertakings which sell goods or services of the same kind at the same time to an identifiable group of customers. Each undertaking having made a commercial decision to place its goods or services on the market, utilizing its production and distribution facilities, will by that act necessarily bring itself into a relationship of potential contention and rivalry with the other undertakings in the same geographical market, whose limits may be a single shopping precinct, a city, a region, a country, a group of countries, the entire European Community, or even the entire world. Whilst competition law tends to focus more on the activities of, and relationship between, sellers, it logically applies equally to the like activities and relationships between buyers, who also find themselves in contention in particular product and geographic markets."[8]

Schmidt/Schmidt[9] in referring to Katzenbach, identify five economic functions, workable competition has to fulfil:

- the safeguarding of allocation of income according to the performance on the market, in other words: the protection against exploitation by market-power
- adjustment of the supply of goods according to consumer preferences
- allocation of resources in the most productive way
- adaptability of products and production capacities on continuously changing demand and production methods
- incentive for producers to invest in research and development and innovation (the strong survive)

Additionally, competition has non-economic goals like the safeguarding of individual freedom of action and widespread market power.[10]
However, the competition process is not self-maintaining, but is menaced by competition-distorting strategies of undertakings, for which it is generally an advantage to elude from the pressure of competition. It is therefore the task of competition policy and laws to protect workable competition with its functions.[11] Accordingly, competition policy not only seeks to retain the existence of competitors, but it envisages the protection of the process of competition, through the prevention of an unfair acquisition of market power by individual undertakings.[12]

---

secrets discounts, better warranties or service, or changes in product specification. See *Goyder*, EC Competition Law[3] (1998) 10-12.

[8] See *Goyder*, Competition 9.
[9] See *Schmidt/Schmidt*, Wettbewerbsrecht 13.
[10] See *Schmidt/Schmidt*, Wettbewerbsrecht 14.
[11] See *Schmidt/Schmidt*, Wettbewerbsrecht 14.
[12] See *Goyder*, Competition 14-15.

The acquisition of market power enables undertakings to exercise strategic power over prices and thus increase their profit markets. What is more, it also grants further advantage over competitors through facilitating successful research and development or economies of scale. Market power puts an undertaking also in the position to overcome adverse economic trading conditions (ie: recession, falls in demand), by which competitors can be further weakened and hence, ultimately strengthens the undertaking possessing market power even more.[13]

Obviously, competition can also be distorted by alliances between competing undertakings. In this context, one has to distinguish between horizontal agreements, which are concluded between undertakings in competition with each other at the same level (ie between manufacturers or between wholesalers)[14] on the one hand and vertical agreements on the other hand. These latter are characterised by the fact that they are entered into between undertakings whose relationship is complementary, such as manufacturer and distributor or licensor and licensee.[15]

Gerber acknowledges that it is not easy to define what is meant by the protection of competition from restraints. Especially in a multi-layered system like the EC competition law a definition of this simple description becomes rather difficult. Gerber outlines 4 basic conceptions. The first one focuses on economic efficiency, in other words, competition law concentrates primarily on optimum resource allocation and wealth-maximisation. Such aims have always been part of the system. A further conception addresses the issue of economic freedom, what means that competition law concentrates on those restraints that limit the decisional opportunities of economic actors. It is shaped along the ideas of classical liberalism and strongly influences competition law in general, and also EC competition law. A next approach centres on economic power and tries to hinder firms from adopting their economic power to weaken competitive structures. Lastly, protecting competition is often related to the destruction and weakening of hitches that hinder economic change and development. Gerber outlines that "the current and future emphasis in Europe on reducing barriers to economic development is likely to reinforce its prominence." See *Gerber*, Modernising European Competition Law, ECLR 2001, 122 (124).

13 See *Goyder*, Competition 13-14.

14 As numbers of undertakings in oligopolistic markets are relatively small, it is easier for them to adjust their commercial and pricing policies so as to achieve the effects of a horizontal agreement covering products, prices, conditions of business. Accordingly, oligopolies can achieve higher prices and profits without agreement and concerted practices and hence, markets may appear at first sight to be competitive, in that prices are closely matched (concept of 'joint dominance'). Goyder emphasises that a strict system of merger control helps to prevent the creation of market structures in which such joint dominance and 'tacit collusion' is possible. See *Goyder*, Competition 14.

15 It is questioned though, whether reciprocal exclusive distributorships should be allowed between manufacturers in potential competition with each other, although not actually competing at that moment. See *Goyder*, Competition 13.

As seen, to function properly, competition needs corrective collaterals. Goyder[16] in referring to the traditional school of economists recommends a two-fold form of intervention:

1. The intervention seeks to prevent distortion of competition by agreements or concerted practices between undertakings. This shall be achieved by rendering them unenforceable, civil or criminal penalties on those who participate in them shall be imposed.[17]
2. The intervention counteracts the undue acquisition of power by undertakings achieved through monopolisation of markets, abuse of dominant positions by exclusionary anti-competitive or predatory practices or merger.[18]

That said, I would like to draw the attention to competition policy of the European Community and more precisely, I will outline how European policy and law have come into being.

2.2 The origins of a European competition policy

Soon after the 2nd world war, there were calls for the creation of a common market for coal and steel in a Europe pursuing a fast recovery of the, at that time, very important markets for these raw materials. The idea of such European economic co-operation was proposed by means of the so-called Schuman-plan in April 1950, which led to the establishment of the European Coal and Steel Community (ECSC[19]) the year after, when the relevant treaty

---

[16] See *Goyder*, Competition 15.

[17] This mechanism is applied under Section 1 of the Sherman Act of the United States, under the UK Competition Act 1998 and under Art 81 of the Treaty of Rome.

[18] This mechanism is applied by Section 2 of the Sherman Act and Section 7 of the Clayton Act of the US, the UK Fair Trading Act (monopolies and mergers provision), Chapter 2 of the new Competition Act and Art 82 of the Treaty of Rome.

[19] This organisation, which was the first bearing a supranational character, was based on the ideas of Jean Monnet and Robert Schuman, the Belgian and French foreign ministers respectively. The ECSC established a common market for iron, steel and coal in Western Europe and pursued the elimination of all customs duties, tariffs, quotas and other market restrictions in the relevant economic fields. The Community was founded by France, Italy, the Benelux and Germany. Referring to Germany it should be said, that this state and its undertakings were linked to the economies of the other Member States of the Community in order to assure that Germany's economy could be stabilised and that through this linkage further war-tendencies could be kept under control.

In the field of competition, the Community was assigned the task to ensure the establishment, maintenance and observance of normal competitive conditions. The reasons for such a pro-competitive approach were two-fold: firstly, it was necessary due to major imperfections or even the absence of competition in Western Europe and

was signed by Belgium, Germany, France, Italy, the Netherlands and Luxembourg. This treaty came into force in 1952 and represents the first real step towards the economic integration of Europe.[20] Responsible for the application of the provisions was the European Commission, whose activities were submitted on the one hand to the judicial control of the European Court of Justice (ECJ) and on the other hand to the political control of the Council of Ministers.[21] The Treaty expired on 23 July 2002.[22]
In the mid-fifties, the political claim of setting economic co-operation on a much broader basis was put forward. The first attempt in this respect was advanced by the governments of Belgium, the Netherlands and Luxembourg. In the so-called Benelux-memorandum they criticised not only that partial or selective co-operation was not enough to push European productivity, but furthermore emphasised the fact that such limited co-operation did not foster enough the creation of European solidarity among each other. In this sense, Germany highlighted the necessity of competition rules to guarantee normal market conditions within an integrated market and of protecting competition both from state intervention and from private monopoly power.
At a meeting held in Messina (Italy) in May 1955, the six foreign ministers of the Member States of the ECSC agreed in principle to the creation of a single market, which went beyond the selective co-operation structure of the ECSC. The Messina Declaration stressed the importance of the establishment of a Common European Market free from all custom duties and quantitative restrictions between its members. As a result, a group of senior officials, under the presidency of the Belgian Foreign Minister Henry Spaak, was assigned the task of seeking a possible international treaty aimed at achieving this goal. The outcome was published in the so-called Spaak-

secondly, the fact that the economic strength of the USA relied on many decades of free competition provided for an example of the economic possibilities of free competition. However, the organisation contained also certain elements of central control. In fact, in case of a serious imbalance between supply and demand, the High Authority was enabled to take the necessary steps to bring the market forces back into closer accord. This body was also empowered to deal with restraints on competition. See *Goyder*, Competition 19-21.

20 See *Schmidt/Schmidt*, Wettbewerbspolitik 2.
Goyder clarifies that the first post-war institution, which acted in the field of economics was the Organisation for European Economic Co-operation (OEEC) with the task to allocate the Marshall-Aid. However, due to the lack of political will to convert this organisation into one with supranational quality, it was not able to foster economic integration of the participating European states. The same is true for the Council of Europe, which is particularly known for its achievements in the field of human rights. See *Goyder*, Competition 17-18.

21 See *Schmidt/Schmidt*, Wettbewerbspolitik 1-2.

22 From there on, the provisions of the 'Treaty establishing the European Community' apply. See *European Commission*, XXXII Report on competition policy, 15.

report, which once more identified the advantages of a common market, such as a common economic policy guaranteeing continuous and stable economic development, fast improving living standards and harmonised relationships among the Community's Member States. In this context, it was also admitted that a prerogative for the pursued advantages was the abolishment of those practices that hinder economic competition. In fact, Art 55 of the report emphasised on the necessity of the adoption of rules, which shall guarantee that monopolistic situations or practices do not contrast the essential aims of the common market.[23] The Spaak-report was approved – with slight modifications – at a meeting of the six foreign ministers in Venice in May 1956.

The final step in this process, and which ultimately launched a new era in the field of competition law of the Six,[24] was the signing of the Treaty establishing the European Economic Community in Rome on 27 March 1957.[25] The treaty[26] founding the European Economic Community (EEC) came into force on 1 January 1958.[27]

---

23 The introduction of the EC competition law was directed by the German Ordoliberal School, known as the Freiburg School. It is highlighted that the Freiburg School represents however only a model of thought, which does not dispose of an analytical model. What initially did not cause serious trouble, became a critical element in the merger control regime, which was enacted in the late 1980s. In order to achieve for the consumers the maximum benefit out of the competition rules it was therefore necessary to develop a school of thought, which includes an analytical framework for proper economic analyses. See *Hildebrand*, The European school in EC competition law, Journal of World Competition 2002, 3 (3-4).
This trend is exemplified by "the shift in the Commission's policy towards vertical restraints from a formalistic approach, provided by numerous, in total inconsistent block exemptions, to an economic viewpoint, mainly based on the market share of the parties [...]." See *Paulweber*, The End of a Success Story? The European Commission's White Paper on the Modernisation of the European Competition Law: A comparative study about the role of the notification of restrictive practices within the European Competition and the American Antitrust Law, Journal of World Competition 2000, fn 8; also see in this context chapter 2.4.1.3.2.

24 The initial Community of the six became more and more enlarged by the accession of Denmark, Great Britain and Ireland in 1972, Greece in 1981, Portugal and Spain in 1986 and Finland, Sweden and Austria in 1995. The EEC later became the EC (1965) and since the Treaty of Maastricht, it is generally known under the denomination of European Union.

25 On the same day, the European Atomic Community (EURATOM) was set up. However, in contrast to the EEC, this organisation concentrates primarily on the promotion and co-operation of nuclear power. See *Mathijsen*, A guide to European Union Law[7] (1999), 15.

26 The treaty is divided into six parts, followed by final provisions, two annexes and the protocols.
Part I contains the principles, part II addresses the citizenship of the Community, part III covers the Community's policies, part IV deals with the association of the overseas

2.3 Competition policy in context of the European Community

According to Art 2 of the Treaty of Rome, the European Community envisages the creation of a common market as well as the establishment of an Economic and Monetary Union. [28] Art 14 ECT depicts the common market as

countries and territories, part V regards the institutions of the Community, and finally, part VI outlines general and final provisions.
Common rules on competition are accommodated in title VI of part III of the Treaty.

[27] For a more detailed explanation of the creation of EC competition law see *Schmidt/Schmidt*, Wettbewerbsrecht 2-3; also see *Goyder*, Competition 24-26.
According to Art 7 ECT, the tasks entrusted to the Community are to be carried out by five institutions - a European Parliament, a Council, a Commission, a Court of Justice and a Court of Auditors. Besides, Art 7 mentions the Economic and Social Committee and the Committee of the Regions. The role of these two bodies is to assist the Council and the Commission by giving advisory opinions.
The founding Treaties endowed each of the 3 European Communities with separate institutions. However, a Convention on certain Institutions common to the European Communities, which came into force at the same time as the EC and EURATOM Treaties, provided for there to be a single Assembly and a single Court of Justice exercising the various powers attributed to those institutions by the three Treaties. This was followed by the establishment (July 1967) of a single Council of the European Communities, replacing the Special Council of Ministers of the ECSC and the EC and EURATOM Councils, and a Commission of the European Communities, replacing the High Authority of the ECSC, the EC and EURATOM Commissions. See *Mathijsen*, European Union Law 15; also see *Schweitzer/Hummer*, Europarecht[5] (1996), 43.
Whereas the Council consists "of a representative of each Minister State at ministerial level" (see Art 203 ECT) and hence, its members directly represent the interests of their governments, the Commission has a vocation to further the interests of the Community as a whole. The members of the Commission are required to be persons "whose independence is beyond doubt," (Art 157 par 1 ECT) and the Treaty provides that they "shall, in the general interest of the Community, be completely independent in the performance of their duties" (Art 157 par 2 ECT). The rule that the Commission acts by a majority of its members (Art 219 ECT) provides a further guarantee that its decisions will not reflect particular national viewpoints.
In 1974 a European Council was instituted bringing together the Heads of State or Government of the Member States, who are assisted by Ministers of Foreign Affairs and the President of the Commission.
Since 1979 the members of the European Parliament are elected directly by the population of the Member States. As to its powers, it has advisory and supervisory powers and participates by means of such as the co-operation procedure and the co-decision procedure also in the legislative process. See *Mathijsen*, European Union Law 62 - 64, 101; also see *Schweitzer/Hummer*, Europarecht 58.
There is no single institution that constitutes the Community's legislature. The different institutions - Council, Commission and European Parliament - are assigned respective roles in the law-making procedures. See *Mathijsen*, European Union Law 59;

[28] Art 2 ECT indicates the general goals of the Treaty and outlines:

a real internal market providing for the free movement of goods, workers, services and capital and payments.[29] This common market has to follow the principles of market economy, which shall, among others, establish a "system ensuring that competition in the internal market is not distorted."[30] In addition, Art 10 of the Treaty obliges the Member States to

> "ensure fulfilment of the obligations arising out of this Treaty or resulting from action taken by the institutions of the Community. [Moreover], they shall facilitate the achievement of the

---

"The Community shall have as its task, by establishing a common market and an economic and monetary union and by implementing common policies or activities referred to in Art 3 and Art 4, to promote throughout the Community a harmonious, balanced and sustainable development of economic activities, a high level of employment and of social protection, equality between men and women, sustainable and non inflationary growth, a high degree of competitiveness and convergence of economic performance, a high level of protection and improvement of the quality of the environment, the raising of the standard of living and quality of life, and economic and social cohesion and solidarity among Member States."

These goals are pursued by different policies and activities, which are outlined in Art 3 ECT. This indicates for instance:

- a common commercial policy;
- an internal market characterised by the abolition, as between Member States, of obstacles to the free movement of goods, persons, services and capital;
- a common policy in the sphere of agriculture and fisheries;
- a common policy in the sphere of transport;
- a system ensuring that competition in the internal market is not distorted;
- the approximation of the laws of Member States to the extent required for the functioning of the common market;
- the strengthening of the competitiveness of Community industry;
- a contribution to the attainment of a high level of health protection;
- a contribution to the strengthening of consumer protection.

29 More precisely, the aim of the common market is to create, on a Community scale, economic conditions similar to those on the market of a single state. This involved the establishment of a customs union, through the elimination of all customs duties and quantitative restrictions in trade between the Member States and the erection of a common external customs tariff, as well as the removal of barriers to the free movement of the factors of production – labour, business and capital.

The aim of the common market is "the elimination of all obstacles to intra-Community trade in order to merge the national markets into a single market bringing about conditions as close as possible to those of a genuine internal market" (ECJ case 15/81 [Schul]). In this respect, a detailed legislative programme for the unification of the market focusing on the removal of physical, technical and fiscal barriers to freedom of movement of goods, persons, services and capital was formally completed by the end of 1992 (also see Art 14 ECT). See *Mathijsen*, European Union Law 191-194; also see *Schweitzer/Hummer*, Europarecht 328 - 329.

Nevertheless, even after that date legislation has continued to be enacted, though at a lower level of intensity. Currently, various programmes attempt to handle the leftovers of the Internal-Market initiative.

30 See Art 3 subpar g ECT.

Community's tasks, [and] [...] shall abstain from any measure which could jeopardise the attainment of the objectives of this Treaty."

As a result, the Member States have the obligation to guarantee that competition is not distorted.

Moreover, the conception of the common market is further concretised through the provisions referring to competition as contained in the Art 81 to Art 90 ECT:[31]

- Art 81 and Art 82 ECT include both the main substantive principles of law that are applicable to undertakings.[32]
- Art 83 ECT [33] empowers the Council, acting by a qualified majority on a proposal from the Commission and after consulting the European Parliament, to adopt implementing regulations or directives.
- Art 84 ECT[34] refers to the responsibilities of the Member States during the transitional period until regulations and directives according to Art 83 ECT are enacted.

---

31 It follows, that the overriding goal of competition law in the European Community has ultimately always been European integration. The planned expansion of the EU ensures that integration will continue to have its importance when talking about EC competition law. See *Gerber*, ECLR 2001, 122.
On the other hand, Salord in citing Wesseling stresses that "from striking down barriers to trade between Member States in order to establish the common market, the Community's interest shifted to regulating the functioning of the market." See *Salord*, Concurrent application, the April 1999 White Paper and the future of national laws, ECLR 2001, 128 (135).

32 For a detailed analysis of their content, see chapter 2.4.

33 Art 83 ECT reads as follows:
1. The appropriate regulations or directives to give effect to the principles set out in Articles 81 and 82 shall be laid down by the Council, acting by a qualified majority on a proposal from the Commission and after consulting the European Parliament.
2. The regulations or directives referred to in paragraph 1 shall be designed in particular:
(a) to ensure compliance with the prohibitions laid down in Article 81 (1) and in Article 82 by making provision for fines and periodic penalty payments;
(b) to lay down detailed rules for the application of Article 81 (3), taking into account the need to ensure effective supervision on the one hand, and to simplify administration to the greatest possible extent on the other;
(c) to define, if need be, in the various branches of the economy, the scope of the provisions of Articles 81 and 82;
(d) to define the respective functions of the Commission and of the Court of Justice in applying the provisions laid down in this paragraph;
(e) to determine the relationship between national laws and the provisions contained in this Section or adopted pursuant to this Article.

34 Art 84 ECT reads as follows:
Until the entry into force of the provisions adopted in pursuance of Article 83, the authorities in the Member States shall rule on the admissibility of agreements, decisions and concerted practices and on abuse of a dominant position in the

- Art 85 ECT[35] emphasises the predominant role of the Commission in the protection of EC competition law.
- Art 86 ECT[36] contains rules regarding problems arising from the relationships between governments, on the one hand, and public undertakings or undertakings which have been entrusted with the performance of certain tasks in the public interest on the other hand.
- Under Art 87 to Art 89 ECT the Community institutions, and in particular the Commission, have supervisory powers over the granting of aid to industry in the various Member States. The general principle is that aid must not be granted if it distorts or threatens to distort competition by favouring certain undertakings or forms of production, in so far as trade between Member States may be affected.[37]

---

common market in accordance with the law of their country and with the provisions of Article 81, in particular paragraph 3, and of Article 82.

35 Art 85 ECT reads as follows:
1. Without prejudice to Art 84 ECT, the Commission shall ensure the application of the principles laid down in Articles 81 and 82. On application by a Member State or on its own initiative, and in cooperation with the competent authorities in the Member States, who shall give it their assistance, the Commission shall investigate cases of suspected infringement of these principles. If it finds that there has been an infringement, it shall propose appropriate measures to bring it to an end.
2. If the infringement is not brought to an end, the Commission shall record such infringement of the principles in a reasoned decision. The Commission may publish its decision and authorise Member States to take the measures, the conditions and details of which it shall determine, needed to remedy the situation.

36 Art 86 ECT reads as follows:
1. In the case of public undertakings and undertakings to which Member States grant special or exclusive rights, Member States shall neither enact nor maintain in force any measure contrary to the rules contained in this Treaty, in particular to those rules provided for in Art 12 ECT and Art 81 to Art 89 ECT.
2. Undertakings entrusted with the operation of services of general economic interest or having the character of a revenue producing monopoly shall be subject to the rules contained in this Treaty, in particular to the rules on competition, insofar as the application of such rules does not obstruct the performance, in law or in fact, of the particular tasks assigned to them.
The development of trade must not be affected to such an extent as would be contrary to the interests of the Community.
3. The Commission shall ensure the application of the provisions of this Article and shall, where necessary, address appropriate directives or decisions to Member States.

37 In fact, Art 87 ECT determines that "any aid granted by a Member State or through State resources in any form whatsoever which distorts or threatens to distort competition by favouring certain undertakings or the production of certain goods shall, insofar as it affects trade between Member States, be incompatible with the common market." Compatible with the common market can be, for example:
- aid having a social character, granted to individual consumers, provided that such aid is granted without discrimination related to the origin of the products concerned;

As mentioned in chapter 1, the provisions regarding restrictive practices of undertakings form an essential part of this paper. Before analysing the relevant articles, I would still like to add two more brief observations in respect of EC competition policy.

Firstly, three essential targets have to be achieved through competition policy:

- Competition policy has to safeguard the unity of the common market. This is because it would be useless to abolish trade hampering barriers like customs, if – on the other side – Member States were allowed to close their national markets by means of state aid or other competition restrictions.
- A further goal consists of upholding competition as a controlling mechanism for economic proceedings, which is mainly menaced through the concentration of economic and financial power.[38] Continuously, the European Commission has emphasised that well-functioning competition creates an environment of a sane and harmonical development of the economy within the Community and for guaranteeing international competitiveness.
- Lastly, European competition policy focuses on economical justice and hence, slightly weakens the afore-mentioned targets. Indeed, the combination of the three goals implies that on the one hand all participants have to be granted the same opportunities on the market. On the other hand, it means that when applying competition rules one has also to consider the economic situation of the single undertakings. In the light of economical justice, small and medium enterprises deserve particular support. Besides, the legitimate interest of employees and consumers has to be taken into account as well.[39]

Secondly, competition policy is not the only policy of the Community, but often stands in a concurrent position to others policies (ie the Industrial

---

- aid to make good the damage caused by natural disasters or exceptional occurrences;
- aid to promote the economic development of areas where the standard of living is abnormally low or where there is serious underemployment;
- aid to promote the execution of an important project of common European interest or to remedy a serious disturbance in the economy of a Member State. See Art 87 par 2 and par 3 ECT.

To accomplish this task, the Commission constantly reviews, in cooperation with Member States, all systems of aid existing in those states. Moreover, it can order aid-granting states to abolish or alter such aid within a determined period of time. See Art 88 ECT.

Furthermore, the Council "may make any appropriate regulations for the application of Articles 87 and 88." See Art 89 ECT.

38 As we have seen in chapter 2.1.

39 See Schmitdt/Schmidt, Wettbewerbspolitik 6.

Policy or the Common Agricultural Policy [CAP][40]). In such cases, the competition policy of the EC does not necessarily hold the primary position, but has to be balanced with these other policies. Indeed, even though the Commission continuously highlights competition as the cornerstone of the common market, it also stresses the importance of industrial policy, by which industry shall be prepared for changing market realities. It is emphasised that the ultimate goal of Industrial Policy is to support new competitive structures and the efficient allocation of resources. In this context, the Commission is referring to active competition policy.[41]

2.4 Explanation of the substantive rules (Art 81 and Art 82 ECT)

As the quality of procedural rules ultimately depends on whether they allow efficient application of the substantial law they aim to implement, I will illustrate in this subchapter the substantial law provisions that are implemented by the procedural rules subjected to the reform. These rules are Art 81 ECT- dealing with cartels - and Art 82 ECT, this latter referring to abuse of dominant positions. In the development of these rules, the European Court of Justice and the Court of First Instance have played a vital role. Indeed, as the Treaty does not provide for definitions of the concepts contained therein, one has to stick to the case law of the European judiciary in order to get an idea about what the substantive rules signify. Moreover, to give a clear profile of these provisions and especially to show their limits, I will further address briefly those economic fields, for which special regimes have been adopted to the restriction of Art 81 ECT and Art 82 ECT. Lastly, I will look into the most important notices of the Commission, which have been issued in order to offer guidance on some elements on the application of the substantive rules.

2.4.1 Cartels

The provisions regarding cartels are contained in Art 81 ECT. This article is structured in order to contain in par 1 the facts that constitute the prohibition, par 2 outlines the legal consequence and par 3 contains conditions for an exemption from the prohibition.
Art 81 ECT states:

---

40 In respect of the CAP also consider chapter 2.4.3.2.
41 See Schmidt/Schmidt, Wettbewerbspolitik 8.

> 1. The following shall be prohibited as incompatible with the common market: all agreements between undertakings, decisions by associations of undertakings and concerted practices which may affect trade between Member States and which have as their object or effect the prevention, restriction or distortion of competition within the common market, and in particular those which:
> (a) directly or indirectly fix purchase or selling prices or any other trading conditions;
> (b) limit or control production, markets, technical development, or investment;
> (c) share markets or sources of supply;
> (d) apply dissimilar conditions to equivalent transactions with other trading parties, thereby placing them at a competitive disadvantage;
> (e) make the conclusion of contracts subject to acceptance by the other parties of supplementary obligations, which, by their nature or according to commercial usage, have no connection with the subject of such contracts.
> 2. Any agreements or decisions prohibited pursuant to this Article shall be automatically void.
> 3. The provisions of paragraph 1 may, however, be declared inapplicable in the case of:
> -any agreement or category of agreements between undertakings;
> -any decision or category of decisions by associations of undertakings;
> -any concerted practice or category of concerted practices,
> which contributes to improving the production or distribution of goods or to promoting technical or economic progress, while allowing consumers a fair share of the resulting benefit, and which does not:
> (a) impose on the undertakings concerned restrictions, which are not indispensable to the attainment of these objectives;
> (b) afford such undertakings the possibility of eliminating competition in respect of a substantial part of the products in question.

In other words, collusive or co-operative market behaviour between undertakings, which tends to preclude competition within the common market, is prohibited. Additionally, it is requested that trade between Member States has to be affected. The violation of the prohibition imposed, makes them automatically void. However, exemptions can be granted by the Commission.

The terminology used by Art 81 ECT has been clarified and interpreted by several decisions from the Commission and rulings from the ECJ and will be illustrated in these following subchapters. To begin with, I will concentrate on the prohibition provision contained in par 1. I will consider the following eight notions:[42] 'agreements', 'decisions by associations of undertakings', 'concerted practices', 'undertaking', 'which may affect trade between Member States', 'which have as their object or effect', 'prevention, restriction and distortion of competition' and 'within the common market'. Afterwards, I will focus on the nullity-provision, then I will consider the exemption-provision and last but not least, I will draw attention to the hierarchical relationship between Community and national competition rules in respect of the application of Art 81 ECT.

2.4.1.1 Art 81 par 1 ECT: the prohibition

2.4.1.1.1 Agreements

An agreement in the sense of Art 81 is a "legally binding and therefore enforceable commitment"[43] based on consensus between the involved undertakings.[44] Concerning the formal prerequisites of an agreement it does not matter whether it is written, verbal or partly verbal and written.[45] In fact, in several cases the ECJ[46] outlined a rather wide interpretation[47] of the stated formula by indicating that such commitments are not limited to certain forms: for instance, it was clarified that already the systematic dispatching by a supplier to his customers of invoices bearing the words 'exports prohibited', constitutes a prohibited agreement. In this case, the customers had accepted the restriction though.[48]

---

42 Anyhow, I would like to make it clear from the beginning that due to the limited space and scope of this paper, the analysis of the terminology cannot reach every level of detail, rather I would say that the analysis pursued only scratches the surface of the various notions. A more detailed description is provided by *Emmerich*, Wettbewerbsregeln: Kartellrecht § 1 Art 81 und 82 EGV in Dauses, Handbuch des EU-Wirtschaftsrechts 2001.

43 See *Mathijsen*, European Union Law 255.

44 See *Goyder*, Competition 93.

45 See *Goyder*, Competition 93.

46 See ECJ case 209/78 (Van Landewijk).

47 The interpretation is independent from any national systematic or qualifications. See *Stockenhuber* in Grabitz/Hilf, Das Recht der Europäischen Union 2001, 16.

48 See ECJ case C-277/87 (Sandoz).

The tendency towards wide interpretation is exemplificatory demonstrated by the Mayer-Melnhof case[49] in which the ECJ defined an agreement as "the faithful expression of the parties' intention to conduct themselves in a certain way." More specifically, in order that an agreement may become void, the clauses of the agreement have merely to show the intention of the parties to distort competition. In other words, it is not relevant whether competition is finally distorted or not.[50] Next, it is also not required that the relevant documents have been signed or dated. In such a case it is required that both parties to the agreement act upon it however.[51]

Quite controversial is the question of whether or not a gentlemen's agreement falls into this category.[52] However, this question shall not be of great importance as ultimately gentlemen's agreements can be encompassed by the category of concerted practices.

The case law of the ECJ also embraces unilateral instructions under the notion of agreements in the sense of Art 81 ECT. Indeed, they may be classified as agreements on the condition that they are acknowledged by the recipient,[53] also by tacit acceptance.[54] Interestingly, also unilateral action can be considered as an agreement in the sense of Art 81 ECT. However, in such a case it is necessary that the unilateral action be closely linked to an agreement in order to form part of a distribution system that eventually fosters the partitioning of national markets.[55]

Lastly, the sphere of applicability of Art 81 ECT covers both horizontal as well as vertical agreements.[56]

2.4.1.1.2 Decisions by associations of undertakings

Concerning the term 'decision', it is held that the expression not only embraces the constitutive act of a trade association and its internal rules,[57]

---

49 See CFI case T-347/94 (Mayer-Melnhof).

50 See ECJ case 56/65 (Société Technique Minière).

51 See the decision of the European Commission in Atka, 1979.

52 See *Eilmannsberger*, Europarecht II (2000) 45; also see *Stockenhuber* in Grabitz/Hilf, Recht, 18; and *Emmerich*, in Dauses, Kartellrecht 30.

53 See the decision of the European Commission in WEA-Filipacchi, 1972: WEA had forbidden its distributors to sell records outside their home country. These latter acknowledged this by affixing their official stamp on the circular containing the instruction.

54 See *Emmerich*, in Dauses, Kartellrecht 31.

55 See ECJ case 107/82 (AEG Telefunken) and case 228-229/82 (Ford); in this latter decision, the ECJ outlined that the Commission does not have to express its opinion on each individual element of the agreement, but can focus on the agreement as a whole.

56 See *Stockenhuber* in Grabitz/Hilf, Recht 17.

but also includes decisions which are taken according to those rules and which are binding upon the members of the association,[58] as well as mere recommendations such as the fixing of target-prices by an association.[59] However, it should be stressed that it is not relevant, if an agreement is one between undertakings or one between associations of undertakings. It is furthermore irrelevant whether there is a determined structure by which the concerned decisions are taken or how national authorities classify that structure.[60]

The second aspect of the concept here dealt with, regards the term 'association'. As stated in Metropole *versus* EBU,[61] this expression is not limited to any particular form of association and one has not even to distinguish between public and private associations.[62] The decisive element is the ambition of the group, which has to be of common interest to the members of the association.[63] The term here analysed includes associations of associations, with or without legal personality and also non-profit-making associations.[64] Again, it becomes clear that the ECJ adopts a rather wide interpretation of Art 81 ECT.

2.4.1.1.3 Concerted practices

More confusing is the concept of concerted practices, which are given in case several undertakings are acting with anti-competitive parallel market behaviour. If this behaviour is the result of 'concertation' between these undertakings, the prohibition of Art 81 par 1 ECT applies.[65] Undoubtedly, concerted practices is the broadest of the three concepts, and as such it is often asserted by the Commission to be an alternative to the concept of agreement, as it focuses on more informal arrangements.[66]

---

57 See *Mahtijsen*, European Union Law 256.

58 See the decision of the European Commission in Bomee-Stichting, 1975.

59 See ECJ case 8/72 (Cementenhandelaren).

60 See ECJ case 123/83 (BNIC).

61 See CFI case T-528/93 (Metropole).

62 See ECJ case 123/83 (BNIC).

63 See *Emmerich*, in Dauses, Kartellrecht 27.

64 Interestingly, a de facto association of associations was considered by the Commission to be an association of undertakings. See the van Landewyck-case (ECJ case 209/78).
An association representing a significant number of manufacturers in a relevant sector can be directly and individually concerned by a decision addressed to another association and is therefore admissible to challenge that Commission decision in court. See CFI case T-380/94 (AIUFASS).

65 See ECJ cases 100/80 (Musique Diffusion Francaise).

66 See *Goyder*, Competition 94 and 98.

A very detailed definition of concerted practices was given by the ECJ, defining it as

> "a form of co-ordination between undertakings which, without having been taken to the stage where an agreement properly so-called has been concluded, knowingly substitutes for the risks of competition practical co-operation between them, which leads to conditions of competition, which do not correspond to the normal conditions of the market having regard to the nature of the products, the importance and number of the undertakings as well as the size and nature of the said market." [67]

Contrary to agreements, in order that concerted practices can become void, one has to focus on the subsequent market behaviour. Only this latter can be caught by the prohibition. Of course, the condition applies that trade between Member States is affected and competition is distorted. Accordingly, the burden of proof for the Commission is double: it has to demonstrate both that the practice violates the Treaty of Rome and secondly, that there was collusion among parties, which finally determined the anti-competitive behaviour.[68]

The complexity and difficulties in determining a possible violation is best shown by parallel price increases conducted by several undertakings. These price increases could be purely coincidental or the result of an oligopoly with price leadership. Consequently, they are not in themselves prohibited. In the Hoffmann-La Roche case,[69] the court talks about "parallel courses of conduct which are peculiar to oligopolies". However, parallel price increases are prohibited when they are the result of a concertation. Evidence in proof of violation can be seen through participation of the undertakings concerned in meetings with an anti-competitive object.[70] As outlined in the ICI case, proof will often be based on circumstantial evidence.[71]

Further important elements that help in confirming the existence of a concerted practice are the existence of intentional communication flows between the parties involved. This goes beyond normal mutual awareness of competitors who become aware of their rivals competition strategy by simply observing their pricing, and it requests not only that the party directing the information to the other party does so with intention, but also that the party receiving the information is aware not by coincidence but by intention.[72]

---

[67] See ECJ case 40/73, (Suiker Unie), the so-called Sugar-Cartel-case.

[68] See *Mathijsen*, European Union Law 256.

[69] See ECJ case 85/76 (Hoffmann-La Roche).

[70] See ECJ case T-327/94 (SCA Holdings).

[71] See ECJ case 48/69 (ICI).

[72] See *Goyder*, Competition 101.

Again, this concept is also not only applicable to horizontal agreements, but to vertical agreements as well.[73]

2.4.1.1.4 Undertakings

Equally to the other terms analysed above, the Treaty of Rome does not provide for a definition of this term either. A first attempt to rectify this omission was made by Deringer who defined an undertaking as

> "any activity aimed at an exchange of economic values (goods and services) that is not limited to an individual fulfilment of personal needs [...], any independent activity of a person that is not purely personal and that is not outside the economic sphere, regardless of its legal form and intention to make a profit." [74]

More briefly, Goyder[75] describes an undertaking as "a body capable of having legal rights and duties and acting in co-operation with other parties".

Generally, the term 'undertakings' encompasses all entities that eventually pursue an economic activity,[76] or better still, entities that comprise every offer of goods or services on the market.[77] It should however be stressed that it is not essential that such undertakings pursue profit-making.[78] In fact, the ECJ[79] specified that also a non-profit organisation, whose duty is the management of old-age insurance schemes in keeping with the rules laid down by the authorities, is an undertaking within the scope of Art 81 ECT. In its reasoning, the ECJ stressed that the involved organisation did compete with private insurance companies and followed the normal principles of insurance contributions. Again, a key element in determining whether an undertaking exists is the nature of its activity. On the other hand, insurance funds based on the principle of solidarity do not constitute an undertaking.[80] The same is true for companies performing central functions of a state in the public's interest.[81]

Nevertheless, this non-profit-making feature cannot be interpreted so broad as to also include activities administered by a State, which form part of its sovereign functions[82] or activities that "neither involve the conduct of any

[73] See ECJ case 100/80 (Musique Diffusion Francaise).
[74] See *Goyder*, Competition 87.
[75] See *Goyder*, Competition 87.
[76] See *Emmerich*, in Dauses, Kartellrecht 24.
[77] See *Emmerich*, in Dauses, Kartellrecht 15.
[78] See *Goyder*, Competition 87.
[79] See ECJ case C-244/94 (Société d'Assurance).
[80] See ECJ case C-159/91 (Poucet and Pistre).
[81] See ECJ case C-343/95 (Diego Cali).
[82] See *Goyder*, Competition 87.

kind of business nor the co-ordination of commercial activities to be carried on by others."[83] Consequently, one can determine that the term undertaking is applicable

> "to state bodies engaged in commerce, nationalised industries operating as separated legal entities, municipalities, federations, trade associations, publicly owned undertakings, undertakings with special rights granted by the state; it also includes private individuals engaged in any form of business, commerce or profession, partnerships, co-operatives, companies and performing rights societies."[84]

Another relevant question in this context is whether the term 'undertakings' encompasses entities without legal personality. An analysis of Art 43 par 2 ECT in combination with Art 48 ECT provides for a positive answer. As the former explicitly refers to "undertakings, in particular companies or firms within the meaning of the second paragraph of Art 48" ECT and the latter states that "companies or firms' means companies or firms constituted under civil or commercial law" one can draw the conclusion that the Treaty uses the terms 'company' or 'firm' for referring to legal persons. Consequently, the term 'undertakings' has to be defined broader in a way also to cover entities without legal personality.[85]

Moreover, as emphasised above, it is necessary that undertakings are able to carry out economic activities; in other words, they must possess legal autonomy. This feature can only be given when undertakings are legal entities. To determine whether this qualification is given, one has to consult the applicable national law.[86]

Lastly, it is important that an undertaking is economically independent.[87] Under certain conditions, this prerequisite might not be given with undertakings that, belonging to the same group or concern, have the status of parent company or subsidiary respectively. In such a case, it has to be taken into consideration whether the parent company controls the subsidiary, or better, whether the subsidiary is free to determine its market behaviour independently of the parent company.[88] If this independency is not

---

83 See *Goyder*, Competition 87.

84 See *Goyder*, Competition 87.

85 Anyhow, it is nevertheless necessary that they must have some kind of recognised legal status (eg with the Dutch 'vennootschap onder firma', the English 'partnership' and the German 'offene Gesellschaft'); see CFI case T-25/96 (Arbeitsgemeinschaft Deutscher Luftfahrt-Unternehmen).

86 See *Mathijsen*, European Union Law 257.

87 See CFI case T-387/94 (Asia Motor France).

88 See the decision of the European Commission in Welded Steel Mesh, 1989, where it was found that a 25% interest held by one company in a competitor does not give rise to a parent-subsidiary relationship.

given, the agreement, which determines the interdependency between parent company and subsidiary, merely constitutes an internal allocation of tasks and hence, both undertakings form a single economic unit. Therefore, when the subsidiary as a part of the single economic unit violates the competition rules, the parent company can be held responsible.[89] It is not even relevant whether the parent company is situated within the Community, as one only has to consider whether the effects of the violation are felt within the common market and hence, can be caught by its rules.[90]

2.4.1.1.5 Which may affect trade between Member States

The wording "which may affect trade between Member States" dictates the field of application of Art 81 ECT.[91] It is

> "to the extent that the agreement may affect trade between Member States, that the interference with competition caused by that agreement is caught by the prohibition in Community law found in Article 85 [now Art 81], while in the converse case it escapes this prohibition."[92]

In several rulings the Court stated that in order to fulfil the condition that trade between Member States is affected, it

> "must be possible to foresee with a sufficient degree of probability on the basis of a set of objective factors of law and fact that [the agreement[93]] may have an influence, direct or indirect, actual or potential, on the pattern of trade between Member States such as might prejudice the realisation of the aim of a single market in all the Member States."[94]

From this wording it becomes clear, that agreements in the sense of Art 81 ECT simply have to be capable of constituting a threat to freedom of trade between Member States in order to be caught by the prohibition.[95] For instance, one should think of an agreement that prevents undertakings from importing certain goods from other Member States as well as of an agreement that prohibits undertakings from re-exporting those goods to other Member States. Obviously, these agreements are against the principle of free movement of goods and hence, against the competition rules, which

---

89 See CFI case T-309/94 (KNP).

90 See ECJ case 48/69 (ICI) and ECJ case 85/76 (Hoffmann-La Roche).

91 See *Stockenhuber*, Europäisches Kartellrecht (1999) 34.

92 See ECJ case 56/65 (Société Technique Minière).

93 In order to facilitate the reading, from now on the word 'agreement' will also include 'decisions by associations of undertakings' and 'concerted practices'.

94 See ECJ case 42/84 (Remia).

95 See ECJ case 56/64 (Consten and Grundig).

aim at guaranteeing the effectiveness of this principle. The same applies to agreements that grant an exclusive right and where a partitioning of the common market in certain product areas between Member States might be the consequence.[96]

Clarification was also necessary in respect of the expression 'trade', which refers to industrial and commercial activities of manufacture and distribution and also includes various commercial services like banking, insurance and financial services or other commercial activities like performing right societies, television programmes or the provision of exhibitions and trade fairs.[97] However, this rather broad qualification does not go so far as to include an agreement that simply encourages an increase in the volume of trade between Member States.[98] On the other hand, the notion of trade is not precluded due to the fact that an agreement does not concern imports nor exports.[99]

The concept of trade-affection between Member States is also limited by the Commission's practice. In fact, by issuing several notices it determined a threshold by means of the so-called '*de minimis* rule'. Herewith, the Commission

> "quantifies, with the help of market share thresholds, what is not an appreciable restriction of competition under Art 81 of the EC Treaty. This negative definition of appreciability does not imply that agreements between undertakings, which exceed the thresholds set out in this notice, appreciably restrict competition. Such agreements may still have only a negligible effect on competition and may therefore not be prohibited by Art 81 par 1 and 2. [However, this notice] does not quantify what does not constitute an appreciable effect on trade. It is however acknowledged that agreements between small and medium-sized undertakings [...] are rarely capable of appreciably affecting trade between Member States. Small and medium-sized undertakings are currently defined in that recommendation as undertakings which have fewer than 250 employees and have either an annual turnover not exceeding EUR 40 million or an annual balance-sheet total not exceeding EUR 27 million."[100]

Currently, this borderline is determined by a market share percentage, which for agreements between competitors is laid down as 10 % and between non-

[96] See ECJ case 56/65 (Société Technique Minière).

[97] See *Goyder*, Competition 115.

[98] See ECJ case 56/64 (Consten and Grundig).

[99] See ECJ case 43/69 (Bilger).

[100] See par 2 and par 3 of *European Commission*, Notice on immunity of fines and reduction of fines in cartel cases, 2002, hereinafter referred to as de-minimis rule.

competitors as 15 %.[101] Still, this notice has to be considered with caution as it does not bind the ECJ nor the Member States' courts.[102]

2.4.1.1.6 Which have as their object or effect

This formula of Art 81 ECT focuses on the one hand
- on the intention of an agreement to distort competition, and, on the other hand, in the absence of this intention,
- on whether the agreement's result is such a distortion.

Let me first explain the former notion. In case the object of an agreement is distortion of competition,[103] one does not have to consider whether competition was actually distorted, rather, the intention of the parties as expressed in the agreement, in its economic context.[104] This intention can result from an analysis of all but also of only some of the agreement's clauses. In this latter case, the whole agreement need not necessarily be caught by the prohibition and consequent nullity, but only those clauses, which specify as their object the interference with competition.[105] Anyhow, as an additional and necessary element in this context, the concerned provision has to be capable of distorting competition. In other words, the sole intention of the parties in this respect does not provoke the violation of the norm.[106]
The second conception considers the situation in which no clause of the agreement shows the intention of distorting competition. In this case, one has to take one step further to consider the consequences of the agreement's implementation. It is up to the Commission or any other investigating authority or court to find factors showing that competition is indeed distorted, or, that there is at least a danger of distortion.[107]

---

[101] See *de-minimis* rule par. 7. However, these thresholds are not applicable to determined hardcore restrictions.

[102] See *Goyder*, Competition 111; also see *Stockenhuber*, Kartellrecht 37.

[103] The notion of 'distortion of competition' is going to be explained in the next subchapter.

[104] See *Goyder*, Competition 120.

[105] See ECJ case 56/64 (Consten and Grunding): The Court annulled the Commission's decision because it considered the whole agreement as void.
Also see ECJ case 319/82 (Société de Vente): The Court reiterated that the consequences of the nullity of certain provisions for other parts of the agreement are not a matter for Community law, but must be determined by the national court on the basis of its own national law.

[106] See *Stockenhuber*, Kartellrecht 24.

[107] See ECJ case 56/65 (Société Technique Minière).

2.4.1.1.7 Prevention, restriction or distortion of competition

To draw a distinction between prevention, restriction or distortion is of no relevance, as the consequences for these forms of impairment of competition are the same.[108] Hence, I will continue to use the term distortion solely. In order to fulfil this condition, it is necessary to analyse the agreement comparing its results with a hypothetical reality that could exist in the absence of the agreement.

By making such a comparison, one has to consider several aspects like

> "the nature and quantity, limited or otherwise, of the products covered by the agreement, the position and importance of the [parties] on the market for the products concerned, the isolated nature of the disputed agreement or, alternatively, its position in a series of agreements, the severity of the clause intended to [limit trade], or alternatively, the opportunities allowed for other commercial competitors in the same product by way of parallel re-exportation or importation."[109]

Certain categories have been established as being *prima facie* restrictions. Of course, the agreements listed under subpar a to subpar e of Art 81 par 1 ECT fall under this category. However, this list is not exclusive.[110] For instance, one can additionally name those agreements, which impose export bans on distributors and hence directly ban parallel imports[111] or those horizontal agreements that inhibit the export of goods to other Member States or into territories outside the common market with the aim to hinder the re-importation of these goods.[112]

Nevertheless, one has to bear in mind that according to the *de-minimis* rule a distortion of competition has to reach an appreciable extent.[113] For instance, an exclusive dealing agreement with a weak position in the market of the products in question and persons concerned does not fulfil the relevant criteria and hence escapes the prohibition.[114]

Lastly, exemptions to the illustrated concept are granted by the notions of 'rule of reason' and of 'ancillary restraints'. Whereas the former envisages the necessity for an exemption from the prohibition in case the agreement concerned constitutes - even if competition is distorted - a precondition for

---

108 See *Eilmannsberger*, Europarecht 48.

109 See ECJ case 56/65 (Société Technique Minière) and ECJ case 99/79 (Lancôme/Etos).

110 See *Stockenhuber*, Kartellrecht 29.

111 See ECJ case 56/64 (Consten and Grundig).

112 See *Goyder*, Competition 121.

113 See ECJ case 56/65 (Société Technique Minière) and the *de-minimis* rule.

114 See ECJ case 5/69 (Volk) and ECJ Case 30/78 (Distillers Company).

the creation of new markets,[115] the latter stresses that a restriction is needed to assure that a benefit gained by one party from the transaction involved will not be to the deprivation of the other party. There are limitations though.[116]

2.4.1.1.8 Within the common market

A further prerequisite for the prohibition to be applied requires the distortion of competition to take place within the common market. Clearly, Community law does not prohibit an agreement between undertakings that are based within the Community, but which restricts competition in an external country only.[117] However, if such an agreement influences the behaviour of the parties in a way resulting in the distortion of competition and trade between the Member States, then the prohibition provision as outlined by Art 81 ECT would remain applicable.[118] What is more, an agreement, which was concluded between undertakings situated outside the Community but which has an effect on trade between Member States and on competition within the Community, is prohibited and prosecutable (extra-territorial application of Community competition law).[119] Of course, the same is true when just one of the parties is situated within the Community.[120]
A last point, which has to be mentioned in this context, is that the formula "within the common market" does not imply that agreements must concern all the Member States or even a few of them. As a matter of fact, the ECJ acknowledged that an agreement, which covers the whole territory of one Member State, might come within the prohibition, since with such an agreement a threshold effect concerning imports is created.[121] This can also be true where an agreement does not cover an entire national market.[122]

---

[115] See ECJ case 56/65 (LTM) and ECJ Case 42/84 (Remia).
[116] See the decision of the European Commission in Reuter/BASF, 1976.
[117] See *Emmerich*, in Dauses, Kartellrecht 13.
[118] See ECJ case 6/73 (Commercial Solvents).
[119] See *Emmerich*, in Dauses, Kartellrecht 13.
Mathijsen doubts, whether the expression 'extraterritorial-effect' is correct in the above mentioned case since it is only in "operating within the Community", territorially speaking, that the behaviour of these undertakings is caught, See *Mathijsen*, European Union Law 262 fn 44.
[120] See the decision of the European Commission in Franco-Japanese Ballbearings, 1974.
[121] See ECJ case 8/72 (Cementhandelaren).
[122] See ECJ case 126/80 (Salonia).

2.4.1.2 The nullity-provision

As Art 81 par 2 ECT outlines, cartels prohibited under par 1, are automatically void and no declaration is needed.[123] However, in this context a distinction has to be drawn between those agreements that were concluded before March 13th 1962 (the date on which Reg 17 came into force and which first implemented Art 81 ECT) - so-called old agreements - and those concluded afterwards, so-called new agreements.[124]

In line with the general principle of contractual certainty, old agreements had provisional validity[125] as long as the Commission did not overturn the agreement by decision. In respect of new agreements, the nullity applies without reservation in case an agreement is prohibited according to the law.[126] A consequence of this regime is that these agreements have to be implemented at the parties' own risk: it is their duty to assess whether an agreement is prohibited and consequently void. This implies the risk that national courts might declare the agreement as void *ab initio* afterwards, if it has been implemented anyway.[127] Under the procedural rules as established by Reg 17, undertakings had the option to ask for negative clearance or an exemption by filing a notification to the Commission and obtaining legal certainty by this means.[128]

2.4.1.3 Exemptions from the prohibition

Reg 17 conferred the power to grant exemptions from the prohibition contained in Art 81 par 1 ECT exclusively to the Commission and more precisely to Directorate General IV (DG IV): the directorate responsible for competition matters within the Commission.[129] Before the adoption of the afore-mentioned regulation, this power lay in the hands of national authorities.[130]

---

[123] See Art 1 Reg 17 and Art 1 Reg 1.

[124] Different dates apply in the Member States (ie: Denmark, Ireland, Greece) that have acceded to the Community after this date.

[125] See ECJ case 13/61 (Bosch). Also see ECJ case C-39/96 (KVBBB), where it states that "provisional validity expires only when the Commission has taken a positive or negative decision on the agreement".

[126] Some of those agreements were exempted from notification; see ECJ case 48/72 (Brasserei de Haecht).

[127] See *Mathijsen*, European Union Law 263.

[128] See chapter 3.1.2.

[129] See Art 9 par 1 Reg 17, and ECJ case 31/80 (L'Oréal); also see *Goyder*, Competition 129.

[130] See Art 84 ECT.

One can distinguish between 2 kind of exemptions: individual exemptions and categories of exemptions (so-called block exemptions). Under Reg 17, the former could only have been granted upon specific notification of the agreement concerned by an undertaking to the Commission.[131] The latter granted exemptions to clearly outlined and specified categories of arrangements.

These exemptions had constitutive power, as they transformed an illegal and prohibited restrictive practice into a legal one.[132]

2.4.1.3.1 Individual exemptions

Art 81 par 3 ECT outlines four conditions all of which have to be met in order for an exemption to be applicable[133]. The first two of them are positive, the other two negative. Before analysing these conditions, it is important to stress 2 points: first it is up to the parties to provide for the proof of all these conditions, and second, there is no principle of *stare decisis,* which has a binding effect on subsequent cases.[134]

The first condition regards the efficiency effects of agreements and states that an "agreement must contribute to improving the production or distribution of goods or to promoting technical or economic progress."[135] Both the improvement as well as the economic or technical progress may arise either immediately or at a later stage. Whereas improvement is a rather loosely interpreted expression so as to contain almost every beneficial alteration, the concept of progress is more obscure. However, it does definitely not go as far as to ask for a "broad social balancing of economic advantages and disadvantages".[136] Besides, it is necessary that improvement and progress also benefit third parties.[137] The Commission also acknowledged that environmental benefits constitute technical and economic progress.[138]

---

[131] See Art 4 par 1 Reg 17.
For details concerning notifications, see Commission Reg 3385/94 of 21 December 1994 on the form, content and other details of applications and notifications provided for in Reg 17.

[132] See chapter 2.4.3.2.

[133] See *Hirsch/Burkert* in Gleiss/Hirsch, Kommentar zum EG-Kartellrecht I[4] (1993), 683.

[134] See *Goyder*, Competition 136 and 138.

[135] See Art 81 par 3 ECT.

[136] See *Goyder*, Competition 138.

[137] See the decision of the European Commission in VNP/Cobelpa, 1977.

[138] See *Goyder*, Competition, 140.

The second condition considers consumer welfare[139] and declares that "consumers must get a fair share of the resulting benefit."[140] This phrasing does not only focus on end consumers or retail purchasers but also refers to the acquisition of goods at any stage of the distribution process. A wide delineation of benefit includes every economic advantage a consumer may experience (ie: increase in the number of outlets, greater range of goods).[141]
Next, for obtaining an exemption it is necessary that an agreement does not impose on the undertakings involved restrictions that are not indispensable to the accomplishment of the previously mentioned goals.[142] In other words, the agreements have to be designed to strictly meet the outlined objectives. This concept is similar to the principle of proportionality.[143]
The last condition refers to the external impact of a restrictive business practice and states that an agreement may "not afford such undertakings the possibility of eliminating competition in respect of a substantial part of the products in question."[144] Hereby, the Commission's analysis is based upon the nature of the market concerned, the size of the companies involved and their market shares.[145]
Generally, the assessment of these conditions is quite complex and requests a deep knowledge in the field of economic theory. Especially due to the vast range of non-defined terminology, a broad sphere of discretion is granted to the applying body.[146] However, a limit is set by the European Court of Justice, who has expressly held that all positive effects must show appreciable objective advantages that would compensate for the disadvantages, caused by the restriction of competition.[147]

139 In the Green paper on vertical restraints in EC competition policy, the Commission acknowledges that "the interest of the consumer is at the heart of competition policy. Effective competition is the best guarantee for consumers to be able to buy good quality products at the lowest possible prices." See *European Commission*, Green paper on vertical restraints in EC competition policy, par 54.

140 See Art 81 par 3 ECT.

141 See *Goyder*, Competition 141.

142 See Art 81 par 3 ECT, these goals are those mentioned in condition one. Also see *Goyder*, Competition 141.

See *Goyder*, Competition 142; also see ECJ case 61/80 (Cooperative Stremseln Kleurselfabriek).

144 See Art 81 par 3 ECT.

145 See *Goyder*, Competition 144.

146 See *Emmerich*, in Dauses, Kartellrecht 70.

147 See ECJ Case 56/64 (Consten and Grundig).

2.4.1.3.2 Block exemptions

A further possibility to be exempted from the cartel-prohibition is a declaration of inapplicability that is valid not for a single specific agreement but for categories of agreements. They are issued in respect of those restrictive practices, which appear with sufficient certainty to be in line with the conditions set out by the Treaty. Such general and rather wide-ranging declarations of inapplicability are granted by the Commission in the form of block-exemptions.[148] The power to adopt such exemptions is based on a Council regulation, setting out the principles of the exemption. Details are implemented by the Commission.[149]

Up to the late 1990's, block exemptions were drafted in line with a certain standard approach. The category of agreements to which the regulation applied, were identified in broad terms containing lists of specific obligations, which could have been included without loosing the benefit of the block exemption (white list). Additionally, it listed clauses that were forbidden to be contained (black list).[150] Other provisions executed the withdrawal of the exemption by the Commission if it found that, despite compliance with the regulation, an agreement had certain effects that did not satisfy the criteria in Art 81 par 3 ECT. Moreover, transitional provisions and the duration of the regulation had also been specified. Some of the regulations included an opposition-procedure to accelerate the process of obtaining exemption on an individual basis. In fact, clauses not covered by the regulation could have been notified to the Commission, which was given a period (normally six months) to express its oppositions. If the clauses had not been opposed by the Commission within the prescribed period, they were catalogued under the scope of the block exemption.

The approach taken by the new block exemptions[151] is somewhat different. It relies upon a black-list only, indicating unacceptable hardcore restraints. This

---

[148] For the discussion regarding the effect of block exemptions under the new regime, see chapter 3.4.3.

[149] This kind of delegation constitutes an example of what is provided for in Art 211 ECT, last indent: in fact, in such cases the Commission exercises "the powers conferred on it by the Council for the implementation of the rules laid down by the latter"; also see *Hirsch/Burkert* in Gleiss/Hirsch, Kommentar 684.

[150] See *Goyder*, Competition 133; for details concerning the legal consequences of block exemptions, see *Hirsch/Burkert* in Gleiss/Hirsch, Kommentar 686-687.

[151] See for instance: Commission Reg 2658/2000 on the application of Art 81 par 3 ECT (specialisation agreements), Commission Reg 2659/2000 on the application of Art 81 par 3 ECT (research and development agreements), Commission Reg 2790/1999 on the application of Art 81 par 3 ECT (vertical agreements and concerted practices), Commission Reg 1400/2002 on the application of Art 81 par 3 ECT (categories of vertical agreements and concerted practices in the motor vehicle sector).

instrument is attached to a market share threshold. The absence of a white-list is intended to avoid some of the more rigid side effects of previous block exemptions. The new regulations adopt a broad umbrella approach, removing the need for the earlier more specialized regulations. This structure reflects the lenient approach to vertical restraints adopted in the Commission's original Green paper. Apart from the prohibited restraints, the other bar is the operation of rules relating to market shares.[152]

2.4.1.4 The relationship between Community and national competition rules

A very important question is, whether Community law and national rules can be applied simultaneously to the same cartel. It is acknowledged that Community law and national rules consider cartels from a different perspective (double barrier theory). Whereas Community law views the cartel as being a possible obstacle which may impede trade between Member States, national law focuses on considerations and priorities, which are specific to a Member State. It results that one and the same agreement may be subjected to two parallel proceedings. However, it was clarified that it is always requested that ultimately the general aims of the Treaty are respected. In other words, the parallel application of the national system can only be permitted to the extent that the uniform application throughout the common market of EC competition law is not prejudiced.[153]
In this sense, the Court ascertained that

> "conflicts between the rules of the Community and national rules in the matter of the law on cartels must be resolved by applying the principle that Community law takes precedence."[154]

It follows that national authorities may act in accordance with their national law, as long as no conflict of laws is generated.[155] This means that a cartel

---

[152] However, one shall bear in mind that agreements, which are not exempted by the means of a block-exemption, may still be exempted by the means of an individual exemption. Also see the decision of the European Commission in Carlsberg, 1984.

[153] See *Hirsch/Burkert* in Gleiss/Hirsch, Kommentar 30.

[154] See ECJ case 14/68 (Wilhelm).

[155] See *Hirsch/Burkert* in Gleiss/Hirsch, Kommentar 30 and 31.
In the Walt Wilhelm Case (ECJ case 14/68), the Court indicated three conditions, which had to be satisfied, in order that simultaneous investigations were allowed:
Firstly, the national application of the law must not prejudice the full and uniform application of Community rules, or of the full effect of the measures adopted in the implementation of those rules (uniformity rule).

that is void under Community law cannot be declared valid under national law by national authorities. On the other hand, this raises the question whether an agreement, which was exempted under Art 81 par 3 ECT by the Commission, may be declared as void by a national authority. If so, a situation could be created in which an agreement would be void in one Member State, but valid in all the other Member States of the Community. Obviously, this appears to be contrary to Community law, which calls for uniform application of Community decisions throughout the Community.[156] Nevertheless, this obligation does not constrain national authorities, when applying national law, to consider possible infringements of Community law, as long as the Commission has not opened proceedings.[157]
To sum up, the principle may be illustrated as follows.

- If a behaviour is contrary to both sets of rules, it may be dealt with under both.
- A behaviour prohibited by Art 81 or Art 82 ECT but permissible under the competition rules of a given Member State, cannot be treated as lawful in that one State.
- A behaviour, which does not satisfy the criteria in Art 81 par 1 or Art 82 ECT, for example, because trade between Member States is not appreciably affected, may nevertheless be prohibited under national law.
- A grant of exemption pursuant to Art 81 par 3 ECT or a block exemption probably overrides any conflicting rules of national competition law, since it presents a positive choice of policy by the Community authorities.[158]

The scope for conflict between national competition laws and those of the EC is reduced further by the tendency among Member States to enact or adopt legislation to match or mirror EC approaches.[159]
Nevertheless, a legal solution clarifying and codifying the principles established still needs to be adopted.[160]

Secondly, to ensure in any conflict between Community and national rules that the Community law takes precedence, Member States should not introduce or retain any measures, which would prejudice this aim (practical effectiveness rule).
Lastly, individual Member States must take appropriate measures to avoid any risk that a national decision on an issue of competition law might conflict with Commission proceedings still in progress (parallel proceeding rule).

[156] See *Eilmannsberger*, Europarecht 44; and *Stockenhuber*, Kartellrecht 135-136.

[157] See *Mathijsen*, European Union Law 299.

[158] Opinion held by the Commission in ECJ case C-266/93 (Bundeskartellamt)

[159] See for instance the UK Competition Act 1998 and particularly the Italian law 287 as analysed in chapter 4 of this dissertation.

[160] See *Emmerich*, in Dauses, Kartellrecht 17.

2.4.2 Abuse of Dominant Position

Besides Art 81 ECT, also Art 82 ECT contains competition rules in respect of undertakings. Both articles have to be considered separately and it is reasonable that

> "the restraint of competition which is prohibited if it is the result of behaviour falling under Art 81, cannot become permissible by the fact that such behaviour succeeds under the influence of a dominant undertaking."[161]

Art 82 ECT reads as follows:

> Any abuse by one or more undertakings of a dominant position within the common market or in a substantial part of it shall be prohibited as incompatible with the common market insofar as it may affect trade between Member States.
>
> Such abuse may, in particular, consist in:
>
> (a) directly or indirectly imposing unfair purchase or selling prices or other unfair trading conditions;
>
> (b) limiting production, markets or technical development to the prejudice of consumers;
>
> (c) applying dissimilar conditions to equivalent transactions with other trading parties, thereby placing them at a competitive disadvantage;
>
> (d) making the conclusion of contracts subject to acceptance by the other parties of supplementary obligations, which, by their nature or according to commercial usage, have no connection with the subject of such contracts.

In other words, competition and interstate trade can also be hampered due to a situation in which one or more undertakings hold a so-called 'dominant position' (a quasi-monopoly situation), which the undertakings involved take abuse of. Similarly to Art 81 ECT, it is requested that trade between Member States has to be affected. There are three notions contained in this article, which have to be analysed: 'dominant position', 'abuse' and 'may affect trade between Member States'. The latter has already been explained in chapter 2.4.1.1.5.

According to Art 83 par 2 subpar e ECT the Council is empowered to adopt a regulation or directive in order to "determine the relationship between national laws and the provisions contained in this Section or adopted pursuant to this Article."

[161] See ECJ case 6/72 (Europemballage and Continental Can).

2.4.2.1 Dominant Position

An undertaking possesses a dominant position when its economic strength on a determined market is such that it

> "enables it to hinder the maintenance of effective competition on the relevant market by allowing it to behave to an appreciable extent independently of its competitors and customers and ultimately of its consumers."[162]

Generally, one can observe that a dominant position consists of holding at least 25 % of the market share by an undertaking.[163] The Commission emphasises especially the element of market share in determining whether a dominant position exists or not. Once it can be demonstrated that 45 % is exceeded, it is nearly impossible to refute the existence of a dominant position, unless another undertaking in the same market is vested with a market share of a similar dimension.[164] However, opposed to this, in the Miller case[165] the Court highlighted the threat that trade between Member States would be appreciably affected due to the market share of the applicant, which was roughly 6 % of the German market.

In addition to market strength, other elements combined with each other can also be requested in order to verify the existence of a dominant position. For instance, the relationship between the market shares of the undertaking concerned and the market shares of its closest competitor, the existence of a highly developed sales network and the absence of potential competition or technological lead.[166] Moreover, from the wording of Art 82 ECT it follows that a dominant position can also be maintained by more undertakings together. In this case one refers to it as joint or collective dominance.[167]

To give relevance to market shares of various undertakings and to make them comparable among each other one has to define the relevant market. Two types of relevant market shall shortly be considered at this point: product/service market and geographic market.[168]

The relevant product/service market is the decisive factor that enables the Commission and courts to determine whether indeed competition is contortable by abuse. Competition between products or services exists when

---

162 See ECJ case 322/81 (Michelin); also see ECJ case 27/76 (United Bands).

163 See *Goyder*, Competition 324.

164 See ECJ case C-62/86 (AKZO).

165 See ECJ case 19/79 (Miller).

166 See particularly ECJ case 85/76 (Hoffmann-La Roche), in which the Court rejected as irrelevant a number of additional criteria mentioned by the Commission, but indicated those, which it considered important.

167 For further information about joint or collective dominance, see the decision of the European Commission in Irish Sugar, 1997.

168 See *Goyder*, Competition 325.

the end consumer can choose between different products/services. More precisely, these different products/services have to be interchangeable [169] in relation to their price, their intended usage and their characteristics.[170] The concept of cross-elasticity of demand between substitutes is a useful means in clarifying interchangeability.[171] Consequently, a relevant product market can hence be defined as comprising

> "all those products and/or services which are regarded as interchangeable or substitutable by the consumer, by reason of the product's characteristics, their prices and their intended use."[172]

What is more, a product with more than one end-use can be considered as belonging to separate product markets.[173]

Difficulties might arise regarding the service market. This is illustrated best by the banking sector. The Commission outlined that a significant number of non-financial companies have subsidiaries that deal in financial services (ie: retail banking subsidiaries of big retailers, payment cards or financing subsidiaries of big car manufacturers).[174] In other words, not only banks offer banking services. Hence, it becomes quite difficult to determine the cornerstones defining this market.

Moreover, abuse in the considered sense can also occur on a market that is distinct from the dominated one and without effects on the latter. In this respect it was clarified that these markets must be closely linked with each other.[175]

To help identifying the relevant product market the Commission issued a notice[176] in 1997, in which it outlines three main competitive constraints. The first one, demand substitution, focuses on consumer preferences and declares that in case a small (5 to 10 percent) but permanent rise in prices

---

[169] An illustrative and often cited example of a product that is not interchangeable is the banana. In fact, the Court ascertained that "the banana has certain characteristics, appearance, taste, softness, seedlessness, easy handling, a constant level of production, which enables it to satisfy the constant needs of an important section of the population consisting of the very young, the old and the sick [...] Consequently, the banana market is a market which is sufficiently distinct from the other fresh fruit markets." See ECJ case 27/72 (United Brands) and ECJ case 85/76 (Hoffmann-La Roche).

[170] See ECJ case 31/80 (L'Oreal).

[171] See ECJ case 27/76 (United Brands).

[172] See *European Commission,* Notice on the definition of relevant market for the purposes of Community competition law, 1997.

[173] See ECJ case 85/76 (Hoffmann-La Roche).

[174] See the decision of the European Commission in Price Waterhouse/Coopers & Lybrand, 1998.

[175] See CFI case T-83/91 (Tetrapak).

[176] See *European Commission,* Notice on the definition of relevant market for the purposes of Community competition law, 1997.

necessitates customers to switch to other suppliers or substitutes, as a consequence the additional suppliers or substitutes become part of the relevant market. However, to be of relevance, enough customers have to take part in this switchover.

Secondly, supply substitutability measures the degree to which suppliers are able to shift their production to new products and markets without bearing relevant additional risks or costs. This has an effect on the price tactics of those suppliers with whom the shifting suppliers have to compete in the new market. In case the suppliers are not able to enter the market without making new substantial investment, this will not be regarded as part of the original relevant product market.

Lastly, potential competition refers to factors that may gain importance in assessing demand and supply, ie information from the principal competitors in respect of their activities, the prices they pay and price-increases, which they are ready to accept from existing suppliers.

As mentioned, in addition to the relevant product/service market a dominant position is also characterised by the relevant geographic market. The above-mentioned notice also contained a definition of a relevant geographic market circumscribing it as

> "the area in which the undertakings concerned are involved in the supply and demand of products or services, in which the conditions of competition are sufficiently homogenous and which can be distinguished from neighbouring areas because the conditions of competition are appreciably different in those areas."

The geographic market is referred to by Art 82 ECT through the wording "within the common market or in a substantial part of it". Indeed, it may cover the whole Community territory, the territory of single Member States but also parts of it[177] and allows even geographic markets that are rather small.[178] However, as statistics are normally available only for the territories of the Member States or of the Community, these territories in general coincide with the limits of geographic markets.[179] Moreover, undertakings also tend to view national territories as separate markets.[180]

Nevertheless, one should bear in mind that dominance alone, even in cases where it reaches 100 %, is never sufficient enough to create a behaviour challengeable under Art 82 ECT. In fact, the abuse of the dominant position also has to be proved.[181]

---

177 See ECJ case 40/73 (Suiker Unie).

178 See the decision of the European Commission in Eurotunnel, 1994.

179 See *Mathijsen*, European Union Law 275.

180 See ECJ cases 27/76 (United Brands) and 322/81 (Michelin).

181 See *Goyder*, Competition 323.

2.4.2.2 Abuse

The concept of abuse can be characterised as an objective that is related to the behaviour of an undertaking that holds a dominant position in a given market. In order for such behaviour to constitute an abuse, it is necessary that the structure of the relevant market is influenced by this behaviour. Such behaviour must hinder the maintenance of growth of existing competition by means of methods that differ from those, which normally condition competition.[182]

To be more precise, an abuse is constituted by a behaviour of an undertaking holding a dominant position that collides

- with the freedom of access to the market or to an essential facility, or
- with one of the basic freedoms of the common market, or
- with the free choice of the purchaser or consumer.[183]

The most obvious criterion is given by the freedom of choice that remains to the other participants in the market.

Various types of abuse can be drafted. For instance, refusal to deal can constitute abuse when certain conditions are met (ie justified delivery-expectations are frustrated[184] or the refusal is motivated by the fact that a long-standing distributor promotes sales of competitors' products[185]).

Further types of abuse exist in discriminatory pricing[186] and excessive pricing. The latter means that there is no reasonable relation to the economic value of the product delivered, which eventually penalises the customer. In other words, "the margin between prices charged and costs involved is not within the normal commercial range of profit".[187] In this context a detailed cost analysis and a comparison between the prices charged and those to be paid to competitors for the same good are used to determine whether a price shall be regarded as excessive or not.[188]

Furthermore, Art 82 ECT is applicable where prices charged for a product are below its average variable costs (so-called predatory pricing) with the

---

[182] See ECJ case 85/76 (Hoffmann-La Roche).
Mathijsen stresses that Art 82 ECT refers to abuse 'of' a dominant position. This does not mean that there must be a link of causality between the dominant position and the abuse. Mathijsen outlines that "the strengthening of the position of an undertaking may constitute an abuse and be prohibited regardless of the means and procedures by which it is achieved." See *Mathijsen*, European Union Law 276 .

[183] See the decisions of the European Commission in Sea Containers/Stena, 1994 and in Landing fees at Zaventem, 1995; also see ECJ case C-55/96 (Job Centre).

[184] See ECJ case 48/69 (ICI).

[185] See ECJ case 27/76 (United Brands).

[186] This is clearly opposed to Art 82 subpar c; also see ECJ case 27/76 (United Brands).

[187] See *Goyder*, Competition 341.

[188] See ECJ case 27/76 (United Brands).

intention of eliminating competitors.[189] Rebates can form part of abuse on the condition that by this normally accepted commercial practice customers shall be urged to purchase all their requirements from one supplier.[190] In order that rebates are acceptable as a normal commercial practice,

> "they must be both clearly known to the purchaser and defined on an objective basis, the sums payable to dealers being commensurate with the task they performed and the services which they actually provided."[191]

Another type of abuse is constituted by denied access to essential facilities. In this case an undertaking refuses to allow access to a facility (ie: a port, harbour, an airport) or to an infrastructure, which it owns or controls, to competitors who require this access to carry out a service to their customers. The abuse also consists of demanding such unfavourable terms that put competitors at a competitive disadvantage.[192] In such cases, access to essential facilities is denied without any objective justification or on terms, which are less favourable compared to those on which services are normally provided, in relation to competitors as well as to customers.[193] Besides, the doctrine of essential facilities requires balancing the interests between the dominant undertaking and its rival. For instance, a refusal of access may be outweighed by a possible damage to the dominant undertaking's customers in case access is granted.[194]

A final type of abuse that shall be briefly considered in this context is the practice of tying. In this case, the dominant undertaking supplies a product on the only condition, that his customers purchase a second product (so-called tied product). Often this product can be purchased elsewhere on better terms. A similar practice is 'full-line-forcing'. In this case, a product will be supplied only on condition that a full range of products is purchased.[195] This kind of abuse is clearly exemplified in subpar d of Art 82 ECT.

2.4.3 Exemption of rules in certain economic sectors

Specific economic sectors are partly or completely exempted from the application of Art 81 and Art 82 ECT and take account of particularly sensitive areas, from a political point of view, where national interests still

[189] See ECJ case C-62/86 (AKZO).
[190] See ECJ case 85/76 (Hoffmann-La Roche).
[191] See *Goyder*, Competition 345.
[192] See ECJ case 311/84 (CBEN); also see the decision of the European Commission in Aer Lingus/British Midland Airways, 1992.
[193] See *Goyder*, Competition 349-350.
[194] See *Goyder*, Competition 349-350.
[195] See *Goyder*, Competition 350.

play a predominant role. These sectors include defence, agriculture, transport, telecommunications, postal services, banking and financial services and mergers.[196] In ordér to sharpen the understanding of the task how to enforce Art 81 and Art 82 ECT and particularly to indicate its limits, I will be briefly consider these sectors in the following subchapters.

2.4.3.1 Defence

Art 296 par 1 subpar b ECT addresses the issues of defence items and allows the exclusion from the application of the EC competition rules of any product, which is included in a list of defence items. This list is prepared by the Council of Ministers. The provision empowers Member States to take measures for the protection of essential security interests in connection with the production of, or trade in, arms, munitions, and war materials. However

> "such measures shall not adversely affect the conditions of competition in the common market regarding products, which were not intended for specifically military purposes."[197]

Arrangements for the supply of boots or thick blankets that can be used by the army as well as civilians come to mind.[198]

2.4.3.2 Agriculture

As Art 36 ECT affirms, rules of competition are applicable in the field of agricultural products only to the extent determined by the Council. In this case, the Council acts within the framework of the Common Agricultural Policy (CAP) and its requirements.[199] The objectives of the CAP are to

---

196 A further category of exclusion referred to the ECSC Treaty. As Art 305 par 1 ECT outlines, the provisions contained in the Treaty of Rome may not affect the ECSC Treaty and 'in particular as regards [...] the rules laid down by that Treaty for the functioning of the common market in coal and steel'. On 22 July 2002, the ECSC Treaty ceased being and since then, the competition rules of the EC-Treaty have to be applied.
Moreover, Art 305 par 2 ECT rules that the Treaty of Rome provisions may not derogate from those contained in the EURATOM Treaty. As the Art 81 to Art 90 ECT have no counterpart in the EURATOM Treaty, it follows that these rules will be applicable in that sector, though. See *Goyder*, Competition 76.

197 See Art 296 par 1 subpar b ECT.

198 See *Goyder*, Competition 77.

199 See Art 37 ECT.

- increase agricultural productivity by promoting technical progress, and by ensuring the rational development of agricultural production and the optimum utilisation of the factors of production, in particular labour;
- thus to ensure a fair standard of living for the agricultural community, in particular by increasing the individual earnings of persons engaged in agriculture;
- to stabilise markets;
- to assure the availability of supplies;
- to ensure that supplies reach consumers at reasonable prices.[200]

Furthermore, the CAP highlights the social function of agricultural activity and acknowledges disparities in this field between different regions.[201]

In line with the mentioned Treaty-provisions, a Council-Regulation[202] was adopted allowing the application of competition rules of the ECT, although with some exceptions.[203] Allowed cartels have to regard the production or sale of agricultural products or the use of joint facilities for the storage, treatment, or processing of agricultural products. However, these agreements may not contain an obligation to charge identical prices, and, what is more, this range of exceptions will not be applicable if such agreements exclude competition or jeopardise the objectives of Art 33 ECT. Which specific cartels do fulfil the required criteria is determined exclusively by the Commission, who published a list of exemptions.

2.4.3.3 Transport

In the field of transport, the Treaty of Rome contains special provisions[204] distinguishing between transport by road, rail, and inland waterway,[205] and additionally, empowering the Council to adopt appropriate provisions for sea and air transport.[206]

---

[200] See Art 33 ECT.
[201] See Art 33 par 2 ECT.
[202] See Council Regulation 26/62.
[203] See Art 2 Reg 26/62.
[204] See Title V, Art 70 to Art 80 ECT.
[205] See Art 80 par 1 ECT.
[206] See Art 80 par 2 ECT.

2.4.3.3.1 Transport by road, rail and inland waterway

Specific rules for transport by road, rail, and inland waterway were implemented by Reg 1017/68,[207] which generally acknowledges that Art 81 and Art 82 ECT are applicable, although with exemptions.
Firstly, an exemption is feasible with agreements that encourage technical and economic progress or foster the quality of transport services. Similarly, given the knowledge that supply and demand can fluctuate widely, exemptions can be granted for agreements that promote greater continuity and stability in satisfaction of transport needs in those markets.[208]
Another exemption is contained in Art 3 of this regulation, which exonerates agreements for standardisation of equipment or other technical matters, including co-operation of timetables and routes, and organisation of combined transport operations. Art 4 of the regulation refers to special exemptions for small and medium-sized undertakings, which are subjected to some maximum carrying capacities. A final possibility of exemption, which is at the discretion of the Commission, is provided for cases were disturbances amount to 'a state of crisis' in transport.
A specific directive facilitates competition by providing[209] for a 'right of access' in one Member State for operators of transport services on railways from other Member States. This right of access includes the establishment of railway undertakings as well as a right of transit.

2.4.3.3.2 Maritime and air transport

The application of EC competition law in the areas of maritime and air transport is quite different from the above-mentioned. This is particularly true for air transport where one can find various international treaties dealing with the matter (ie the Chicago Convention). The opening up of this sector was strongly opposed by some Member States. Hence, the Commission looked for alternatives to make competition rules applicable to the air and sea transport sector.[210] Interestingly, in the *Nouvelles Frontières* case,[211] the Court, by acknowledging that no regulation existed for air and sea transport under Art 83 ECT, drew the conclusion that Art 84 and Art 85 ECT remained

[207] See Council Reg 1017/68 of the Council of 19 July 1968 applying rules of competition to transport by rail, road and inland waterway,
[208] See Art 5 Reg 1017/68.
[209] See Council Dir 440/91 of 29 July 1991 on the development of the Community's railways.
[210] See *Goyder*, Competition 81-82.
[211] See ECJ case 209/84 (Ministère Public).

applicable. In this context, one should bear in mind that Art 84 ECT obliges national authorities to apply Art 81 (including par 3) and Art 82 ECT, when no specific relevant regulation had been adopted.
A first regulation[212] was adopted in 1986 and concerned sea transport services. To be more precise, it regulates international maritime transport services from or to a Community port with the exclusion of tramp vessel services. This regulation encloses block exemptions for certain categories of agreements if certain conditions are met. The conditions refer to safeguards of publicity, state that rates have to be charged on a non-discriminatory basis, and declare that the Commission supervisory rights do not have to be touched. A further block-exemption[213] exonerates liner shipping consortia, whose goal is to co-operate in joint operations of maritime transport services between liner shipping companies.
Regarding air transport, the Council passed a first package of measures implementing Art 81 and Art 82 ECT in 1987. This package contained two regulations (Reg 3975/87[214] and Reg 3976/87[215]), a directive and a decision. The aim of these measures was to limit the route- and capacity-sharing agreements between airlines, facilitating new discount fares, and entitling the Commission to adopt block exemptions[216] for agreements with minor effect on competition. Reg 3975 and Reg 3976 deal with domestic and international transport between Community airports, but do not cover transport between non-Community airports.[217]

2.4.3.4 Telecommunications

In the 1990s, a legislative framework was created consisting of a package of legislative measures of which one should pay particular attention to the 'Full Competition Directive,'[218] aiming to introduce competition in the telecommunication markets of the EC by requiring the Member States to

212 See Council Reg 4056/86, laying down detailed rules for the application of the Community competition rules to maritime transport.
213 See Commission Reg 823/2000 on the application of Art 81 par 3 of the Treaty to certain categories of agreements, decisions and concerted practices between liner shipping companies (consortia).
214 See Council Reg 3975/87, as amended by Reg 1284/91 and Reg 2410/92.
215 See Council Reg 3976/87, as amended by Reg 2344/90 and by Reg 2411/92.
216 See Commission Reg 1617/93, as amended by Reg 1105/2002,.
217 Goyder stresses the importance of filling this gap. See *Goyder*, Competition 85.
218 See Commission Dir 96/19/EC of 13 March 1996 amending Dir 90/388/EEC with regard to the implementation of full competition in telecommunications markets.

abrogate the existing monopoly rights in this area. Further provisions[219] focus on the transition to full liberalisation and lastly, the 'Interconnection Directive'[220] enables market players to be interconnected with other networks, provided certain conditions are met.

2.4.3.5 Banking and Financial Services

Since the mid 1980s, lots of restrictions between groups of national banks have been scrutinised by the Commission, and, as a result, agreements that fix common interest rates or commission payments have been banned. The same applies to various common rates that were agreed for collecting cheques or bills or for providing safe-deposit facilities.[221] In 1995, the Commission published a notice referring to cross-border credit transfer services, outlining the principles upon whereby it would apply Art 81 ECT. The Commission analysed agreements between participating banks and other financial institutions and ordered a withdrawal of clauses restricting competition, which impose restrictions both on their members and on retailers that participate in such schemes.

As regards insurance services, directives enable insurers to establish branches or agencies in other Member States. Due to Art 81 ECT, agreements that fix common or minimum rates for policy holders have been declared void. The leading principle in this field is that each insurance company must eventually decide on the total premium that it will charge.[222] Moreover, Council Reg 1534/91[223] authorised the Commission to adopt block exemptions that also address forms of co-operation between insurance companies. Co-operation in this field has to focus on the establishment of common-risk premium tariffs which are founded on collectively ascertained statistics, and shall also allow the introduction of certain common standard policy conditions, the establishment of common coverage of certain types of

[219] See Council Dir 92/44/EEC of 5 June 1992 on the application of open network provision to leased lines, and Dir 95/62/EC of the European Parliament and of the Council of 13 December 1995 on the application of open network provision (ONP) to voice telephony.

[220] See Dir 97/33/EC of the European Parliament and of the Council of 30 June 1997 on interconnection in Telecommunications with regard to ensuring universal service and interoperability through application of the principles of Open Network Provision (ONP).

[221] See the decisions of the European Commission in Belgian Banks, 1987 and Dutch Banks, 1989.

[222] See the decision of the European Commission in Nuovo Cegam, 1984.

[223] See Council Reg 1534/91 of 31 May 1991 on the application of Art 85 par 3 of the Treaty to certain categories of agreements, decisions and concerted practices in the insurance sector.

risk, and finally, mutual assistance on the settlement of claims. Exemptions are established in respect of public undertakings that fulfil various governmental or quasi-governmental duties. These public undertakings have to be granted special or exclusive rights by the Member States.

2.4.3.6 Mergers

The Merger Regulation[224] attempts to provide a system of unitary control for mergers with a significant Community impact. It is based on pre-notification to the Commission for evaluation and sanction and seeks to provide business with a one-stop-shop for clearance of large mergers. Herewith, the need to obtain multiple authorisations from different national authorities shall be avoided. To trigger the application of the Merger Regulation there must be a concentration of undertakings[225] having a Community dimension.[226] The former requirement is concerned with the structural alteration that is in progress, whereas the latter is directed towards the economic significance and international character of the parties' activities.[227]

2.4.4 Commission notices of a general nature

To provide undertakings with information concerning the correct application and interpretation of Art 81 and Art 82 ECT, the Commission issued several notices, which have, however, no binding effect. To complete this rather short introduction into the complexity and particulars of the application of Art 81 and Art 82 ECT, I will, at this point, illustrate the most important ones.
One of the first notices, which deals with exclusive agency contracts made with commercial agents, was published in 1962[228] and declares that certain commercial practices adopted by commercial agents are not prohibited under Art 81 par 1 ECT. More precisely, commercial agents are empowered to negotiate or conclude contracts on behalf of an enterprise for a specified part of the common market.

---

[224] See Council Reg 4064/89 on control of mergers.
[225] See Art 3 Reg 4064/89.
[226] See Art 1 Reg 4064/89.
[227] Also in this sector, a reform is on its way though. See for instance, *European Commission*, Information related to merger control activity.
[228] See *European Commission*, Notice on exclusive agency contracts made with commercial agents, 1962.

A further notice,[229] focusing on co-operation agreements, stresses the importance of co-operation between small and medium-seized enterprises (SMEs)[230] in which productivity and competitiveness should be supported. It lists eight categories of agreements that do not restrict competition, which are, among others, joint market research, co-operation in accounting matters, R&D, and joint advertising.

A Notice on the Import of Japanese products[231] was published in 1972 and concentrates on undertakings that conclude arrangements with Japanese firms with the intention of restricting imports of Japanese products into the Community. It states that such practices do not fall outside of the EC competition law just because of the mere fact that one of the parties is not situated within the EC.

In 1979 the Commission focused its attention on subcontracting agreements.[232] In a notice, the Commission indicated various types of agreements that concentrate on work distribution, primarily between SMEs, with the aim of making technology available. These agreements are not prohibited by the Treaty.

A next notice is the already mentioned *de-minimis* rule.[233]

Moreover, the ECJ recognised that EC competition rules also apply to the postal sector.[234] It was within this context that a notice[235] was published delineating guiding principles concerning the application of EC competition rules to the postal sector and considering safeguards for a universal service. The notice contains rules that, among others, refer to the duties of dominant postal operators, public undertakings and exclusive rights, services of general economic interest and freedom to provide services.

Next, the Commission has adopted notices to seek to establish some transparency and certainty in the calculation of fines as well as to offer incentives to undertakings, which co-operate with it.[236] In fact, co-operation

---

229 See *European Commission*, Notice concerning agreement, decision and concerted practices in the field of co-operation between enterprises, 1968.

230 Concerning the definition of SMEs, see *European Commission*, Recommendation of 3 April 1996 concerning the definition of small and medium-sized enterprises, 1996.

231 See *European Commission*, Notice on Import of Japanese imports, 1972.

232 See *European Commission*, Notice of 18 December 1978 concerning its assessment of certain subcontracting agreements in relation to Art 85 par 1 of the EEC Treaty.

233 See chapter 2.4.1.1.5.

234 See ECJ case C-48 (Nederlandse and Koninklijke) and ECJ case C-320/91 (Corbeau).

235 See *European Commission*, Notice from the Commission on the application of the competition rules to the postal sector and on the assessment of certain state measures relating to postal services, 1998.

236 See for instance *European Commission*, Notice on immunity of fines and reduction of fines in cartel cases, 2002.

For example, key elements of this notice are: full immunity from fines is available to the first company that comes forward, the evidence supplied should be enough for the

should be achieved by granting immunity of fines on the condition that undertakings involved in a cartel provide qualified evidence.
Finally, there is a notice, which considers the internal rules of procedure for processing requests for access to the files of cases pursuant to Art 81 and Art 82 ECT.[237] It grants a right of access to files distinguishing between 'communicable' and 'non-communicable' files.
Having explained first competition theory and then, how competition law has been phrased, evolved and interpreted in the EC – both in order to facilitate the understanding of the new division of tasks due to the reform process and more precisely the fulfilment of these tasks – I will now turn to the core of my dissertation, which is the modernisation process of the procedural rules in competition matters. In other words, I will stick to those rules that dictate how the now-clarified substantive rules have to be applied within the Community and how these procedures are going to be changed.

Commission to order an inspection though, or with a view to introducing more certainty with respect to reductions, the Commission takes a preliminary decision on the band of reduction to be applied as soon as possible.

237 See *European Commission*, Notice on the internal rules of procedure for processing requests for access to the file in cases pursuant to Art 85 and Art 86 of the EC Treaty, Art 65 and Art 66 of the ECSC Treaty and Council Reg (EEC) No 4064/89.

3 Reform of the rules implementing Art 81 and Art 82 ECT

Starting point is the fact, that Reg 17 conferred the power to grant exemptions from the prohibition as contained in Art 81 ECT, exclusively to the Commission.[238] For years though, academics, lawyers, industry and the Member States debated about whether Art 81 par 3 of the EC Treaty might become applicable in a decentralised way, in other words, the discussion concentrated on the pro's and contras of whether national courts and authorities should be empowered to apply Art 81 ECT as a whole. Rather unexpectedly, the European Commission accelerated the debate by publishing on 28 April 1999 a 'White Paper on modernisation of the rules implementing Art 85 and Art 86 of the EC Treaty':[239] a paper which summarises the problems and their reasons relating to the practical enforcement of Art 81 and Art 82 ECT and recommends solutions in response to illustrated problems.

Indeed, until then the Commission's attitude towards the application of Art 81 par 3 ECT, was strictly contrary to a possible decentralised application of it. Besides, the White Paper does not stop at this point, but goes further. Basically, it accommodates three main aspects:[240]

- the application of par 3 shall finally become decentralised,
- the authorisation system should be substituted by a legal exemption system, and as corollary,
- restraints of competition shall be controlled *ex post*.

It is generally acknowledged, that a reform of the EC competition procedural law is overdue because of a backlog in controlling restraints of competition, created by the modest resources available to the Commission to effectively enforce competition law and to protect the postulates of free competition.[241] Accordingly, it is little wonder that the White Paper and its suggestions were more than warmly welcomed. In fact, comments on the White Paper used adjectives like revolutionary[242] or highlighted its importance by declaring it as being "the most important policy paper the Commission has ever published in more than 40 years of EC competition policy."[243]

---

[238] See chapter 2.4.1.3.

[239] *European Commission*; White Paper on modernisation of the rules implementing Articles 85 and 86 of the EC treaty, 1999; hereinafter referred to as 'White Paper'.

[240] See *Bourgeois/Humpe*, The Commission's draft "New Regulation 17", ECLR 2002, 43.

[241] See *Paulweber*, Journal of World Competition 2000, 3-4; in this context, also see chapter 3.3.

[242] See *Wißmann*, Decentralised enforcement of EC Competition Law and the new policy on cartels, Journal of World Competition 2000, 123.

[243] See *Ehlermann*, The modernisation of EC Antitrust policy: a legal and cultural revolution, CMLR 2000, 537.

In less gushing words, the White Paper may clearly be seen as a cornerstone for a process that pinpoints to remodelling the application of Art 81 and Art 82 ECT. As the White Paper openly invited interested parties to comment on the proposed suggestions, it triggered a discussion surrounding a wide range of issues that were raised in this context. Various bodies (ie the EU institutions,[244] Member States and other third parties) were involved: at the closing stage of this consultation process, observations by 14 Member States and 104 formal position papers from other institutions (ie EFTA countries, ESA and competition authorities from applicant countries) had been handed in.[245]

In 2000, the White Paper was followed up by a draft regulation,[246] which replaced over, with some modifications, the main ideas of the White Paper.[247] However,

> "given the number of issues raised, it [was] unfortunate that the Commission [had] moved on to the next stage of publishing a draft regulation without either itself holding a public hearing or holding a second period of wide consultation on its revised proposal."[248]

The proposed regulation concerned itself with the preoccupations expressed during the discussion process,[249] but did not entirely reach a satisfying outcome in order to tackle the doubts highlighted during the consultation process. Finally, on 17 December 2002, the final version was adopted as Reg 1, but the outcome still is – in my opinion – not yet adequate as not all the doubts in respect of the reform that were raised since the publication of the White Paper have found a suitable solution. Reg 1 enters into force 1 May 2004.[250]

Before beginning to analyse the various matters, I want to focus on the existing procedural framework as contained in Reg 17 and afterwards clarify the motives that were put forward in order to sustain the envisaged reform. Afterwards, I will illustrate how the legal exemption system works. As the main protagonist in the modernisation process is the Commission, it seems

---

[244] The European Parliament organised a public hearing on 22 September 1999 and adopted a resolution on 18 January 2000 (the Von Wogau Report). The Social and Economic Committee adopted an opinion on 8 December 1999. See *European Commission*, White Paper on reform of Reg 17, Summary of observations, 2000.

[245] This submissions were published in the summary of observations. See fn 244.

[246] The Proposal.

[247] See *Bartosch*, Von der Freistellung zur Legalausnahme: Der Vorschlag der EG-Kommission für eine "neue Verordnung Nr. 17", EuZW 2001, 101.

[248] See *Holmes*, The EC White Paper on modernisation, Journal of World Competition 2000, 51 (52).

[249] See Explanatory Memorandum of the Proposal, 3.

[250] This is the date of the enlargement of the European Union to include 10 new Member States.

useful to begin with by outlining the Commission's role in drafting the reform, but also in working out Reg 17.

3.1 Reg 17: the 1st regulation implementing Art 81 and Art 82 ECT

3.1.1 The path that led to the adoption of Reg 17

Art 211[251] ECT grants the Commission the vest of basic executive body responsible for effectuating the implementation of the Treaty and outlines, among others, the following two tasks:
Firstly, the Commission is obliged to warrant the application of the provisions of the Treaty as well as the application of the measures that are taken by the Community bodies under the Treaty's authority. Secondly, it has to exercise those powers that are necessary to implement subordinate legislation that the Council would subscribe. These powers had to be conferred by the Council.
In the context of competition law and more precisely anti-competitive behaviour of undertakings, these obligations, which are of a rather general nature, are supplemented by Art 83 ECT,[252] and, first of all, by par 1 of this article, which is the *sine qua non* for the adoption of suitable regulations and directives by the Council. Moreover, par 2 subpar a and 2 subpar b mention two specific objectives, which have to be addressed when regulations and directives are adopted: namely, to include rules for sanctions in case of non-compliance with Art 81 par 1 and Art 82 ECT and rules for a possible exemption from the prohibition as outlined by Art 81 par 3 ECT. The appropriate implementation of these rules requires balancing effective supervision against the necessity to keep administrative procedures as simple as possible. As mentioned, the first regulation "to give effect to the principles set out in Art 81 and Art 82 ECT"[253] was Reg 17.

---

[251] Art 211 ECT reads as follows:
In order to ensure the proper functioning and development of the common market, the Commission shall:
- ensure that the provisions of this Treaty and the measures taken by the institutions pursuant thereto are applied;
- formulate recommendations or deliver opinions on matters dealt with in this Treaty, if it expressly so provides or if the Commission considers it necessary;
- have its own power of decision and participate in the shaping of measures taken by the Council and by the European Parliament in the manner provided for in this Treaty;
- exercise the powers conferred on it by the Council for the implementation of the rules laid down by the latter.

[252] For the complete text of Art 83, see fn 33.

[253] Art 83 par 1 ECT.

It is the Commission's task, and more precisely, those of DG IV to establish the detailed content of these rules as well as its exemptions. In other words, it was DG IV's duty to find the appropriate procedural instrument enabling the proper enforcement of these Treaty-articles throughout the Community.
Before Reg 17 was adopted, DG IV evaluated the existing national competition laws of the Member States and considered particularly two mainstream: one reflecting the French approach of competition rules, which comprehended a legal exemption system and another one favouring the German approach with its notification system. The French approach considered the possibility for undertakings to decide themselves, whether the agreement concerned was in line with the competition law and hence followed the idea of a legal exemption system. On the other hand, the German solution envisaged a notification system, providing for an individual or group exemption to be pronounced by competition authorities. This method was the approach adopted by the ECSC.[254]
Besides, a committee of the European Parliament charged with the evaluation of the proposed Regulation, examined a third possible method, which the Commission could consider in implementing Art 81 and Art 82 ECT. This followed the system as adopted by the Dutch national legislation and specified that all restrictive agreements have to be notified. This notification implied a presumption of validity, which, in order to be refuted, had to be opposed by evidence put forward by the competition authority outlining that the agreement constitutes an abuse. This presumption of validity had only prospective effect. Eventually, the Parliamentary Committee approved the German solution and declared that this approach was the most consistent with the actual terms of the Treaty. Moreover, this system provided the Commission with the widest knowledge regarding the various types of agreements, which were concluded by undertakings within the Community. Furthermore, the Parliament's report proposed the insertion of a negative clearance procedure.[255] Herewith, the Commission should be given the power to certify that the competition provisions concerned did not apply in an individual case, because of the missing requirements as asked by Art 81 and Art 82 ECT. Nevertheless, this negative clearance automatically lost its validity where the circumstances and conditions, under which it had been granted, changed subsequently. This procedure became part of the final version of Reg 17.[256]

---

[254] See *Goyder*, Competition 36.
[255] Although not part of German competition law.
[256] See *Goyder*, Competition 37-38.
An alternative method to deal with the agreements was proposed by the so-called Deringer Report, which favoured an opposition procedure comparable to the one used in German law. This procedure allowed a provisional validity of agreements, in case no specific opposition is raised within six months from the date of the notification.

Eventually, the French procedure outlining that no prior decision of the Commission was needed before a restrictive agreement could be declared void, was considered as not reconcilable with the text of Art 81 ECT. The final wording, which was adopted for Reg 17, contained a mechanism allowing notified agreements to be declared valid, after being contemplated by the Commission.[257]

The Commission's position towards the proposed regulation was rather ambivalent: on the one hand it feared the sheer size and scope of the jurisdiction, and hence, it appreciated to share it to some extent with Member States. On the other hand, it did not assign Member States and their national courts the power to apply the exemption provisions. In fact, the Commission feared, that a divided application of these latter competencies could signify the loss of control over the system and would eventually weaken the system's effectiveness as well as its consistency.[258]

However, the conviction succeeded that such a procedure would move too far away from the prohibition principle, which is the cornerstone of the cartel law. It was also found, that an administrative body which does not have any adequate case law experience might not be able to operate such a system. Nevertheless, the opposition procedures have been adopted by block exemptions. In this context, Goyder emphasises that "it is a characteristic of a mature competition authority that it has such experience upon the basis of which decisions can be issued more speedily than is possible in its early days." See *Goyder*, Competition 37.

[257] See *Goyder*, Competition 36.

[258] See *Goyder*, Competition 38-39.
Moreover, the Commission explains that in the early sixties, national competition authorities had only been recently instituted or did not even exist. Hence, no significant experience existed in this field, neither on national level, nor on Community level, as the case law of the ECJ was rather humble. See White Paper par 15.
Moreover, a coherent development of the Competition policy called upon the granting of centralised control and a monopoly in applying Art 81 par 3 ECT to the Commission: a system that was eventually realised by Reg 17 whose aim consisted in guaranteeing a uniform and coherent development of competition policy throughout the Community and ultimately envisaged market integration. See *Wißmann*, Journal of World Competition 2000, 124-125; see White Paper par 16 and par 17; see *Ehlermann*, CMLR 2000, 540.
According to Art 83 par 2 subpar e, Art 84 and Art 85 ECT, enforcement of competition policy requires co-operation between the Commission and Member States. Goyder highlights that it is remarkable that the Treaty provided for such co-operation, as in the late fifties competition law in the six Member State was in a rather primitive state or did not even exist. In fact, neither Italy, nor Belgium nor Luxembourg had adopted competition laws. The legal system of the Netherlands enclosed an Economic Competition Act, which required registration of restrictive agreements but contained the possibility of granting exemptions on quite a liberal basis. The French Competition Law's concern focused on vertical agreements. It can be said that the only Member State that had relatively comprehensive competition law, was Germany. However, due

On 6 February 1962 the Council approved Reg 17. It also embraced Art 82 ECT, although initially not intended. Reg 17 was published in the Official Journal on 21 February of the same year and it became effective on the following 13 March.

That said, I want to consider the various provisions of Reg 17. For a comprehensible understanding of the law it seems useful to me to begin by delineating those provisions that refer to investigations in the field of infringements of Art 81 and Art 82 ECT, then I will lay down the exemption regime contained in Reg 17 and which implements Art 81 par 3 ECT, afterwards I will outline the various decisions the Commission is empowered to adopt with particular concern to possible informal instruments.

3.1.2 The detailed provisions of Reg 17

Reg 17 declared that agreements, decisions, concerted practices and the abuse of a dominant position within the meaning of Art 81 and Art 82 ECT respectively were prohibited, and no prior notification being required.[259] In order to protect this prohibition, the Commission could initiate an investigation into suspected business practices that might run counter to the prohibition of Art 81 and Art 82 ECT. This could be done by the Commission *ex officio* or due to a complaint submitted by a natural or legal person.[260] In this context, Art 3 Reg 17[261] indicated that a possible complaint had to be based on a legitimate interest.[262]

It was questioned whether the Commission was allowed to reject a complaint. In this respect, the Community courts ascertained that this lay at the discretion of the Commission in case the issue at stake did not justify further investigation due to a lack of sufficient Community interest.[263] This means that the Commission might apply different degrees of priority in respect of cases submitted to it. Such discretion is consistent with the Commission's obligation under Community law, which obliges the Commission to draw its attention to the Community interest. More illustrative, it had to take into consideration the claimed violation in respect of the proper

---

to the fact that this law was adopted recently, the German legal system lacked experience in its application. See *Goyder*, Competition 32.

259 In this respect, Art 1 Reg 17 determined that "[...] agreements, decisions and concerted practices of the kind described in Article 85 (1) of the Treaty and the abuse of a dominant position in the market, within the meaning of Article 86 of the Treaty, shall be prohibited, no prior decision to that effect being required."

260 See Art 3 Reg 17.

261 See Art 3 par 2 subpar b Reg 17.

262 Also see in this context ECJ case 792/79 (Camera Care).

263 See CFI case T-114/92 (Industries Musicales).

functioning of the common market, the scope of the investigation required or the probability of determining the existence of the violation.[264]

The proceedings of investigations were formally opened by a 'Statement of Objections', that the Commission sent to the undertaking in question and by which the latter got informed about the points to which the Commission objected. In addition, the undertaking concerned had to be heard at its own request, by the Commission.[265]

The competencies to accomplish the duties effectively were indicated in Art 10 to Art 14 Reg 17. Indeed, Art 14 empowered the Commission to commence all necessary investigations and granted officials the following competencies:[266]

They were enabled

- to inspect books and other business records,
- to take copies of books or business records, to interrogate on the premises of the undertaking investigated and
- to enter any premises or vehicle or land belonging to the undertaking under investigation.[267]

These powers could be exercised with the consent of the undertaking or in the absence of such a consent, due to a decision of the Commission and hence in a compulsory manner.[268] To decide how these competencies were adopted was at the discretion of the Commission.[269]

---

264 See CFI case T-24/90 (Automec II).

265 See Art 19 par 1 and par 2 Reg 17.
See also Commission Reg 99/63 governing procedures of hearings of individual cases by the Commission, as replaced by Commission Reg 2842/98.

266 "The officials of the Commission authorised for the purpose of these investigations shall exercise their powers upon production of an authorisation in writing specifying the subject matter and purpose of the investigation and the penalties provided for in Article 15 (1) (c) in cases where production of the required books or other business records is incomplete. [...]." See Art 14 par 2 Reg 17.

267 However, the confidentiality of written communications between lawyer and client is preserved in case (i) such communications aim to and are in the interest of the client's defence and (ii) they derive from independent lawyers, ie lawyers who are not bound to the client by a relationship of employment. See ECJ case 155/79 (AM & S).

268 See Art 14 par 2 and par 3 Reg 17.
"[...] The decision shall specify the subject matter and purpose of the investigation, appoint the date on which it is to begin and indicate the penalties provided for in Article 15 (1) (c) and Article 16 (1) (d) and the right to have the decision reviewed by the Court of Justice." See Art 14 par 3 Reg 17.
Moreover, these decisions must only be taken "after consultation with the competent authority of the Member State in whose territory the investigation is to be made." See Art 14 par 4 Reg 17.

269 See ECJ case 136/79 (National Panasonic).

Moreover, investigation made on the spot, necessitated co-operation with national authorities. This was illustrated in the Hoechst-case,[270] which determines that the Commission officials have no right to use force to enter business premises, when they want to examine documents, but they are requested to ask for appropriate authorisation from national courts.[271] A power, which was not included in Art 14 Reg 17, is one by which employees or directors of undertakings can be ordered to attend a hearing and to submit relevant documents for that purpose.[272]

Art 11 and Art 13 Reg 17 contained the obligation of national governments and their competent authorities to co-operate with the Commission. This included that

> "the Commission [might] obtain all necessary information from the Governments and competent authorities of the Member States and from undertakings and associations of undertakings."[273]

In respect of the latter, only

> "the owners of the undertakings or their representatives and, in the case of legal persons, companies or firms, or of associations having no legal personality, the persons authorised to represent them by law or by their constitution [should] supply the information requested."[274]

Penalties were provided for supplying incorrect information.[275] In case an undertaking did not supply the information requested or supplied incomplete

---

[270] See ECJ case 46/87 (Hoechst).

[271] Moreover, in respect of co-operation between the Commission and national authorities, Art 14 Reg 17 provided for the following rules:
"[...] In good time before the investigation, the Commission shall inform the competent authority of the Member State in whose territory the same is to be made of the investigation and of the identity of the authorised officials." See Art 14 par 2.
"Officials of the competent authority of the Member State in whose territory the investigation is to be made may, at the request of such authority or of the Commission, assist the officials of the Commission in carrying out their duties." See Art 14 par 5.
"Where an undertaking opposes an investigation ordered pursuant to this Article, the Member State concerned shall afford the necessary assistance to the officials authorised by the Commission to enable them to make their investigation. Member States shall, after consultation with the Commission, take the necessary measures to this end before 1 October 1962." See Art 14 par 6.

[272] See *Goyder*, Competition 44.

[273] More specifically, "when sending a request for information to an undertaking or association of undertakings, the Commission shall at the same time forward a copy of the request to the competent authority of the Member State in whose territory the seat of the undertaking or association of undertakings is situated." See Art 11 par 1 Reg 17.

[274] See Art 11 par 4 Reg 17.

[275] See Art 11 par 3 Reg 17.

information, the Commission could adopt a decision ordering the information to be supplied, indicating the penalties for non-compliance.[276]
Next, the necessary investigations could be assisted or even undertaken by the competent authorities of the Member States.[277]
Mandatory co-operation demanded that copies of the most important documents in each individual case in possession of the Commission had to be sent to the Member States.[278] This procedure had to be conducted in close and constant *liaison* with competent authorities also providing the authorities with the right to express their view.[279] The idea of co-operation furthermore established an Advisory Committee that was composed of representatives of the Member States. It was only enabled to express its views in respect of the application of Art 81 and Art 82 ECT and accordingly had no power of veto. The proceedings were strictly confidential.[280]
In the spirit of Art 81 par 3 ECT, Reg 17 also contained an exemption system, based on the notification of the agreement concerned.[281] The exemption granted could not come into force on a date earlier than the date, on which the cartel was notified to the Commission[282] and its validity had to be for a specific period. It was also possible, that conditions and obligations were attached to it; provisions also dealt with a renewal of the exemption and also

[276] See Art 11 par 5 Reg 17.
[277] See Art 13 Reg 17.
[278] In fact, in this respect, Art 10 par 1 Reg 17 declared that "the Commission shall forthwith transmit to the competent authorities of the Member States a copy of the applications and notifications together with copies of the most important documents lodged with the Commission for the purpose of establishing the existence of infringements of Articles 85 or 86 of the Treaty or of obtaining negative clearance or a decision in application of Article 85 (3)."
[279] See Art 10 par 2 Reg 17.
[280] Art 10 par 3 Reg 17 determined that "an Advisory Committee on Restrictive Practices and Monopolies shall be consulted prior to the taking of any decision following upon a procedure under paragraph 1, and of any decision concerning the renewal, amendment or revocation of a decision pursuant to Article 85 (3) of the Treaty." Also see par 4 to par 6 of this article.
[281] The relevant provisions were contained in Art 4 Reg 17 par 1, which reads as follows: "Agreements, decisions and concerted practices of the kind described in Article 85 (1) of the Treaty which come into existence after the entry into force of this Regulation and in respect of which the parties seek application of Article 85 (3) must be notified to the Commission. Until they have been notified, no decision in application of Article 85 (3) may be taken."
As mentioned in chapter 2.4.1.3.1, a specific Commission regulation specifies the form, content and other details of applications and notifications under Reg 17.
Interestingly, in the Koelman-case (CFI Case T-575/93), the CFI found that Art 81 ECT does not grant a person who files an application the right to receive from the Commission a decision within the meaning of Art 249 ECT.
[282] See Art 6 par 1 Reg 17.

contained the possibility of revoking it.[283] Furthermore, once notified, an agreement could no longer serve as ground for the imposition of a fine by the Commission.[284]

It is clear that an exemption can only be granted when the detailed conditions as set out by Art 81 par 3 ECT are met. Detailed rules for implementation of the exemption under par 3 could be found in Art 6 and Art 8 Reg 17. Due to the fact that the submission of the notification was, at the end, at the discretion of the undertaking, a possible grant of an exemption could enter into force from the date of the notification and not with effect of the date when the agreement had been made.[285] Next, for the application of an exemption a concrete period had to be specified.[286] This rarely exceeded 10 years.[287] Moreover, the exemption might be renewed[288] and under determined circumstances be amended or revoked.[289]

Next, with the adoption of Reg 17 the jurisdiction over the application of Art 81 par 3 ECT had been removed from national authorities to the exclusive competence of the Commission.[290] Additionally, Art 9 par 3 Reg 17 clarified that the application of the Art 81 par 1 and Art 82 ECT by the Member States was possible only until the Commission actually initiated a procedure against an undertaking.[291] In the Delimitis-case[292] the ECJ confirmed the inability of

---

283 See Art 8 Reg 17.

284 See Art 15 par 5 Reg 17.

285 In this concern, Art 6 Reg 17 clarified that "whenever the Commission takes a decision pursuant to Article 85 (3) of the Treaty, it shall specify therein the date from which the decision shall take effect. Such a date shall not be earlier than the date of notification."

286 Also obligations might be attached thereto. See Art 8 par 1 Reg 17.

287 See *Goyder*, Competition 43.

288 "[...] if the requirements of Article 85 (3) of the Treaty continue to be satisfied." See Art 8 par 2 Reg 17.
The ECJ clarified that in case circumstances had changed since the date of the original exemption, these renewal conditions were adaptable by DG IV to the new reality. See ECJ Case 17/74 (Transocean Marine Paint Association).

289 Indeed, "the Commission may revoke or amend its decision or prohibit specified acts by the parties:
(a) where there has been a change in any of the facts which were basic to the making of the decision;
(b) where the parties commit a breach of any obligation attached to the decision;
(c) where the decision is based on incorrect information or was induced by deceit;
(d) where the parties abuse the exemption from the provisions of Article 85 (1) of the Treaty granted to them by the decision. In cases to which subparagraphs (b), (c) or (d) apply, the decision may be revoked with retroactive effect." See Art 8 par 3 Reg 17.

290 The Commission's decision was only subjected to review by the Court of Justice. See Art 9 par 1 Reg 17.

291 In fact, Art 9 par 3 Reg 17 determined that "as long as the Commission has not initiated any procedure under Articles 2, 3 or 6, the authorities of the Member States shall remain competent to apply Article 85 (1) and Article 86 in accordance with Article

national courts to grant individual exemptions to agreements under Art 81 par 3 ECT and also addressed the possibility of the Commission to attach obligations to the exemption. A breach of these conditions resulted in the withdrawal of the exemption.

Reg 17 also dealt with the notification for already existing agreements at the date of entry into force of the regulation.[293] However, for this kind of agreement rather short time limits were scheduled. This fact was criticised by US and European industrial and commercial concerns as it was feared that the Commission, given its limited resources, might not have time enough to consider these agreements in an adequate manner. The raised criticism proved to be well founded.[294]

Explicitly excluded from this notification procedure were those business practices, which, because of their very nature, were considered to distort competition between Member States less likely.[295]

Three categories could be identified:

- Firstly, those agreements were exempted, in which the parties were undertakings from one Member State and the agreements did neither refer to imports nor exports between Member States.[296]
- Secondly, also excluded were agreements, which limited the freedom of one party in fixing prices or setting certain conditions of business. This limitation had to refer to goods purchased from a party "at a different level of the production or distribution chain", which were to be resold. Moreover, this category also referred to restrictions on the

---

88 of the Treaty; they shall remain competent in this respect notwithstanding that the time limits specified in Article 5 (1) and in Article 7 (2) relating to notification have not expired."

In the BRT/Sabam-case the ECJ clarified that a national judge is no longer able to decide on the application of Community competition law, once the Commission has initiated the procedure.

Moreover, Art 9 par 3 Reg 17 demanded for a formal procedure-initiation before the Commission is allowed to adopt any decision. This initiation was not a separate act, which could be tackled in Court. See ECJ case 60/81 (IBM).

[292] See ECJ case C-234/89 (Delimitis).

[293] See Art 5 par 1 Reg 17, which reads as follows:

1. Agreements, decisions and concerted practices of the kind described in Article 85 (1) of the Treaty, which are in existence at the date of entry into force of this Regulation, and in respect of which the parties seek application of Article 85 (3) shall be notified to the Commission before 1 November 1962. However, notwithstanding the foregoing provisions, any agreements, decisions and concerted practices to which not more than two undertakings are party shall be notified before 1 February 1963.

[294] See *Goyder*, Competition 42.

[295] See *Goyder*, Competition 41.

[296] See Art 4 par 2 subpar 1 Reg 17.

exercise of industrial property rights or which concerned the use and application of industrial processes.[297]

- The last category regarded agreements, whose sole object was the standardisation or joint research and development or specialisation agreements. The products of such specialisation could not have more than 15 % of the volume of business done in the common market. Moreover, the total annual turnover of the parties to the agreement could not exceed 200 million units of the account.[298]

In all these 3 cases, notification for being granted an exemption according to Art 81 par 3 ECT, was voluntary. As a result, "the grant of an exemption at a later stage [could] be retrospective to the date when the agreement was made."[299]

The final and closing stage of the investigation-proceeding was formally reached by a decision, either declaring that Art 81 and Art 82 ECT were not applicable in a specific case[300] or that an ascertained legal infringement had to be put to an end.

Additionally, a so-called 'comfort letter' (or 'administrative letter') provided for the same result, although with some limitations especially concerning the binding effect of these letters. The Commission could issue two kinds of comfort letters: an enhanced[301] and an informal one. Whereas with the former the Commission outlined that there are no reasons for intervention, with the latter it stated that it saw no reason to issue a formal decision. Before an enhanced comfort letter was sent, the Commission had to publish a notice in the Official Journal in which it briefly illustrated the cartel and with which it invited the interested parties to submit comments on the issue.

Concerning the missing binding effect, the Court affirmed in the Lancôme case[302] that the letters in question were issued neither by the means of the publication as laid down in Art 19 par 3 Reg 17, nor published pursuant to Art 21 par 1 Reg 17. However, even though they were informal, national courts had to take them into account as important indications.[303] A further

---

297 See Art 4 par 2 subpar 2 Reg 17.

298 See Art 4 par 2 subpar 3 Reg 17.

299 See *Goyder*, Competition 42.

300 So-called 'negative clearance'. The concerned rules were contained in Art 2 Reg 17, which reads as follows:
"Upon application by the undertakings or associations of undertakings concerned, the Commission may certify that, on the basis of the facts in its possession, there are no grounds under Article 85 (1) or Article 86 of the Treaty for action on its part in respect of an agreement, decision or practice."
As EC law did not apply, national rules remained applicable. See *Hirsch/Burkart* in Gleiss/Hirsch, Kommentar 35.

301 See Art 19 par 3 Reg 17.

302 See ECJ case 99/79 (Lancôme).

303 See ECJ case 37/79 (Marty).

reason for their non binding effect can be found in the fact that these comfort letters were emanated from a top official of the Commission and hence, they did not bind the Commission itself. Since such letters involved much less delays than a formal decision, more and more undertakings had asked for it. The Court ascertained that such a letter was based only upon the facts, which were in possession of the Commission and that the procedure of examination was brought to an end by the department of the Commission that is responsible for this. Consequently, national courts before which the agreements concerned were claimed to be contrary to Art 81 ECT, were not prevented from seeking a different conclusion regarding the agreements concerned, due to the information available to them.[304] As will be seen, comfort letters and their missing binding effect have been an important motive for the reform.

Even though not explicitly mentioned in Reg 17, the Commission was also empowered to adopt interim measures. In fact, in the Camera Care case,[305] the ECJ concluded that the Commission was entitled under Art 3 Reg 17 to take interim measures that are indispensable for the efficient effective exercise of its function.

> "However, the Commission could not take such measures without having regard to the legitimate interests of the undertaking concerned by them. For this reason it is essential that interim measures be taken only in cases proved to be urgent in order to avoid a situation likely to cause serious and irreparable damage to the party seeking their adaptation, or which is intolerable for the public interest. A further requirement is that these measures be of a temporary and conservatory nature and restricted to what is required in the given situation."[306]

Further articles of Reg 17 contained clauses of value to the Commission in its administrative task and imposed substantial fines and penalties.[307] A fine could be imposed for past conduct where undertakings had taken part in agreements or practices, which were prohibited under Art 81 and Art 82

---

304 See *Hirsch/Burkart* in Gleiss/Hirsch, Kommentar 35.

305 See ECJ case 792/79 (Camera Care); also see ECJ Case 228/82 (Ford Werke), where interim measures were suspended.

306 See ECJ case 792/79 (Camera Care).

307 In 2002 the Commission adopted nine decisions imposing fines totalling about 1,000,000,000.– EUR: Austrian Banks, Methionine, Industrial and medical gases, Fine art auction houses, Plasterboard, Methylglucamine, Concrete reinforcing bars, Specialty graphites and Food flavour enhancers. See *European Commission*, XXXIInd report of competition policy, 19-23.

ECT,[308] but also where incorrect or misleading information had been given during the course of the investigation.[309]
As already mentioned, fines were not imposed though in respect of acts conducted after notification had been made unless preliminary warning had been given.[310] Moreover, the Commission produced a Notice on the non-imposition or reduction of fines for those enterprises that do co-operate with the Commission during an investigation concerning a cartel.[311]
Art 16 Reg 17 dealt with penalties. They had to be paid for each subsequent day where an undertaking did not stop the infringement condemned by a decision[312] or in case it did not supply the information, which had to be put forward throughout the course of an investigation. [313] In this context, one shall be aware that according to Art 229 ECT the ECJ may challenge every decision of the Commission. Accordingly, the ECJ can cancel, reduce, and increase fines or penalties respectively.
Next, Art 19 Reg 17 dealt with natural justice and gave undertakings the possibility to be heard on matters, which the Commission intended to raise. Such rights were also given to other natural or legal persons having sufficient interest.[314]

---

[308] In this case, "the Commission [might] by decision impose on undertakings or associations of undertakings fines of 1,000 to 1,000,000 units of account, or a sum in excess thereof but not exceeding 10 % of the turnover in the preceding business year of each of the undertakings participating in the infringement." See Art 15 par 2 Reg 17.

[309] In this case, "the Commission may by decision impose on undertakings or associations of undertakings fines of 100 to 5,000 units of account." See Art 15 par 1 Reg 17.

[310] See Art 15 par 5 and par 6 Reg 17.

[311] See chapter 2.4.4.
However, the conditions asked for are very strict and the 'co-operating' undertaking will not get information about whether a reduction will be granted, before the end of the procedure.

[312] See for instance the decision of the European Commission in IMA-Statuut, 1980.

[313] According to Art 16 par of Reg 17, a fine could amount from "50 to 1,000 units of account per day, calculated from the date appointed by the decision" and compel businesses
(a) to put an end to an infringement of Article 85 or 86 of the Treaty, in accordance with a decision taken pursuant to Article 3 of this Regulation;
(b) to refrain from any act prohibited under Article 8 (3) [Reg 17];
(c) to supply complete and correct information which it has requested by decision taken pursuant to Article 11 (5) [Reg 17];
(d) to submit to an investigation which [the Commission] has ordered by decision taken pursuant to Article 14 (3) [Reg 17].

[314] See Art 19 par 2 Reg 17.
See also ECJ case 26/76 (Metro) in which competitors and customers were acknowledged of having sufficient interest and hence empowered them to object to decisions by the Commission, which were claimed to have prejudiced them.

According to Art 19 par 3 Reg 17, the Commission was obliged to publish any proposed decisions, which concerned either a negative clearance or an exemption in the sense of Art 81 par 3 ECT. These statements had to be published in the Official Journal in order to enable interested parties to put forward their observations within a time-period that did exceed at least one month. This publication consisted of a summary of the cartel or abuse, which was the object of the decision. As the Court found, respect for the rights of the defence

> "requires that any person who may be adversely affected by the adoption of a decision should be placed in a position in which he may effectively make known his views in the evidence against him, which the Commission has taken as the basis for the decision at issue."[315]

Lastly, Art 21 Reg 17 determined that final decisions had to be published thoroughly in the Official Journal whilst being obliged to consider requirements of business secrecy. In this context, two delicate subjects were discussed controversially and were also at stake at the European courts: one concerned the theme of 'business secrets', another one regarded the right of access to the Commission files by the undertakings, which are involved in proceedings. Concerning business secrets the Court outlined that the obligation of professional secrecy is laid down in the Treaty itself.[316] In respect of the right of access to files, one shall know that this is - although not explicitly provided for by Reg 17 - generally admitted and recognised by the Court. It is the result of 'due process' requiring that undertakings are enabled to have access to the files, which are in possession of the Commission.[317]

3.2 Objectives and reasons for the process of modernisation

As described above, the system under Reg 17 compelled an undertaking to file a notification to the Commission exclusively if the undertaking concerned intended to adopt measures that *prima facie* contrasted EC competition rules. It was also emphasised the motives (lack of competition culture in the Member States, creation of the common market[318]) behind the approach adopted in 1962. Nowadays, it is acknowledged that this system proved to be successful in helping to shape a European culture of open markets and of free competition through "the implementation of a modern competition policy

[315] See CFI case T-450/93 (Lisrestal).

[316] See ECJ case 53/85 (Akzo).

[317] See ECJ case 85/76 (Hoffmann-La Roche).

[318] See also chapter 3.1.1.

in Member States that did not have considerable competition laws before"[319] and by establishing a body of rules that is accepted by Member States and industry as essential for the appropriate functioning of the internal market.[320] However, the system of prior notification as designed by Reg 17 was also seen as the root for the enormous administrative burden that lay upon the Commission in acting upon the notifications. In fact, due to this obligation, the Commission and more precisely DG IV was - and still is - confronted by masses of notifications filed by undertakings thus creating an enormous administrative burden on the European Commission in the field of competition surveillance and thereby handicapping its efficiency.[321]

The massive submission of notifications with its hampering effect on the work-capacities of the Commission had already emerged in the sixties. In fact, by the end of 1967, more than 37,000 cases had already been submitted.[322] Quite interestingly, at the time that Reg 17 came into force, a high number of notifications had been predicted.[323] Over the years, the number of cases has increased progressively due to factors like ongoing market integration and expansion of the European Community. This trend has been inverted in the late 90's, even though the number of notifications is still at a high level. Moreover, it is correctly outlined that the reform of law of vertical restraints fosters this tendency.[324] In fact, from 1999 to 2002 the numbers of submitted notifications per year has declined from 162 to 101.[325]

The crisis is a direct result of the fact that Art 81 ECT was continuously interpreted in a rather extensive way,[326] thus considerably enhancing the possibilities for exemptions under Art 81 par 3 ECT.[327] Even though Art 4 Reg 17 tried to limit the number of agreements notified to the Commission

---

319 See *Paulweber*, Journal of World Competition 2000, 11.

320 See *European Commission*, White Paper, executive summary par 4.

321 See *Paulweber*, Journal of World Competition 2000, 3; also see Immenga, Eine Wende in der gemeinschaftsrechtlichen Kartellpolitik?, EuZW 1999, 609.

322 See *Paulweber*, Journal of World Competition2000, fn 42.
One shall also bear in mind that a formal adoption of an exemption decision is proceeded by several steps, involving a consultation procedure with the Advisory Committee and publication of a notice of the initiated procedure and the adopted decision in the Official Journal in the 11 official languages.

323 By the end of 1961, the Economic and Social Committee warned that Reg 17 with its obligatory notification and authorisation system might overload the Commission with administrative work. See White Paper par 43.

324 See *Paulweber*, Journal of World Competition 2000, 12-13

325 See *European Commission*, XXXIInd Report on competition policy 2002, 46.

326 See also chapter 2.4.1.1., in which this fact was described.

327 See *Holmes*, Journal of World Competition 2000, 54; also see *Rittner*, Kartellpolitik und Gewaltenteilung in der EG, EuZW 2000, 129.

(particularly agreements in the field of vertical co-operation), too many of them were registered.
A further aspect that circumvented effective supervision and which also hampered decentralisation was found in Art 9 par 3 Reg 17: by applying an exemption under Art 81 par 3 ECT undertakings could shift the jurisdiction from a national authority to the Commission. This was quite popular in case the national competition authority might adopt a prohibition under Art 81 par 1 ECT. In fact, the number of these so-called 'obstructive notifications' had steadily increased.[328]
Besides, other factors have increased the Commission's tasks and therefore inhibited its performance in the field of competition monitoring as well. For instance, due to the increasing penetration of national markets and the subsequent creation of the common market, the Commission's duties in the field of competition have been expanded considerably. In addition, co-operation agreements with third countries as well as the economic globalisation in general, have widened the Commission's sphere of activities in this context[329] and will ultimately present new challenges in order to keep markets open and preserve competitive structures.[330]
Moreover, one has to bear in mind that the European Community was founded by six Member States: consequently, the initial rules and laws were tailored to meet the demands of six states only. Nowadays, the Community has 15 members and will soon reach a number of 25.[331] The envisaged enlargement of the Union could especially exacerbate the current problems, as accession states might present a higher number of competition issues due to their relatively recent transition to free market economies and principles. Hence, the work to be accomplished by DG IV is more likely to be increased than decreased.[332]
In order to gain control over this flood of notifications and to speed up the Commission's proceedings, various instruments were adopted (ie block exemptions, notices aimed to clarifying the content of Art 81 and Art 82 ECT, comfort letters).[333]

---

[328] See *Paulweber*, Journal of World Competition 2000, 15.
[329] See White Paper par 19.
[330] See *Ehlermann*, CMLR 2000, 545.
[331] See White Paper par 21.
[332] See *Holmes*, Journal of World Competition 2000, 54; and *Wißmann*, Journal of World Competition 2000, 127.
[333] In respect of comfort letters, the Commission acknowledges that due to their informality, the principle of publication and transparency is watered down. Its informality is further underlined by the fact, that neither national courts nor national competition authorities are bound by comfort letters which are degraded to simple elements of fact. See White Paper par 35; also see ECJ case 99/79 (Lancôme).

In the 1990's, the Commission also tried to persuade undertakings to turn their complaints to national courts or authorities, first by adopting a Notice on co-operation with national courts in February 1993,[334] and later by publishing a Notice on co-operation with national competition authorities in October 1997.[335] However, both notices did not affect the exemption monopoly, which the Commission has in applying Art 81 par 3 ECT. As a result, even these endeavours did not prove to be successful.[336] Indeed, the Commission stresses that complainants are not eager to apply to national courts and/or authorities in case they were damaged by an infringement of EC competition law. [337]

The whole dilemma of work-overload is better illustrated by the following figures: as a result of the usage of comfort letters to tackle the issues raised through notifications, by 1999 only 222 decisions had been adopted since the entry into force of Reg 17 in 1962.[338] In the period from 1990 to 1999 only 5 formal exemption decisions were issued on average per year.[339] Moreover, the backlog that had been generated since the first notifications were handed in, was never totally eliminated. By the end of the 1990's it amounted to about 1,000 notifications.[340] The Commission has to deal with

On the other hand, Paulweber outlines that "despite these indisputable drawbacks and the massive critique, the comfort letter system worked very well and won general acceptance. The critique, although theoretically and systematically convincing, has turned out to be largely academic. Some legal uncertainties, however, have always remained, thereby distorting incentives to invest and the like." See *Paulweber*, Journal of World Competition 2000, 14.

334 In 1993, the Commission issued a Notice on co-operation between the Commission and the national judges in order to take account of several judgements of the ECJ (ie case C-234/89 [Delimitis]). It shall be mentioned that it is primarily the national judge who is responsible for the application of the Community competition law. See ECJ case 127/73 (BRT). In such cases, the national rules of procedure and admissibility apply to appeals (See ECJ case 158/80 [Rewe]). See *European Commission*, Notice on co-operation between national courts and the Commission applying Art 85 and Art 86 of the EEC Treaty, 1993.

335 Hereby, the Commission stressed that national authorities should normally deal with cases that primarily affect their territories and which also do not seem, on preliminary examination, to qualify for exemption under Art 81 par 3 ECT. See *European Commission*, Notice on co-operation between national competition authorities and the Commission in handling cases falling within the scope of Articles 85 and 86 of the EC Treaty, 1997.

336 See *Wißmann*, Journal of World Competition 2000, 136.

337 See White Paper par 39.

338 Ehlermann in referring to Forrester, see *Ehlermann*, CMLR 2000, fn 10.

339 See *Ehlermann*, CMLR 2000, 541.

340 See *Ehlermann*, CMLR 2000, 541.
However, these figure also seem to be in decline. In fact, whereas in 1999 there were still 1,013 cases pending, in 2002 this figure had shrunk to 805. See *European Commission*, XXXIInd Report of competition policy, 47.

about 200 notifications each year of which 90% are closed informally. For the remaining 10 % it takes generally two to three years from notification to reach a formal decision.[341] Furthermore, Holmes[342] indicates that roughly 1 percent of notifications concern real competition problems. It results that the limited resources of DG IV mainly deal with inoffensive agreements diverting their attention away from serious cartels that significantly harm competition in the European Union. This opinion is in line with the Commission's arguments, which admits that most serious restrictions are generally not notified and thus have to be scrutinized *ex officio*.[343] Obviously, the fact that the massive notification-stream hindered the Commission to initiate procedures on own initiative (for instance, in 1998-1999 only 13 % of the Commission's work consisted of own-initiative procedures) or to adopt formal decisions (these reached a percentage of only 6 % of the Commission's work in 1998-1999) constitutes a huge problem.[344] Of course, one can argue that the Commission's task force should simply be increased in numbers: however, there is "no realistic prospect of the Competition DG's resources being significantly increased, other than in relation to merger."[345] This fact has to be taken into account when considering reform proposals under Art 81 and Art 82 ECT.

The indicated figures are not undisputed though. In fact, the German Monopolies Commission argued that at the time being the approximately 1,200 unsettled cases could be worked through with a single concerted effort. Moreover, it emphasised that the total number of notifications in relation to the total number of new cases came down from 70 % to 40 %. Lastly, in the years 1997 and 1998 there were about 500 new cases recorded compared to 517 cases concluded in 1997 and 581 cases

---

341 See *Holmes*, Journal of World Competition 2000, 53.
In 2002, there have were 321 cases submitted and 363 closed, 330 of them informally. See *European Commission*, XXXIIst Report of competition policy, 46-47.

342 See *Holmes*, Journal of World Competition 2000, 53.

343 See White Paper par 40; also see *Bogdandy*, Legal Equality, Legal Certainty and subsidiarity in transnational economic law – decentralised application of Art 81 par 3 and WTO law: why and why not, European integration and international co-ordination 2000, 13 (16)

344 See White Paper par 44.
In this respect Goyder also stresses that the regulation brings "within coverage for notification too many routine and relatively innocuous agreements, without enabling DG IV to focus its attention on the kind of horizontal market-sharing and other cartels which are normally considered to have most effect on the health of the competitive process." See *Goyder*, Competition 47.

345 See *Holmes*, Journal of World Competition 2000, 54. Unfortunately Holmes does not put forward any evidence or reasons for this assumption.
Also see *Wißmann*, Journal of World Competition 2000, 137; and *Goyder*, Competition 498.

concluded in 1998. Considering these figures it was argued that the extent of exemption applications had reached a level, which could have been handled, in other words, there was no need to change the entire system. Nevertheless, the German Monopolies Commission has also been aware of the fact that 90 % of submitted notifications were closed informally by the means of comfort letters, also highlighting the fact that hardcore cartels are not submitted, affirming thus that *ex-officio* investigations are indispensable. Moreover, it has also been aware of the fact that the eastward enlargement will provide an increase in notifications.[346]

Besides the mentioned arguments that focus on the 'flood of notification' and the decentralised application of the exemption provision of Art 81 ECT, it was underlined that the diverging application of par 1 and par 3 of Art 81 ECT constituted an artificial splitting that run counter to the integral nature of Art 81 ECT, which ultimately necessitates an economic analysis of the overall impact of restrictive practices.[347] What is more, as every imaginable prohibition case can also be a case for exemption, the potential for decentralisation was kept strictly limited since the adoption of Reg 17.[348]

In respect of decentralisation, several arguments were put forward in support of this goal. To begin with, one has to consider that due to their acquaintance with local markets as well as with national operators, national competition authorities are in a good position to ensure effective action. One simply has to consider that their infrastructure might affect their whole country. Hence, investigation can be carried out more rapidly. They also have the human and legal resources at their disposal to ensure that infringements of EC competition rules in their territory can be pursued. Next, national bodies are closer to the complainants and national courts and authorities can consider both, national competition law as well as EC competition law. Additionally, national courts are empowered to react rapidly by means of interlocutory proceedings and they can grant damages to the victims of an infringement.[349] A further advantage of the new system is that undertakings can obtain immediate execution of contracts before national courts. Moreover, as a result of the application by national courts and authorities of EC competition law, the White Paper has predicted the convergence between EC competition law and national competition law. Such an effect will eventually ease the adopting of commercial strategies by undertakings.[350]

---

346 *German Monopolies Commission*, Cartel policy change in the European Union? – On the European Commission's White Paper of 28th April 1999, par 57 – par 59.

347 See *Paulweber*, Journal of World Competition 2000, 15; also see White Paper par 49; and ECJ case 13/61 (Bosch) and ECJ case 59/77 (de Bloos).

348 See *Paulweber*, Journal of World Competition 2000, 15.

349 See White Paper par 46.

350 See White Paper par 78; also see chapter 3.4.4.

Anyhow, the Commission was and still is aware of the fact that decentralisation might inhibit consistent enforcement of EC competition law, as more institutions are involved in the enforcement of the law.[351] In order that a decentralised enforcement system may work effectively, Wißmann identifies four main prerequisites that have to be met:

- "the authorities of all Member States have to have the power to enforce the EC competition rules,
- they have to be given the appropriate material resources to do so,
- there have to be instruments which ensure coherence and a high level of uniformity in the application, and finally,
- criteria for the allocation of cases between the Commission and national authorities have to be found in order to avoid a duplication of procedures."[352]

Lastly, as it is clear that the legal environment also determines the competitiveness of an undertaking, the Commission criticised that the notification procedure produced major costs to undertakings due to the administrative burden it caused:[353]

Hence, one can agree that

> "there [was] an obvious need to refocus the Commission's implementation of Art 85,[354] allowing it to use its resources to combat cartels, particularly in concentrated markets and in markets which are being liberalised."[355]

To solve these problems, the Commission has instituted a system bringing with it decentralised application of the EC competition rules and the abolition of the notification procedure. As seen, in order to get the new system to work properly, there have to be mechanisms put in place which guarantee uniform interpretation of the law and to avoid the risk of possible contradictory decisions as a consequence of decentralisation. Eventually though, the primary objective of a reform has to be the maximisation of efficiency in the implementation of the Community competition rules by guaranteeing the balance between sufficient legal certainty, wide-spread enforcement, ease of administrative constraints and transparent decision-making.[356]

---

[351] See White Paper par 42.
[352] See *Wißmann*, Journal of World Competition 2000, 137.
[353] See White Paper par 50 and par 76; also see in this respect chapter 3.4.7.
[354] Art 81 ECT as of today.
[355] See White Paper par 45.
[356] See *Wißmann*, Journal of World Competition 2000, 136; also see White Paper par 42.

3.3 The legal exemption system as proposed by the reform

As already mentioned, decentralisation is only one part of the reform, which additionally replaces the notification regime with a legal exemption system based on *ex-post* control. The Commission argued that there is no need for an authorisation system by stressing that there are other systems, which are not based on notification and authorisation.[357] Moreover, after more than 35 years of application, EC competition law has been clarified in so far as the initial doubts of application did not exist anymore.[358] This should guarantee the necessary predictability for undertakings. Quite true, an enlarged Union does also stand for 1,000s of notifications of restrictive practices.[359]
As described, the notification procedure is characterised by the fact that it allows the lifting of a prohibition on a restrictive practise only by way of an act of an empowered public authority (ex *ante* control). Such a decision is constitutive in nature, which on the other hand implies that before such a decision is granted, the restrictive practice is void. There exists a *prima facie* invalidity in respect of such practices.[360]
Contrary to this, the new system of legal exemption incorporates the rule that the prohibition of a restrictive practice does not have to be applied without any further decision, given the criteria of Art 81 par 3 ECT are met.[361] This exception is an exception by law. This means that a decision confirming the exception can only be declaratory in nature. It is also clear that due to the fact that no constitutive decision has to be granted in respect of the exemption, there is no *prima facie* invalidity of the practice concerned.[362] Obviously, as no authorisation is needed, notification of restrictive practices is neither required and enforcement of the law concentrates on mere *ex-post* control.
The Commission presents this system of legal exception as the problem solving means, stressing that it is in line with the prohibition system accommodated in the Treaty.[363] According to the Commission, this new system can be based on a Council Regulation, which is adopted pursuant to

---

357 See White Paper par 48. In respect of the mentioned other systems Paulweber suggests that the Commission refers to the US antitrust law, see *Paulweber*, Journal of World Competition 2000, 5; and *German Monopolies Commission* par 80. For more details in this respect, see chapter 3.4.6.4.

358 See White Paper par 48. Of this opinion is also *Ehlermann*, CMLR 2000, 545.

359 See White Paper par 48.

360 See *Wißmann*, Journal of World Competition 2000, 138.

361 See Art 1 Reg 1.

362 See *Wißmann*, Journal of World Competition 2000, 138.

363 The Commission highlights that such mechanism constitutes an exception to the principle of prohibition and hence, does not create a new rule. See White Paper par 53.

Art 83 ECT and it becomes clear, that according to the Commission's view no amendment of the Treaty is necessary. The new approach enables national courts and authorities to apply Art 81 par 3 ECT in cases in which Art 81 par 1 ECT is applied. With it, Art 81 ECT becomes a unitary norm. Under the new regime, an agreement that fulfils the conditions of Art 81 par 3 ECT is exempted without prior notification and becomes unlawful once these conditions are no longer met.[364]

3.4 A critical appraisal of the reform

As mentioned, the whole process of modernisation was not just pursued by the Commission alone, but also considered opinions of other parties who responded to the initiative of the Commission in a quite distinguished way. In fact, the replies ranged from full agreement with the suggestions of the Commission to scepticism and rejection. The following subchapters outline the different arguments. Even though the various issues are interrelated to each other, and therefore a sharp clear-cut between the various points in question is often not easily accomplished, one can cluster them into eleven captions:

- The compatibility of the proposed legal exemption system with the Treaty of Rome
- The abolition of the notification system and its implications
- What might be the purpose and usage of block exemptions, individual decisions, guidelines and notices under the new regime?
- A new relationship between EC competition law and national competition rules
- What complexities might arise for national authorities due to decentralisation,
- and to national courts?
- Which problems might arise for undertakings under the new regime?
- The proposal in the light of the Eastern enlargement of the European Union
- Consequences for the European Court of Justice and the Court of First Instance
- Further critical remarks
- Discussed (and not discussed) alternatives

[364] See Art 1 par 2 Reg 1; also see White Paper par 69.

3.4.1 Compatibility of the legal exemption system with the Treaty

As mentioned in chapter 3.3, the Commission argues that the switch from an authorisation system to a legal exemption system can be achieved without amending the EC Treaty. Generally, one can observe that the compatibility issue was not of great concern for the parties who submitted their observations to the Commission. Whereas the European Parliament, the Economic and Social Committee and most of the Member States agreed on the compatibility of the proposed system with primary EC law, only one Member State has expressed doubts. Two Member States underline that a Treaty amendment is necessary in order to implement the proposed new system.[365] Interestingly, this latter position is shared by several primarily German authors.[366]

The arguments, which emphasise incompatibility, focus on the wording of Art 81 par 3 ECT, the structure of Art 81 ECT, on the question of whether par 3 is directly applicable and as further hints of incompatibility of the new regime with primary law, on Art 83 par 2 subpar b and Art 84 ECT.

3.4.1.1 The wording of Art 81 par 3 ECT: "may be declared inapplicable"

In order to sustain the adoption of a legal exemption system, the Commission starts its argumentation with a comparison between Art 65 par 2 ECSC Treaty[367] and Art 81 EC Treaty. Whereas the former uses the word 'authorise'

---

[365] Summary of observations, 29.02.2000, 6.

[366] See for instance the various comments of Mestmäcker, Deringer, German Monopolies Commission and Wißmann.

[367] As mentioned in chapter 2.2, the ECSC-Treaty has expired and the norms of the ECT apply. Hence, also in the field of cartels regarding steal and coals a legal exemption system will be introduced in 2004.
Art 65 par 1 and par 2 ECSC-Treaty read as follows:
1. All agreements between undertakings, decisions by associations of undertakings and concerted practices tending directly or indirectly to prevent, restrict or distort normal competition within the common market shall be prohibited, and in particular those tending:
a. to fix or determine prices;
b. to restrict or control production, technical development or investment;
c. to share markets, products, customers or sources of supply.
2. However, the Commission shall authorise specialization agreements or joint buying or joint selling agreements in respect of particular products, if it finds that:
a. such specialization or such joint buying or joint selling will make for a substantial improvement in the production or distribution of those products;

and hence, undoubtedly requires a prior decision of the Commission, the necessity of the adoption of such an administrative act is in the Commission's view not uncontested in respect of Art 81 par 3 ECT, which uses the words "may be declared applicable". During the preparatory works for the Rome Treaty the national delegations which took part at the Conference of Messina for the preparation of the 'new' Treaty of Rome, backed a system that is clearly based on the prohibition principle - which is uncontested - but, as the Commission states, were not in concurrence with respect to the question under which conditions the prohibition of Art 81 ECT might be lifted.[368]

Two different approaches were under discussion: an authorisation system, which asked for a constitutive act in order to lift the prohibition and a directly applicable exemption system.[369]

The Commission emphasises that the discussions surrounding these two opposing approaches, by the wording "may be declared inapplicable", culminated in a compromise,[370] which ultimately enables the Community legislator to choose between the afore mentioned systems. Furthermore, as

---

b. the agreement in question is essential in order to achieve these results and is not more restrictive than is necessary for that purpose; and

c. the agreement is not liable to give the undertakings concerned the power to determine the prices, or to control or restrict the production or marketing, of a substantial part of the products in question within the common market, or to shield them against effective competition from other undertakings within the common market.

368 As seen in chapter 3.1.1.
The Commission considered this historical argumentation in the White Paper only, though. Apparently, the criticism raised during the consultation procedure pushed the Commission to neglect these historical observations.

369 Also see White Paper par 11.

370 Similarly, also Wißmann describes Art 81 ECT as having a neutral character, which tries to consolidate the two opposing approaches put forward by the French delegation (system of "exception légale") on the one hand and by the German delegation (authorisation procedure) on the other. See *Wißmann*, Journal of World Competition 2000, 139; also see *Mestmäcker*, The Modernisation of EC Antitrust Policy: Constitutional Challenge or Administrative Convenience, in Ehlermann/Atanasiu, European Competition Law Annual 2000 (2001), 223 (228).
In this context, Schaub emphasises that the word 'declare' does not say anything about the nature of the declaration. I agree with him, when he outlines that such a declaration can be of declaratory nature and as will be seen in chapter 3.4.3.1, the new system only allows declarations having declaratory power. Anyhow, in my opinion, this raises the question, why Art 81 par 1 ECT should have been phrased in such an ambiguous way to allow declarations that ultimately are bare of any legal effect. Hence, the argument of Schaub is in my opinion not very convincing. See *Schaub*, The reform of Regulation 17: The issues of compatibility, effective enforcement and legal certainty, in Ehlermann/Atanasiu, European Competition Law Annual 2000 (2001), 241 (247).

the Commission stresses, the adoption of an authorisation system would be stringent only in case Art 81 par 3 ECT uses a formula like "restrictive agreements may be declared valid,"[371] or, in other words, a formula that uses a positive statement. The Commission draws the conclusion that the negative formula "provisions of Art 81 par 1 may [...] be declared valid" arguably implies that the choice concerning the question which system should finally be adopted is left to secondary legislation.[372] Accordingly, acting under Art 83 par 1 ECT, the Council may adopt either approaches: the authorisation system or the directly applicable exemption system.[373]

Whereas nothing is to say against the fact that in the early sixties no experience existed in the field of competition policy and hence, from that point of view it seemed to be wise to institute a notification system,[374] the arguments put forward by the Commission to sustain an open interpretation of Art 81 par 3 ECT, should be observed rather cautiously.

Opponents[375] to the idea of an open meaning of the formula in discussion, stick to the Bosch case, in which the French Advocate-General Lagrange, highlighted that the requirement of a prior authorisation

> "accords best with the terms of Art 81 par 3. [...] The theory depending on 'l'exception légale' would have required a different text, for example: 'The provisions of paragraph 1 shall be deemed not to apply [...] or simply 'shall not apply'"[376]

In my opinion this argument seems to be correct. Indeed, the fact that the requirement is phrased in a negative way, as opposed to positive wording, does not alter the substance of the provision, which undoubtedly asks for a declaration.[377] More precise,

> "the need for an additional 'declaration' suggests that the exception does not have effect by virtue of law, ie the Treaty, but rather by virtue of the authoritative act. Thus, meaning that it is not Art 81 par 3 ECT but the authoritative act granting exemption from the rule of prohibition which is constitutive."[378]

---

371 See White Paper par 12.

372 See White Paper par 13. As shortly illustrated in chapters 2.3 and 3.1.1, Art 83 empowers the Council to frame rules for the implementation of Art 81 par 3 ECT.

373 See White Paper par 13.

374 See chapter 2.2.

375 See for instance *Deringer*, Stellungnahme zum Weißbuch der Europäischen Kommission über die Modernisierung der Vorschriften zur Anwendung der Art 85 und 86 EG-Vertrag, EuZW 2000, 5 (5-6).

376 See ECJ case 13/61 (Bosch).

377 See *German Monopolies Commission* par 15; and *Deringer*, EuZW 2000, 5.

378 See *Wißmann*, Journal of World Competition 2000, 139.

Also Ehlermann correctly affirms that the formula "may be declared inapplicable" suggests a positive action.[379]
Moreover, it should be stressed that the Commission does not put forward any clear evidence in order to rectify its assumption. Indeed, there is no clear indication that the final choice was left to the Community legislator. As Deringer, the reporter for the European Parliament for Reg 17 in 1961, specifies, the discussion, whether Art 81 par 3 ECT allows a legal exemption system or rather, gives no other choice than the adoption of an authorisation system, was raised not before the debate was held in the Parliamentary Committee for the common market for the later adopted Reg 17.[380]
A further aspect in this discussion concerns the editing of the EC Treaty as an international treaty aiming at a political goal. According to Geiger, due to such a political motivation that lies beneath the EC Treaty, a textual interpretation has to be pursued very cautiously. Moreover, he stresses that because of the controversies surrounding the correct interpretation of Art 81 par 3 ECT - which according to him do not provide any clear answers - one shall not rely on the formula when choosing between an authorisation system and a legal exemption system. Accordingly, the wording of par 3 does not lead anywhere and should not be overvalued. Geiger outlines that the goal of the negotiations for the Treaty of Rome was ultimately a diplomatic one, which aimed to make sure that every party was satisfied with the outcome. Therefore, he doubts that the wording of par 3 did ultimately decide which system had to be adopted.[381]
Even though this argument that focuses on the EC Treaty as a political instrument makes some valid points, - especially from the historical point of view - in my opinion it does not to give a helpful answer to the question concerned. It opens the door to literally turn every norm an international treaty contains upside down, as ultimately every norm might be a compromise and hence encompasses opposing and contrasting ideas. Moreover, also the Vienna Convention on the law of Treaties firstly focuses on the textual interpretation of an international treaty. The preparatory works of the treaty and the circumstances of its conclusion gain importance only in

[379] See *Ehlermann*, CMLR 2000, 555.
[380] See *Deringer*, EuZW 2000, 5-6.
Also Forrester indicates that the drafters did not concern about which system to adopt. Rather, they looked to reach a compromise between the negotiating parties. Accordingly, "what they produced was an amalgam of several countries preferences." As a result, the answer to the point in question lies first of all in the Treaty itself. See *Forrester*, The Modernisation of EC Antitrust Policy. Issues for Courts and Judges, in Ehlermann/Atanasiu, European Competition Law Annual 2000 (2001), 75 (93-94).
[381] See *Geiger*, Das Weißbuch der EG-Kommission zu Art. 81, 82 EG - eine Reform, besser als ihr Ruf, EuZW 2000, 165 (166-167).

case the textual interpretation does not deliver a satisfying outcome.[382] However, in this case the wording is quite clear.[383]
Opponents to the new system, invoke further references to the wording "any agreement, decision, concerted practice or category of agreement, decision or concerted practice". A switch to a legal exemption system would deprive these limitations of its meaning, as a directly applicable exemption system would not only allow categories, but, to the contrary, automatically allows all agreements, and hence extends far beyond the exemption as contained in par 3 of Art 81 ECT.[384] However, this is not quite correct. I agree with Geiger who observes that the proposed system, by defining a 'black list' (group exemption regulations[385]) of prohibited cartels, limits the possible exemption to those agreements, which are not contained in this list. In fact, this system does not contain an unlimited legal exemption, even though it has to be admitted that this negative definition turns the existing system upside down.[386] Anyhow, this argument eventually does not help to determine whether a declaration in the meaning of an authoritative act can be neglected.

3.4.1.2 Control of abuse?

As explained, the new system does not envisage a *prima facie* presumption that restrictive practices run counter to Art 81 ECT and are accordingly void.
It is argued that such an approach means that all cartels are legal from their beginning, until they are declared incompatible with Art 81 ECT, or better, these practices are deemed to be valid, until a court or authority declares otherwise. As a result, enforcement focuses primarily on the abuse of an

---

382 See Art 31 par 1 of the Vienna Treaty Convention, which reads as follows:
A treaty shall be interpreted in good faith in accordance with the ordinary meaning to be given to the terms of the treaty in their context and in the light of its object and purpose.
Art 32 explains that "recourse may be had to supplementary means of interpretation, including the preparatory work of the treaty and the circumstances of its conclusion, in order to confirm the meaning resulting from the application of Article 31, or to determine the meaning when the interpretation according to Article 31:
(a) leaves the meaning ambiguous or obscure; or
(b) leads to a result which is manifestly absurd or unreasonable."

383 Also see *Mestmäcker*, Versuch einer kartellpolitischen Wende in der EU: Zum Weißbuch der Kommission über die Vorschriften zur Anwendung der Art. 85 und 86 EGV a.F., EuZW 1999, 523 (525).

384 See *German Monopolies Commission* par 16.

385 Also consider in this context chapter 3.4.3.1.

386 See *Geiger*, EuZW 2000, 166.

acknowledged freedom of contract.[387] Accordingly, it is argued that the new system eliminates the structural difference between Art 81 ECT addressing the existence of an agreement or practice and Art 82 ECT, which focuses on the abuse of a dominant position. Such an innovation that radically changes the substantive foundations of Art 81 ECT should only be realisable by means of a Treaty amendment.[388] Apart from the fact that the new regulation still formally works on the assumption of a principle of prohibition,[389] such criticism is not convincing. In fact, the White Paper carefully states that

> "under a directly applicable exception system, the prohibition on restrictive practices is not applicable to those which satisfy certain conditions defined by law. Taken as a whole, such conditions may be regarded as an exception to the prohibition principle. [Only] restrictive practices which satisfy the conditions are therefore valid as soon as they have been concluded."[390]

It results, that restrictive practices that do not satisfy the conditions remain prohibited from the very moment they are concluded.[391]

3.4.1.3 Direct applicability of paragraph 3 of Art 81 ECT

Another issues that has been raised in the discussion surrounding the formal requirements of the EC Treaty, is whether Art 81 par 3 ECT is sufficiently precise to be directly effective.[392] As Ehlermann outlines,

> "the importance of this question cannot be overestimated. If, in effect, the answer were to be negative, it would not be sufficient to substitute the word 'declare' by another term. Instead, it would be necessary to amend the substance of par 3, in order to make it 'justiciable'."[393]

---

[387] See *Wißmann*, Journal of World Competition 2000, 140; and *Mestmäcker*, EuZW 1999, 525

[388] See *Wißmann*, Journal of World Competition, 2000, 140; also see *Immenga*, EuZW 1999, 609.

[389] See Art 1 par 1 and par 3 Reg 1.

[390] See White Paper par 11.

[391] See *Marenco*, Does a legal exemption system require an amendment of the treaty?, in Ehlermann/Atanasiu, European Competition Law Annual 2000 (2001), 145 (147).
If ever, one can "talk of an approximation to a *de facto* principle of abuse control insofar as the need for preventive authorisation decisions no longer generally applies." See *German Monopolies Commission* par 6.

[392] In the Van Gend & Loos case (ECJ Case 26/62), the ECJ ruled that the condition for direct applicability is that the provisions are clear, unambiguous, unconditional and not dependent on further action.

[393] See *Ehlermann*, CMLR 2000, 557.

As seen in chapter 2.4.1.3, par 3 calls for a complex economic assessment of often opposing interests. These interests vary from strictly economic, competition-oriented considerations, to non-economic values, such as the protection of the environment. This balancing of different interests helps the Commission to develop and pursue its competition policy: a task to fulfil for which an administrative authority seems, upon first glance, to be more appropriate than a court of law.[394] On the other hand, directly applicable norms by their very nature, produce rights between individuals, which ultimately have to be safeguarded by national courts. It becomes evident, that directly applicable norms have to be justiciable. [395]

Moreover, opponents to the reform highlight that of as a consequence, Art 81 ECT would become an unitary norm, and consequently, reference would always have to be made to Art 81 ECT as a whole.[396] In other words, Art 81 par 1 ECT could be assessed only in combination with par 3. Direct applicability of Art 81 ECT would hence depend on the justiciability of par 3. Ultimately, that means that failing justiciability of par 3 would eliminate the direct applicability of Art 81 par 1 ECT.[397]

It is argued that the Court of Justice implicitly decided against the direct effect of Art 81 par 3 in its 1962 Bosch judgment.[398] However, one has to recognise that in the Bosch case, the ECJ was not confronted with the question of prior administrative authorisation versus the direct effect of Art 81 par 3 ECT.[399] In addition, at that time Reg 17 had recently been adopted. From this fact, Ehlermanns draws the conclusion that the Court was alleviated from the need to examine the potential direct effect of Art 81 par 3 ECT.[400]

Moreover, it is stressed that indications denying a possible direct effect of Art 81 par 3 ECT can be found in a statement of the Court of First Instance.[401] In

---

394 See *Ehlermann*, CMLR 2000, 557.
Marenco in this regard outlines, that "paragraph 3 is the European codified form of the American 'rule of reason', and that in America the 'rule of reason' is a judicial invention." See *Marenco*, European Competition Law Annual 2000 (2001), 167.

395 See *German Monopolies Commission* par 18.

396 In this context, Marenco stresses that one cannot deny a separation between the 2 paragraphs. But whereas par 1 is directly applicable, par 3 can be rendered directly applicable by the legislator. See *Marenco*, European Competition Law Annual 2000 (2001), 168.

397 See *German Monopolies Commission* par 18; also see *Mestmäcker*, EuZW 1999, 526.
In ECJ case 127/73 (BRT) the ECJ interpreted par 1 of Art 81 ECT as producing direct effect and hence, being directly applicable.

398 Ehlermann in referring to Mok, *Ehlermann*, CMLR 2000, 556 fn 56.

399 See *Mestmäcker*, EuZW 1999, 527; also see *Ehlermann*, CMLR 2000, 556.

400 See *Ehlermann*, CMLR 2000, 556.

401 See CFI case T-29/92 (SPO).

fact, it limited its review of the complex economic assessments carried out by the Commission as requested by par 3

> "to ascertaining whether the procedural rules have been complied with, whether proper reasons have been provided, whether the facts have been accurately stated and whether there has been any manifest error of appraisal or misuse of powers"

Therefore, critics of the proposed reform highlight that the Court itself is not empowered and not able to balance the advantages and disadvantages of restrictive agreements called for in Art 81 par 3 ECT;[402] therefore, how should national courts be able to do so? In other words, this case law shall prove that par 3 accommodates elements of administrative discretion incompatible with the notion of direct effect.[403] As a result, the German Monopolies Commission concludes that

> "a regulation that obliged the courts of the Member States to apply Art 81 par 3 EC Treaty would, in contradiction to the case-law of the ECJ, invalidate the direct applicability of Art 81, par 1 EC Treaty. Such a regulation would have to be declared null and void pursuant to Art 230, par 2 in conjunction with Art 231 of the EC Treaty on the grounds of an infringement of the EC Treaty. "[404]

Admittedly, these standards of review are hardly compatible with the concept of a provision that has direct effect. But nothing stands against the possibility that the Court includes in its standards of review of decisions, an evaluation of economic circumstances. This would be in line with the type of control adopted in respect of Art 81 par 1 and Art 82 ECT.[405]

Anyhow, lastly the necessity for such a standard of review depends on whether Art 81 par 3 ECT as such is phrased precise enough in order to become directly applicable. As Wißmann, by referring to the van Gend & Loos case,[406] correctly highlights,

> "only those provisions which are clear, unambiguous, unconditional and not dependent on further action may be directly applicable. Yet, whether an agreement falls under Art 81 par 3 necessarily entails complex economic assessments and implies wide discretionary power."[407]

---

402 See *German Monopolies Commission* par 18.

403 See *Ehlermann*, CMLR 2000, 559.

404 See *German Monopolies Commission* par 18; in this sense also see *Mestmäcker*, European Competition Law Annual 2000 (2001), 230.

405 See *Ehlermann*, CMLR 2000, 559. In this sense, also see *Deringer*, EuZW 2000, 5 (8). In this respect, one is referred to chapter 3.4.8, which specifically analyses the effects the reform might have on the ECJ.

406 ECJ case 26/62.

407 See *Wißmann*, Journal of World Competition 2000, 140.

He concludes, that it is doubtful that the ECJ may interpret Art 81 EC Treaty as having direct effect as a whole, neither could a regulation grant such effect.
However, there are good arguments to be found, which support the opposite.[408] In fact, the ECJ recognised the direct effect of the Art 82[409] and Art 86 par 2 ECT. Their applicability is concluded to be at least as 'imprecise' and difficult as the applicability of Art 81 par 3 ECT. In fact, Art 86 par 2 ECT exempts undertakings entrusted with the operation of services of general economic interest from obliging to the rules on competition "in so far as the application of those rules does [...] obstruct the performance, in law or in fact, of the particular tasks assigned to them."[410] The exception is qualified by the proviso that "the development of trade must not be affected to such an extent as would be contrary to the interest of the Community." If one considers the open phrasing of Art 81 par 3 ECT, one might suggest that it would have been reasonable to also have denied such an effect to Art 86 par 2 ECT. However, this was not the case.[411]
The same is true for Art 30 ECT,[412] which contains a prohibition, exception, conditions and qualifications that - similar to Art 81 par 3 ECT - require a balancing of opposing interests, some of them are also of non-economic

---

408 It is clear though, that one shall not mix up the conditions for directly applicability of the norm with the actual capacities of judges to handle such cases. This issue will be dealt with in chapter 3.4.6.1.

409 See *Ehlermann*, CMLR 2000, 557-558.
Marenco adds that "while the national courts now dispose of no regulation or notice to guide them as to the manner of interpreting Art 82, a long sets of regulations, guidelines and notices assist them in the application of Art 81." See *Marenco*, European Competition Law Annual 2000 (2001), 165; also see Bogdandy, European integration and international co-ordination 2000, 23

410 For the whole text of Art 86 ECT, see fn 36.

411 See *Ehlermann*, CMLR 2000, 558.
Similar to Art 81 ECT, Art 86 ECT contains a prohibition, an exception and a provision that provides for the adaptation of decisions and instruments of a general nature. In the Corbeau case a national court had to assess whether cross-subsidisation between different sectors of activity was necessary in order to preserve the economic equilibrium of the Belgian postal service, and thus the court had to perform a proportionality test. See ECJ case C-320/91 (Corbeau).

412 Art 30 ECT reads as follows:
The provisions of Articles 28 and 29 shall not preclude prohibitions or restrictions on imports, exports or goods in transit justified on grounds of public morality, public policy or public security; the protection of health and life of humans, animals or plants; the protection of national treasures possessing artistic, historic or archaeological value; or the protection of industrial and commercial property. Such prohibitions or restrictions shall not, however, constitute a means of arbitrary discrimination or a disguised restriction on trade between Member States.

nature.[413] Considering these facts, one can draw the conclusion, and rightly, so in my opinion, that a difficult application of Art 81 par 3 ECT may not constitute an argument against the potential direct effect of this paragraph,[414] and hence, cannot be a valid argument for a possible illegitimacy of the reform in discussion.
According to the outlined arguments, Art 81 par 3 ECT seems to be directly applicable. Remaining doubts[415] can be clarified by means of a regulation,[416] or as Ehlermann suggests, in the course of an intergovernmental conference.[417]

3.4.1.4 The argument of Art 83 par 2 subpar b ECT

As explained in a previous chapter, Art 83 ECT[418] deals with the realisation of the principles set out in Art 81 and Art 82 ECT by means of the adoption of appropriate regulations or directives. More precisely, par 2 subpar b of the mentioned article outlines that these directives or regulations shall

> "lay down detailed rules for the application of Art 81 par 3, taking into account the need to ensure effective supervision on the one hand, and to simplify administration to the greatest possible extent on the other."

According to opponents of the reform, this wording indicates that a separate administrative procedure is necessary in order to make Art 81 par 3 ECT applicable. Hence, it is argued that such an approach seems to be

---

[413] Besides, Ehlermann mentions that there are further provisions that have direct effect despite the lack of earlier administrative or judicial practice and decisions, without outlining any examples though. See *Ehlermann*, CMLR 2000, 558.

[414] See *Ehlermann*, CMLR 2000, 558.

[415] The application of Art 81 par 3 ECT will certainly be difficult. Ehlermann points out "there is still considerable doubt about the correct interpretation of the notion of 'restriction of competition' in the first paragraph. However, even greater is the uncertainty about the interpretation of the third paragraph. The scope of Art 81 (3) is largely unexplored, if only because of the relatively few formal exemption decisions taken by the Commission, and the even smaller number of Court judgments reviewing these decisions. It will be one of the great merits of the abolition of the Commission's exemption monopoly that more formal decisions interpreting Art 81 (3) can be expected. These will contribute to progressively clarifying the scope of this key provision of the EC Treaty." See *Ehlermann*, CMLR 2000, 577.

[416] Such is considered by Art 3 par 2 Reg 1. Moreover, on 10 October 2003 the Commission has published the so called "Modernisation Package", which includes a number of notices and guidelines clarifying the rules under the new Reg 1. See Official Journal C243/3.

[417] See *Ehlermann*, CMLR 2000, 559-560.

[418] For the whole Art, see fn 33.

incompatible with a directly effective exemption system, as under such a regime, an agreement would be authorised or prohibited from its inception, without any authority granting any decision. Opponents to the reform highlight that as a consequence these words would become largely obsolete.[419]

First of all I want to add in this respect that it is not quite clear to me why par 2 subpar b should be understood as referring to a separate administrative procedure.[420] Secondly, mechanisms aimed at reducing the risks resulting from the direct effect of Art 81 par 3 ECT could be based on Art 83 par 2 subpar b.[421] In fact, Reg 1 mentions the possibility to issue a separate regulation for the application of Art 81 par 3 ECT.

Lastly, as an additional and systematic indication for a commitment under primary law to a preventive control, it is argued that one has to take into consideration that both Art 81 par 3 and Art 83 par 2 subpar a and subpar b ECT distinguish between the prohibition norm of Art 81 par 1 ECT and the exemption of par 3. Arguably, it follows that one can draw a clear separation between prohibition and exemption, which, at least with respect to procedural rules, has to be maintained.[422] In my opinion, this argument should not be overvalued, though and be only observed to foster stronger arguments that give a clearer indication for such a presumed separation.

3.4.1.5 The argument of Art 84 ECT

A last argument put forward in order to put in question the admissibility, or better still, the compatibility of the proposed system with the EC Treaty, is based on Art 84 ECT,[423] which stipulates that

> "the authorities in the Member States shall rule on the admissibility of agreements, decisions and concerted practices and on abuse of

[419] See *German Monopolies Commission* par 17; see also *Mestmäcker*, EuZW 1999, 525-526.

[420] As the German Monopolies Commission does. See *German Monopolies Commission* par 17.

[421] See *Ehlermann*, CMLR 2000, 556.
Moreover, Marenco correctly highlights, that "in any event, the White Paper does not claim that the legal exemption system flows from the Treaty itself. In order to achieve that result, legislative intervention is necessary, precisely on the basis of Art 83 paragraph 2 b: a new regulation replacing Reg 17 would have to lay down that the application of paragraph 3 takes place at the same time as the application of paragraph 1." See *Marenco*, European Competition Law Annual 2000 (2001), 170.
Of course, the validity of this statement ultimately depends on the notion of 'declare' and whether this terminology allows a legal exemption system or not.

[422] See *German Monopolies Commission* par 16.

[423] For the whole Art, see fn 34.

> a dominant position on the common market in accordance with the law of their country and with the provisions of Art 81, in particular paragraph 3, and of Art 82",

until provisions, which are adopted according to Art 83 ECT, enter into force. The analysis concentrates on the phrasing "shall rule on the admissibility".[424] It is argued that the norm is based on the assumption that the admissibility of restraints of competition requires an authorisation by competition authorities in Member States. Accordingly, Art 84 ECT refers to a procedure of *ex ante* control.[425] However, this argument ultimately depends on the interpretation of the wording 'declare' as contained in Art 81 par 3 ECT and does not have autonomous meaning.[426]

3.4.1.6 Is a Treaty amendment necessary?

It seems that Reg 1 is based on a weak foundation, at least from the view of compatibility with EC primary law. As we know, Art 83 par 1 of the EC Treaty gives the Council the power to lay down all appropriate regulations and directives, which it considers necessary in order to give effect to the principles set out in Art 81 and Art 82 ECT. It is also well known that secondary law can neither change nor extend primary law. It follows that the decisive factor that determines whether a directly applicable system may be implemented is whether Art 81 ECT leaves the choice between the two systems open or whether it is based on the assumption of preventive control

---

[424] Regarding Art 84 ECT it is further considered that it refers exclusively to national authorities and does not mention national courts at all. This shall imply, that Art 81 par 3 ECT cannot be applied by national courts. According to the case law of the ECJ (case 127/73 [BRT]), the word 'authority' as contained in Art 84 ECT also includes "courts especially entrusted with the task of applying domestic legislation on competition or that of ensuring the legality of the application by the administrative authority." Hence, a legal exemption system entrusting national courts with the application of Art 81 par 3 ECT seems hardly compatible with the Treaty. See *Stillfried/Stockenhuber*, Der Entwurf einer neuen Verfahrensordnung zum EG-Kartellrecht, Zeitschrift für österreichisches und europäisches Wirtschaftsrecht 2001, 145 (152).
Contrary to this opinion, Marenco stresses that although Art 84 ECT could well work as a guide to the legislator when choosing between the two systems in discussion (granted that there is a possibility to choose), one shall be aware that Art 84 ECT is a transitional provision, which loses its purpose when a regulation according to Art 83 ECT is adopted. See *Marenco*, European Competition Law Annual 2000 (2001), 170-171.

[425] See *German Monopolies Commission* par 17.

[426] See *Stillfried/Stockenhuber*, Zeitschrift für österreichisches und europäisches Wirtschaftsrecht 2001, fn 49.

by the relevant authorities.[427] Even though several arguments that have been put forward in order to conclude that a treaty amendment is necessary have to be neglected, the one focusing on the wording of Art 81 par 3 ECT seems to establish a hint of the new reform, which can scarcely be opposed. In fact, in my opinion, the language is quite clear and no real opposing argument has been found to tackle it. Wißmann emphasises that

> "the Commission stresses in its White Paper that the objective of the reform proposed is to be achieved by alteration of the procedural rules only. This fails to acknowledge that the proposals [and so Reg 1] in fact change the competition policy with regard to cartels as a whole. The White Paper [and ultimately the whole modernisation process] [...] fails to address the impact on the underlying Treaty provision, Art 81 ECT, as the substantive cornerstone."[428]

Nevertheless, Reg 1 has been adopted even though the European legislative bodies have been aware of this problem. As a result, this question will eventually only be resolved through the ECJ due to a preliminary ruling according to Art 234 ECT.[429]

Obviously, the analysis pursued in these following subchapters has to be based on the assumption that Reg 1 is legally valid, as otherwise the whole discussion could be stopped at this point.

3.4.2 Abolition of the notification system and its implications

As mentioned, notifications are regarded as the primary cause for the malfunctioning of the system as implemented by Reg 17. On the other hand, there are admittedly also advantages, which the old system contains. Indeed, the old system admittedly helped to gain information about business practices and general business information.

In this respect, the German Monopolies Commission highlights that it is

> "on the basis of notifications that the existing structural information deficits facing competition authorities *vis-à-vis* market participants can be offset. This system not only gives relevant authorities knowledge concerning specific agreements that would have possibly remained undetected without notifications, but also provides them with a general overview of business branches and markets. This information enables the relevant authorities to set

---

[427] See *German Monopolies Commission* par 14.

[428] See *Wißmann*, Journal of World Competition 2000, 140-141.

[429] See *Hossenfelder/Lutz*, Die neue Durchführungsverordnung zu den Artikeln 81 und 82 EG-Vertrag, WuW 2003, 118 (119).

appropriate priorities, take proper decisions in specific proceedings, as well as consistently supervise and keep track of the practices of undertakings relevant to competition independent of individual cases. [...] Furthermore, the notifications play a key role for the public interest and for other market participants. On their basis, consumers, buyers, suppliers and competitors can obtain an overview of the horizontal agreements in markets relevant to their activities."[430]

Indeed, notifications as an information-provider were surely a success. Forrester in this respect correctly comments that

"notifications were not bad in principle. They were bad inasmuch as they were used (or abused) for the wrong purpose. Thus the vice is not that notifications were available, but that the reasons for filing a notification were a consequence of the Commission's absurdly over-inclusive interpretation of its jurisdiction. Since everything was prohibited, nothing was not at risk. The Commission was the only one who could dispel the risks."[431]

Moreover, the German Monopolies Commission elucidates that notifications primarily identified horizontal agreements in the 'grey area', which are agreements between cartels that are clearly admissible and those clearly inadmissible. Eventually, due to the information gained, the Commission was in the position to detect hardcore cartels more easily, as detailed information about practices in the same branch was provided.[432]

In this respect, it is doubted whether the new system will really lead to a relief in the work overload, as the Commission, in order to guarantee effective competition control under the new regime, has to initiate proceedings based on own market observations or on complaints by third parties. Indeed, it can no longer rely on market data as provided by notifications under the old regime, but has to expand substantially its own investigations.[433]

However, in my opinion such criticism is rather artificial as own investigations pursued by the Commission or any other supervising institution should be a

---

430 See *German Monopolies Commission* par 28 and par 29.

431 See *Forrester*, The reform of the implementation of Articles 81 and 82 following publication of the draft regulation, Legal Issues of Economic Integration 2001, 173 (177).
He continues by stressing that, "notifications commonly elicited no reply from the Commission. The attraction of notifying was (to a modest extent) immunity from fines and (to a larger extent) the higher moral or ground, making it more difficult to the other party to wriggle out of his contract by invoking spurious competition law fears." See *Forrester*, Legal Issues of Economic Integration 2001, 177-178.

432 *German Monopolies Commission* par 30.

433 *German Monopolies Commission* par 60.

normal task of an authority and not be considered as burdensome. Hence, it is a question of the right techniques and instruments to gain information and to look into a case, and not primarily a question of case-allocation. Accordingly, as notifications, which were convincing as an information-provider, are abolished, other mechanisms have to be found, in order that the necessary market-data can be retrieved. In relation to this issue, the reform focuses on the one hand on better co-operation between the involved bodies and on incentives of private litigation.[434] Realistically, more authorities involved in the process signify work sharing and ultimately less work for one authority.[435]

3.4.3 Block exemptions, individual decisions, guidelines, and notices under the new regime

It is widely known that the existing legislative framework has been fostered by the European Courts' case law as well as by Commission's practices since the adoption of Reg 17. Also national bodies and undertakings have acquired knowledge in the field of competition policy, helping to assess whether an agreement is in line with the law. In addition, under the new regime possible new uncertainties in respect of the EC competition policy and the application of EC competition rules shall be clarified through the adoption of new-styled block exemptions, individual (positive) decisions, notices and guidelines.[436] The main issues regarding these instruments will be analysed in these following subchapters.

3.4.3.1 Block exemptions

Discussions arose concerning the legal nature of block exemptions under the new regime. The starting point is the fact that under the new system no prior authorisation has to be granted in order to make the exemption regime applicable, which means that restrictive practices are deemed lawful from their conclusion onwards, once it is concluded that the conditions of Art 81 par 3 ECT are fulfilled. As explained, under the old regime block exemptions were constitutive in nature by granting the exemption.[437] Hence, they seem

---

[434] See White Paper par 105 to par 108.
[435] In this context, see particularly chapter 3.4.5.4.
[436] See White Paper par 85 and par 86. Clarifying notices and guidelines are going to be issued. See fn 416.
[437] See chapter 2.4.1.3.2.

hardly compatible with the self-executing character of Art 81 par 3 ECT in which the exemption is granted by virtue of law.[438]

It is therefore interesting that the Commission continues to use the concept of block exemptions.[439] However, one might doubt whether the use of block exemptions - in its traditional meaning - can be consistent with the new directly applicable exemption system. The fact, that under this system an exemption is directly derived form Art 81 par 3 ECT and not from a prior decision, raises the question of how such an additional decision can be embedded in this new system.

This issue was clarified during the debate preceding the publication of the Proposal. In fact, under the new regime

> "block exemption regulations, while containing abstract rules, do not create new law for undertakings, but codify and clarify the interpretation of Art 81 par 3 ECT."[440]

In other words, the objective of a block exemption under the new regime, is to outline more clearly the scope of application of par 3, and no longer to grant an exemption. This is definitely within the spirit of Art 83 par 2 ECT, which, as Wißmann[441] correctly highlights, empowers the definition of the scope of the exemption. Whether the terminology is still useful is another question though. In this respect, Deringer[442] talks about a 'block negative clearance', as this merely includes certifying that there is no reason for action in respect of certain agreements. Such an approach might clearly be less irritating.

More problematic seems to be the risk that these new - non-binding - block exemptions could be counteracted by national laws and hence do not give legal certainty to undertakings. However, this risk can be avoided by adopting a Community regulation based on Art 83 par 2 subpar e ECT,[443] which hinders national legislation from prohibiting or varying the outcome of agreements that were 'exempted' by block exemptions.[444] That should ensure that block exemptions could continue to be binding.[445]

---

[438] See *Ehlermann*, CMLR 2000, 566-567; also see *Wißmann*, Journal of World Competition 2000, 142; and *Mestmäcker*, EuZW 1999, 526. Contrary to this opinion *Schaub*, European Competition Law Annual 2000 (2001), 249.

[439] See recital 10 Reg 1.

[440] See Proposal 16; also see *Schaub*, Die Reform der Regeln zur Durchführung der Artikel 81 und 82 EG-Vertrag, in Baudenbacher, Neueste Entwicklungen im europäischen und internationalen Kartellrecht (2002), 3 (8).

[441] See *Wißmann*, Journal of World Competition 2000, 142.

[442] See *Deringer*, EuZW 2000, 7: 'Gruppennegativattest' instead of 'Gruppenfreistellung'.

[443] For Art 83 par 2 subpar e ECT, see fn 33.

[444] See White Paper par 85.

On the other hand, Schaub stresses that "Art 81 par 3 contains two techniques for applying the exception rule to individual agreements and to categories of agreements. Art 83 empowers the Council to devise an enforcement system that is different for

Ultimately though, block exemptions cannot authorise behaviour that is prohibited by Art 81 ECT. Hence, the benefit of a block exemption can be left aside where it is found, that in an individual case an agreement is incompatible with Art 81 par 3 ECT.[446]

3.4.3.2 Individual decisions

As a consequence of the new regime, the Commission will no longer be obliged to issue negative clearances or individual exemptions upon the request of an undertaking. However, for reasons of Community interest[447] the Commission may issue decisions of non-applicability, also referred to as 'positive decisions'.[448] They differ from the old decisions in so far as they are issued only on the Commission's own initiative, and hence cannot be requested by undertakings.[449] They may pertain to the application of Art 81 or Art 82 ECT. In respect of the former, it is clarified that a positive decision may be issued because the conditions of Art 81 par 1 ECT are not met or because the conditions as set out by Art 81 par 3 ECT are satisfied.[450] For the same reasons as for block exemptions, positive decisions can be

---

each technique. There is nothing incompatible with the Treaty to give a declaratory nature to individual applications of Art 81 (3) while maintaining a constitutive power to block exemption regulations." See *Schaub*, European Competition Law Annual 2000 (2001), 247.
In this sense, also see Marenco, who explains that under the new regime, block exemptions "legislatively circumscribe a portion of the field where Art 81 is not applicable. [...] The applicable law is the regulation itself and the only residual question is whether a concrete agreement meets the legislative description or not." See *Marenco*, European Competition Law Annual 2000 (2001), 173.

445 See *Ehlermann*, CMLR 2000, 567.
Contrary to this Deringer, who mentions that under the new system it will not be possible to adopt binding block exemption regulations. See *Deringer*, EuZW 2000, 7.

446 See Art 29 par 1 Reg 1.

447 For the concept of 'sufficient Community interest' see chapter 3.1.2.

448 Such decision can gain importance in respect of those agreements, which contain new issues and hence, establish guidelines for the market following a criteria of general interest. See White Paper par 88; also see *Schaub*, European Competition Law Annual 2000 (2001), 251.

449 In this context, it was proposed to install a system of voluntary notifications and requests for positive decisions. Yet, it was suggested not to give undertakings a right to obtain such a positive decision, as this could eventually hinder the Commission in focusing on *ex officio* procedures and complaints. It must be at the discretion of the Commission to take such a decision. See *Ehlermann*, CMLR 2000, 568; also see *Marenco*, European Competition Law Annual 2000 (2001), 172.

450 See Art 10 Reg 1.

declaratory in nature only,[451] and hence, will no longer have the authority to transform an illegal agreement into a legal one. Due to their lack of constitutive power, they have the same legal standing as a negative clearance.[452]

In this context, Ehlermann suggests that even if the decisions are of declaratory nature only, a binding effect on national competition authorities and courts could be justified if procedures were installed that investigate the facts completely and allow the participation of all interested parties. The introduction of such procedures could be based on Art 83 par 1 ECT.[453] However, one might question what might be the sense of such a procedure as the decisions - even if 'binding' - do not transform an illegal agreement into a legal one. The agreement itself is legal from the beginning onwards (or it is not), and as such it has binding effect. Moreover, a further appraisal by a national authority or court respectively of the agreement concerned could be unduly impeded due to the binding effect granted by such a procedure.

Furthermore, it was advocated that positive decisions of the Commission should be temporarily limited with the possibility of revocation in case of a change of circumstances, which make the initial decision no longer justifiable.[454] However, it is opposed - quite correctly in my opinion - that, similar to a binding effect, a time limit for exemption decisions can hardly be introduced, as these decisions are not, by nature, constitutive but rather are declaratory, whose legality is based on a correct legal appraisal of the underlying facts. Only a change of these facts to such an extent that the conditions of Art 81 par 3 ECT are no longer justified, makes such a Commission's decision illegal. This logical consequence cannot be modified by a temporal indication in the decision.[455]

Next, as seen, positive decisions are adoptable only on the grounds of Community interest. Accordingly, it has been questioned how the

---

451 See recital 14 Reg 1, in which it is stated that these decisions are applied "with a view to clarifying the law and ensuring its consistent application throughout the Community, in particular with regard to new types of agreements or practices that have not been settled in the existing case-law and administrative practice."

452 See White Paper par 89.

453 See *Ehlermann*, CMLR 2000, 567. In respect of binding effect of positive decisions, also see *Marenco*, European Competition Law Annual 2000 (2001), 172.
In this context, Schaub precises that "when applying Community law, national courts are considered Community courts of general jurisdiction and are bound to co-operate with the Court of Justice and with the Commission with a view to maintaining the coherence of the Community legal system. Conflicts with prior Commission decisions must therefore be avoided." See *Schaub*, European Competition Law Annual 2000 (2001), 251.

454 See *Bourgeois/Humpe*, The Commission's draft "New Regulation 17", ECLR 2002, 43 (50).

455 See *Ehlermann*, CMLR 2000, 568; also see *Deringer*, EuZW 2000, 7.

Commission can provide legal certainty if positive decisions are only issued in exceptional cases. On the other hand, regularly issued positive decisions would not provide for the desired relief of the burden of the workload. The same is true for informal inquiries, whether a legal obligation to handle it existed or not.[456] However, in my opinion such comments seem to neglect that the legal framework has been clarified to the extent, that non-exceptional cases may be consolidated within it.
Another aspect concerned whether national competition authorities may adopt positive decisions. The new regulation does not consider positive individual decisions to be taken by national competition authorities, but mentions only prohibition decisions, which these authorities are empowered to adopt.[457] Hence, one can draw the conclusion that such a possibility for national authorities is excluded. Ehlermann raises the question whether such a new approach might be in line with the pursued idea of decentralisation of decision-making, which arguably calls for sharing of responsibility for the adoption of positive decisions. A reason for it might be the Commission's fear of divergent positive decisions taken by the various national authorities. This risk is considered

> "to be much greater than those resulting from incoherent treatment of complaints (the treatment of which is already decentralised today). For the Commission, the risks of divergences of positive decisions are higher. National authorities might be tempted not to apply Art 81 with sufficient rigour if national interests are at stake. Moreover, positive decisions might have a broader effect than negative decisions. Finally, positive decisions are less likely to be submitted to the control of a judge, as the parties to the agreement, who benefit from it, will certainly not attack these decisions."[458]

Lastly, comfort letters are not considered anymore in the reform and one can assume that the Commission does not want to continue this practice. According to Ehlermann, comfort letters are seen to be even more justified in this new system, though, as a formal decision to set aside the legal effect of Art 81 par 2 ECT is not needed anymore.[459] However, in my opinion he fails to consider that the system of comfort letters produces a substantial amount of the work-overload in the actual system. Hence, there are good reasons to abandon this instrument.

---

[456] See *German Monopolies Commission* par 35.
[457] See Art 5 Reg 1; also see chapter 3.4.5.
[458] See *Ehlermann*, CMLR 2000, 569-570.
[459] See *Ehlermann*, CMLR 2000, 573.

3.4.3.3 Guidelines and notices

To provide further guidance on the application of Art 81 and Art 82 ECT and especially to interpret the rules in an economic nature, the Commission intends to issue guidelines and notices.[460] As Bishop correctly observes,

> "the application of Community competition law is therefore likely to evolve and may entail some seemingly radical departures from previous case law. Indeed, it is the proposed change in the analytical approach that warrants the need for such publications."[461]

Nevertheless, it has been criticised that notices and guidelines are not part of the secondary Community law and hence, they bind neither national courts nor authorities. It is correctly stressed that uncertainties in individual cases are eventually not eradicated.[462] As a result, whether these instruments might prove helpful remains yet to be proven.

3.4.4 A new relationship between the EC law and national law

As explained in chapter 2.4.1.4, the question of which law has to be applied by national bodies is governed by the principle of primacy of Community law over national law.[463] However, this principle leaves a broad margin for parallel proceedings and consequently, bears the risk of contradicting decisions.[464] Moreover, national authorities are not constrained to consider possible infringements of EC competition law, when applying national rules. Therefore, as the possibility of concurrent application was still given there was great concern that decentralisation could produce a renationalisation of competition policy.[465]

---

460 See White Paper par 86. Also see fn 416.

461 See *Bishop*, Modernisation of the rules implementing Article 81 and 82, in Ehlermann/Atanasiu, European Competition Law Annual 2000 (2001), 55 (60-61).

462 See *German Monopolies Commission* par 35. In respect of the missing binding effect, also see White Paper par 86.

463 According to Mestmäcker, "this ruling implies the preservation of national competence for competition law and policy. [...] The supremacy of Community law is thus not defined by its jurisdictional reach in the abstract, because the Court recognises the important complementary role of national competition law, particularly in cases where national law is stricter than Community law." See *Mestmäcker*, European Competition Law Annual 2000 (2001), 238.

464 Also see in this context *Mestmäcker*, European Competition Law Annual 2000 (2001), 239.

465 See *Bourgeois/Humpe*, ECLR 2002, 44.

In this respect the new regulation intends to create a level playing field within the common market by establishing mandatory parallel application of the two sets of rules.[466] In situations where trade between Member States is affected, national courts or authorities that deal with cases referring to collusive behaviour in the meaning of Art 81 ECT have to apply EC law in addition to national rules.[467] The same is provided for abuses as determined by Art 82 ECT. As a consequence, national law can be applied only in conjunction with EC law.[468] This new approach is not as radical as the one contained in the proposal determining that trade distorting practices as defined by the Art 81 and Art 82 ECT are exclusively ruled by Community competition law to the exclusion of national laws.[469]

---

466 applying thus Art 83 par 2 subpar e ECT. In fact, Art 3 par 1 of Reg 1 determines that "where the competition authorities of the Member States or national courts apply national competition law to agreements, decisions by associations of undertakings or concerted practices within the meaning of Article 81 (1) of the Treaty which may affect trade between Member States within the meaning of that provision, they shall also apply Article 81 of the Treaty to such agreements, decisions or concerted practices. Where the competition authorities of the Member States or national courts apply national competition law to any abuse prohibited by Article 82 of the Treaty, they shall also apply Article 82 of the Treaty."
See also *Klocker*, "Fit machen für den Kulturwechsel!", WuW 2002, 1151.

467 In respect of the Proposal, it was criticised that it remained silent in respect of what could be meant by 'national competition law' and it was proposed to define it as national "laws that deal with conduct regulated by Articles 81 and 82." See *Bourgeois/Humpe*, ECLR 2002, 44.

468 *Hossenfelder/Lutz*, WuW 2003, 120.
Weitbrecht in this context, uses the term of ‚factual repression effect' of EC law in respect of national competition rules. See *Weitbrecht*, Das neue EG-Kartellverfahrensrecht, EuZW 2003, 69 (70).

469 See Art 3 Proposal.
Such a solution would have overhauled the parallel applicability of national as well as Community cartel law in favour of EC competition law. See *Stillfried/Stockenhuber*, Zeitschrift für österreichisches und europäisches Wirtschaftsrecht 2001, 148.
Mavroidis/Neven observed that Art 3 of the Proposal - contrary to the final provision as contained in Reg 1 -omitted any explicit reference to the wording 'restriction of competition', but *expressis verbis* referred to trade between Member States. Accordingly, they concluded that arguably the sole condition for the exclusive application of Art 81 ECT is when trade between the Member States becomes affected. As a consequence of this reasoning, the application of national law would have been excluded even where an agreement does not restrict competition but still affects trade between the Member States. As the ECJ has traditionally interpreted this latter concept rather extensively, it would have been "a quixotic test to try to imagine, which cases do not affect trade among Member States. It would [have] thus appear[ed] that the ambit of EC law with respect to national law [increased] as a consequence of the Proposal and as such the proposal should [have been] considered from the perspective of subsidiarity." See *Mavroidis/Neven*, From the White Paper to

Moreover, whereas stricter national law can be applied in respect of Art 82 ECT,[470] this is prohibited in respect of Art 81 ECT.[471] Obviously, the primary condition that trade between Member States has to be affected, still has to be met. An exception is possible for unilateral conduct though.[472]
The new rules do also not preclude the application of national merger law and national laws, which pursue an objective that is different from that pursued by Art 81 and Art 82 ECT.[473]
As a concluding remark one can observe that this enhanced supremacy of EC law will primarily repress those national laws, which differ from EC rules,[474] whereas the rules of the other Member States will not be particularly affected.[475]

---

the Proposal for a Council Regulation: How to treat the new kids on the block?, Legal Issues of Economic Integration 2001, 151 (155).
However, in my opinion Mavroidis/Neven failed to consider that Art 3 Proposal explicitly linked its meaning to Art 81 and Art 82 ECT respectively. Ultimately, this would have meant that competition had to be distorted in order to make Art 3 Proposal applicable. Support for this reasoning can be drawn from the observations of Bourgeois/Humpe who considered the possibility that stricter national law might remain applicable. In my opinion, such a conclusion could not have been embedded in a reasoning that excludes national law *a priori*. Anyhow, the new regulation clarifies these doubts. What remains is the criticism from a point of view of subsidiarity. See *Bourgeois/Humpe*, ECLR 2002, 44.

470 See *Klocker*, WuW 2002, 1151.

471 In fact, Art 3 par 2 Reg 1 indicates that "the application of national competition law may not lead to the prohibition of agreements, decisions by associations of undertakings or concerted practices which may affect trade between Member States but which do not restrict competition within the meaning of Article 81 (1) of the Treaty, or which fulfil the conditions of Article 81 (3) of the Treaty or which are covered by a Regulation for the application of Article 81 (3) of the Treaty."
Hossenfelder/Lutz stress that according to an acknowledged doctrine, supremacy of EC law up to now concentrated on the condition that the conditions of Art 81 par 3 ECT are met. The new system extends this principle to the whole of Art 81 ECT. See *Hossenfelder/Lutz*, WuW 2003, 120.

472 See Art 3 par 2 Reg 1.

473 See Art 3 par 3 Reg 1. This guarantees that national laws dealing with the abuse of market power below market dominance may still be allowed by national competition laws. See *Weitbrecht*, EuZW 2003, 72.

474 As for instance in Germany, see *Weitbrecht*, EuZW 2003, 71; also see Petsche, Das neue EG-Kartellverfahrensrecht, ecolex 2003, 304 (305).

475 See *Weitbrecht*, EuZW 2003, 71.
Bogdandy in this context outlines, that „in particular the principle of equal treatment will make it difficult to maintain another set of competition rules for purely national cases. Yet it must be born in mind that a harmonisation of competition standards represents an increase of legal certainty for the constantly rising number of corporations operating transnationally." See *Bogdandy*, European integration and international co-ordination 2001, 19.

3.4.5 Decentralisation to national authorities

Under the new regime, the Commission as well as national authorities and courts together shall guarantee the maintenance of the system of undistorted competition. In fact, in recital 4 Reg 1 declares that

> "the competition authorities and courts of the Member States have the power to apply not only Art 81 par 1 and Art 82 of the Treaty, which have direct applicability by virtue of the case-law of the Court of Justice of the European Communities, but also Art 81 par 3 of the Treaty."[476]

The relevant provision in respect of national authorities is contained in Art 5 of Reg 1, which states that "the competition authorities of the Member States shall have the power to apply Art 81 and Art 82 ECT in individual cases." Moreover, it contains a catalogue of decisions that the authorities may apply. These are decisions:

- which require that an infringement is brought to an end,
- that adopt interim measures,
- that accept commitments or
- that impose fines and penalties.

As already stated in chapter 3.4.3.2, there is no indication that national authorities can adopt a decision that exempts an agreement, which fulfils the conditions of Art 81 par 3 ECT, and there is also no indication that this catalogue is open, rather it seems that no other decisions than the one indicated can be adopted.[477] An exemption to the prohibition can hence only be applied insofar as the information in the authority's possession reveal that the conditions for prohibition are not met. As a result "they may [...] decide that there are no grounds for action on their part." Anyhow, such an

---

[476] Such was not given by Art 5 Proposal.
In fact, Art 5 Proposal reads as follows:
"The competition authorities of the Member States shall have the power in individual cases to apply the prohibition in Article 81 (1) of the Treaty where the conditions of Article 81 (3) are not fulfilled [...]."
In this regard, it was correctly emphasised that according to such a provision, national competition authorities had been able to apply Art 81 ECT only where the conditions of Art 81 par 3 ECT were not fulfilled. Hence the sharing of enforcement with domestic competition authorities was limited to a 'negative-review' only. A reason for this approach might have been that national competition authorities do not have a mechanism – as courts have by means of Art 234 ECT – for questions relating to the interpretation of EC law. As a result, it is not very likely that EU instances are also involved: a fact that might have inhibited the Commission in deepening devolution in this respect. See *Mavroidis/Neven*, Legal Issues of Economic Integration 2001, 156 and 166-167.

[477] Compare the phrasing of Art 81 par 3 ECT, which uses the wording 'however' to indicate that the list is not exclusive.

evaluation does not reach the extent as a decision according to Art 81 par 3 ECT.[478]

Moreover, as there are still Member States, which do not have competition authorities,[479] the new regulation makes it mandatory for Member States to designate those authorities that shall be responsible for the application of Art 81 and Art 82 ECT.[480] Interestingly, courts shall also be allowed to fulfil the duties of authorities.[481] That seems quite strange as normally courts protect the single interest and not the general interest, which is the task of an administrative authority. However, this solution is justified by the necessity to "recognise the wide variation, which exists in the public enforcement systems of the Member States."[482]

Apart from the said, in respect of decentralisation to national authorities the following issues have been discussed. Firstly, it was asked whether national judges are able to handle the task, secondly, it was considered what consequences the territorially limited effect of national decisions might have, thirdly, concern arose in respect of the allocation of cases between the various national authorities and lastly, doubts appeared in respect of the efficiency of the co-operation-mechanism for national authorities.

3.4.5.1 Can national authorities handle the task?

As we have seen, the application of Art 81 par 3 ECT is not the most simple task in the world, but nevertheless manageable.[483] In respect of fears that political considerations of a Community dimension, which go beyond competition issues, might have to be assessed by national authorities,[484] one can correctly oppose that competition policy must

> "maintain and [...] promote effective competition and market integration following an assessment of the conditions laid down by

---

[478] See Art 5 par 2 Reg 1.

[479] Until 2000, only eight out of 15 Member States had enabled their competition authorities to apply the Art 81 and Art 82 ECT, see *Ehlermann*, CMLR 2000, 581.

[480] See Art 35 Reg 1.

[481] In fact, Art 35 Reg 1 explicitly states that "the effects of Art 11 (6) apply to the authorities designated by the Member States including courts that exercise functions regarding the preparation and the adoption of the types of decisions foreseen in Art 5. The effects of Art 11 (6) do not extend to courts insofar as they act as review courts in respect of the types of decisions foreseen in Art 5."

[482] See recital 35 Reg 1.

[483] See chapter 3.4.1.3.

[484] See *Wesseling*, The Commissions White Paper on Modernisation of EC Antitrust law: unspoken consequences and incomplete treatment of alternative options, ECLR 1999, 420 (425-426).

> the EC competition rules [and] not be influenced by overall political considerations."[485]

Moreover, there are national competition regimes that are modelled along the lines of EC competition law. Thus, Community principles in the field of antitrust have been already incorporated into some nations legislation. This advantage will be rather helpful in applying Art 81 par 3 ECT correctly in order to guarantee consistent application of the law.[486] Therefore,

> "the ideal solution would be to have domestic provisions modelled on EC competition rules, as well as a domestic practice developed along the lines of the EC competition practice."[487]

A further aspect considers whether national authorities are equipped with sufficient staff.[488] Truly, whether these conditions can be fulfilled from all Member States and especially from the new accession states should be considered carefully.[489] On the other hand, increased power of national authorities will force Member States to equip their authorities both from a legally as well as from a personnel perspective.[490] This necessity can draw support directly from Reg 1, which states that Member States when designating the competition authority, shall pursue this target "in such a way that the provisions of this regulation are effectively complied with."[491] In this regard, Forrester stresses that,

> "it is, sadly, true that some national agencies are not yet either well-regarded or well-equipped. There is a remarkable contrast between the *Autorità Garante della Concorrenza e del Mercato* and the

---

485 See *Wißmann*, Journal of World Competition 2000, 143-144.
Burrichter states that "if in the past such considerations have played a role in the practice of the Commission, it would be more than an advantage to return to a strict 'rule of law' in the application of Art 81 par. 3 [...]." See *Burrichter*, Modernisation of EU competition law: the application of Art 81 (3) by national courts. Remarks from the point of view of a practitioner, in Ehlermann/Atanasiu, European Competition Law Annual 2000 (2001), 539 (539-540).

486 Todino observes in this context, that "most of the Member States have now enacted competition law closely modelled on Art 81 par 1 ECT. These countries are: Belgium, Denmark, Finland, France, Greece, Ireland, Italy, Luxembourg, Netherlands, Portugal, Spain, Sweden." See *Todino*, Modernisation from the perspective of national competition authorities: impact of the reform on decentralised application of EC competition law, ECLR 2000, 348 (353 and fn 19). Also see *Immenga*, Harmonisierung des Wettbewerbsrechts als Aufgabe?, EuZW 1997, 449.

487 See *Todino*, ECLR 2000, 353.

488 Wißmann outlines in this context, that some Member States favoured the centralised system, as they feared that the current deplorable state of affairs could be created at national level. See *Wißmann*, Journal of World Competition 2000, 143.

489 For issues referring to the Eastern Enlargement, see chapter 3.4.9.

490 See *Wißmann*, Journal of World Competition 2000, 143.

491 See Art 35 par 1 Reg 1.

> Belgian *Conseil de la Concurrence/Raad voor de Mededinging.*[492] [However], Europe is a large continent with many languages, cultural differences and commercial traditions. A Finnish controversy and a Portuguese controversy regarding similar agreements about the termination of an agency relationship may arrive at a different result. Is this to be regarded as a 'disintegrating' consequence of the decentralisation of enforcement? Or as the consequence of the cultural diversity which Europe honours and by which Europe is marked? I submit it should be the latter. Better that we have some divergence in the application of European competition law reflecting local traditions of commerce and administration than that we have non-existent enforcement, weakened in credibility by having at its heart the fiction that many normal agreements depend for their formal validity on the theoretical availability of practically unavailable Commission blessing."[493]

In this respect, nothing more can be said.
Lastly, Reg 1 concerning the competencies of authorities also deals with the situation in which a national territory or part of it constitutes a separate market.[494] In this case, the concerned national authority is empowered to withdraw the benefit of a block exemption in respect of this territory. Indeed, at the end of the day, national authorities should – in such circumstances – be better placed to determine whether or not the conditions for Art 81 par 3 ECT are fulfilled.[495]

3.4.5.2 Territorial effect of national decisions

Since the publication of the White Paper, the binding effect of decisions taken by national competition authorities has been a regularly discussed issue and often requested matter.[496] However, Reg 1 does not provide for such an effect. In fact, Art 13 par 2 Reg 1 states that

> "where the competition authority of a Member State or the Commission has received a complaint against an agreement, decision of an association or practice which has already been dealt with by another competition authority, it may reject it."

---

[492] See *Forrester*, Legal Issues of Economic Integration 2001, 182.
[493] See *Forrester*, Legal Issues of Economic Integration 2001, 188.
[494] More precisely, Art 29 par 2 Reg 1 refers in this context to a territory having "all the characteristics of a distinct geographic market."
[495] See White Paper par 95.
[496] See for instance *Mestmäcker*, EuZW 1999, 16-17.

It is clear that a national decision that can be rejected by another competition authority or the Commission respectively, cannot be binding on the latter.[497] In line with this reasoning, Bourgeois/Humpe accurately highlight, that

> "the possibility thus left open to the Commission suggests that the drafters consider the preventive measures of the draft regulation[498] insufficient to exclude the adoption by national competition authorities of decisions with which the Commission is not satisfied. Should this be the case then the answer lies - it is submitted - with reinforced preventive measures rather than with the adoption of corrective measures undermining the principle of legal certainty." [499]

Moreover, the fact that decisions taken by one national authority are not binding on another national authority inevitably bears the risk of multiple jurisdiction. Eventually this might lead to conflicting decisions, the risk of double jeopardy[500] for undertakings and obviously the restricted effectiveness of national decisions[501]. Lastly, Mavroidis/Neven[502] fear that national authorities, which are accountable to their constituencies, might only consider the interests of their constituencies and hence will probably not take into account the effects of a case outside their territory.

To tackle this problem the signing of multilateral agreements between the Member States, which enable enforceability of national decisions throughout the Community, was proposed. Of course, the new regulation could also be amended in order to guarantee that national decisions are Community-wide recognised.[503] Other solutions advocate that the decision taken by a national authority shall be attributed to the Commission or propose to adopt the principle of mutual recognition, by which a decision that corresponds to certain minimum standards in term of publicity, due process and judicial

---

[497] See Proposal 17.

[498] Reg 1 did not alter this provision.

[499] See *Bourgeois/Humpe*, ECLR 2002, 49.

[500] "The possibility that a citizen may be tried twice for the same crime", see Collins Paperback English Dictionary[4].

[501] See *Bourgeois/Humpe*, ECLR 2002, 49;
Also see Bovis, who states that "decisions of domestic competition authorities do not produce legally binding effects outside the territory of the relevant member states. Thus, the decentralised application of Art 81 (3) EC would be at the very least ineffective, possibly resulting in a segmented and fragmented application of Community anti-trust law and policy." See *Bovis*, Transforming the application of EC competition laws: the case of decentralisation, European Business Law 2001, 102.

[502] See *Mavroidis/Neven*, Legal Issues of Economic Integration 2001, 161.

[503] See *Wißmann*, Journal of World Competition 2000, 144.

protection would automatically be recognised within the whole Community. A provision that introduces this principle, might be based on Art 83 ECT.[504]

3.4.5.3 The allocation of cases

The pursuit of decentralisation to national competition authorities raises the question of which authority should deal with a case involved, each time EC competition rules are applicable.[505] In this respect, the Commission in referring to Art 13 par 1 of the Proposal, which was completely reiterated by Reg 1,[506] emphasises that this provision shall "serve the purpose of effective case allocation within the network of competition authorities."[507] According to the wording of Art 13 par 1 Reg 1, national authorities have a right[508] and an obligation to suspend or reject a case that is already dealt with by another national authority. Such an observation can clearly be drawn from the fact that Art 13 par 1 Reg 1 uses the wording "shall be sufficient grounds" and hence does contain an obligation on the authorities to suspend or to reject.[509] On the other hand, an existing national decision does not hinder

---

504 See *Ehlermann*, CMLR 2000, 572 and *Bourgeois/Humpe*, ECLR 2002, 49.
For examples, where the mutual recognition principle has been applied, see for instance the Second Banking Directive (Second Council Directive 89/646/EEC of 15 December 1989 on the coordination of laws, regulations and administrative provisions relating to the taking up and pursuit of the business of credit institutions and amending Directive 77/780/EEC).

505 "The principle must be that cases are dealt with by the authority best placed to act. The aim is to avoid multiple control, duplication of work or inefficient actions. In the Community context multiple control means parallel procedures with each authority acting within its own jurisdiction." See *Schaub*, European Competition Law Annual 2000 (2001), 255.

506 Art 13 par 1 Reg 1 reads as follows:
Where competition authorities of two or more Member States have received a complaint or are acting on their own initiative under Art 81 or Art 82 of the Treaty against the same agreement, decision of an association or practice, the fact that one authority is dealing with the case shall be sufficient grounds for the others to suspend the proceedings before them or to reject the complaint. The Commission may likewise reject a complaint on the ground that a competition authority of a Member State is dealing with the case.

507 See Proposal 21.

508 See Proposal 21.

509 See also *Mavroidis/Neven*, Legal Issues of Economic Integration 2001, 160-161; contrary to this opinion *Bourgeois/Humpe*, ECLR 2002, 47; also see *Stillfried/Stockenhuber*, Zeitschrift für österreichisches und europäisches Wirtschaftsrecht 2001, 148. However, *Bourgeois/Humpe*, as well as *Stillfried/Stockenhuber* fail to recognise that "shall" indicates an obligation, especially in official documents. As a matter of fact, "the usual rule given to the use of shall [...] is that where the meaning is one of simple futurity, shall is used for the first person of

another national competition authority to deal with the case once more. In fact, Art 13 par 2 Reg 1 contains no requirement to reject a case already dealt with.[510]

Nevertheless, the regulation does not go further and does not contain precise rules for the allocation of cases. Hence, undertakings may be tempted to put their agreements for scrutiny to those authorities that are more likely to adopt a favourable outcome in respect of their agreements (forum shopping[511]).[512] Moreover, uncertainty in this respect could also generate the lodging of multiple complaints before different domestic authorities.[513]

Various criteria have been put forward to combat this problem. For instance it was suggested to install a 'centre of gravity test', which determines the competence of an authority according to the position of dominance of an undertaking. Another solution was inspired by the Merger Regulation that adopts a turnover criteria. Finally, it was suggested to set a up clearing-house system, under which the Commission will attribute cases to national competition authorities.[514] Anyhow, it seems that no completely satisfying approach has been found yet. It has correctly been emphasised that the proposal, and accordingly the regulation, should be amended in order to contain an efficient mechanism for case allocation.[515]

---

the verb and will for the second and third. I shall go tomorrow, they will be there now. Where the meaning involves command, obligation, or determination, the positions are reversed: it shall be done; I will definitely go. See Collins Paperback English Dictionary[4] (1999); further support for this reasoning can be found in Art 13 par 1 Reg 1 itself, which, for indicating a mere possibility, opposes 'may' to 'shall' in respect of the Commission.

510 In fact, Art 13 par 2 Reg 1 reads as follows:
Where a competition authority of a Member State or the Commission has received a complaint against an agreement, decision of an association or practice, which has already been dealt with by another competition authority, it may reject it.

511 "The process of shopping round the world's courts until one finds a court where one is likely to obtain the most successful outcome", see *Clarkson/Hill*, Jaffey on the conflict of laws (1997), 5.

512 See *Ehlermann*, CMLR 2000, 570; also see *German Monopolies Commission* par 47.

513 See *Bourgeois/Humpe*, ECLR 2002, 47.

514 See *Bourgeois/Humpe*, ECLR 2002, 47; also see *Wißmann*, Journal of World Competition 2000, fn 18.

515 See *Bourgeois/Humpe*, ECLR 2002, 47.
Ehlermann highlights that the problem of attribution arises also in the context of complaints. Such rules do not have to be as precise as for positive decisions but clear enough to balance predictability and flexibility. See *Ehlermann*, CMLR 2000, 571.

3.4.5.4 Co-operation in the network

Decentralisation implies the risk of inconsistent decision-taking by the various bodies involved. To limit this risk, the regulation concentrates on the strengthening of co-operation within a network of the various competition authorities and the Commission.[516]

Art 11 of the new regulation, which is the central provision regarding co-operation between the Commission and the single national authorities,[517] contains for instance the request of informing the Commission of cases involving Art 81 and Art 82 ECT at an early stage,[518] supporting measures like the transferring of important documents collected by the Commission to national authorities[519] and facultative consultation mechanisms.[520] Moreover, a specific provision gives the Commission the possibility to withdraw a case from the jurisdiction of a national authority to initiate an own

---

516 Detailed rules will be determined in an implementing Commission regulation and in a specific notice on co-operation. See Proposal 19 and Art 33 Reg 1.
In this regard, Schaub outlines that "this network with the supporting rules and instruments for co-operation will in itself greatly enhance predictability compared to the present situation where 16 authorities apply 16 sometimes different sets of rules and procedures, each subject to its own autonomous system of judicial control. Taken as a whole, the present system [as established under Reg 17], that incorporates both Community and national elements, leaves room for significant inconsistencies, and reduces the level of predictability within the internal market." See *Schaub*, European Competition Law Annual 2000 (2001), 254-255.

517 Indeed, Art 11 par 1 Reg 1 demands for close co-operation between the Commission and the competition authorities of the Member States when applying EC competition rules. Also see *Stillfried/Stockenhuber*, Zeitschrift für österreichisches und europäisches Wirtschaftsrecht 2001, 149.

518 See Art 11 par 3 Reg 1.
According to the Commission, this mechanism shall help to "facilitate case allocation, to initiate co-operation on cases at an early stage, and to ensure effective handling of multiple complaints", see Proposal 20.
Moreover, Art 11 par 4 precises that "no later than 30 days before the adoption of a decision requiring that an infringement be brought to an end, accepting commitments or withdrawing the benefit of a block exemption Regulation, the competition authorities of the Member States shall inform the Commission." All this information shall also be made available to the competition authorities of other Member States and be exchanged among themselves.

519 Likewise to Art 10 par 1 Reg 17, Art 11 par 2 Reg 1 demands:
The Commission shall transmit to the competition authorities of the Member States copies of the most important documents it has collected with a view to applying Art 7, Art 8, Art 9, Art 10 and Art 29 (1). At the request of the competition authority of a Member State, the Commission shall provide it with a copy of other existing documents necessary for the assessment of the case.

520 See Art 11 par 5 Reg 1. To the contrary, the consultation mechanism as provided for by the Proposal was mandatory. See Proposal 21.

proceeding.[521] However, and this is new, "if a competition authority of a Member State is already acting on a case, the Commission shall only initiate proceedings after consulting with that national competition authority."[522]
In this context, the Commission affirms that

> "this provision is of crucial importance in the new system; it serves to ensure effective case allocation and consistent application of Community competition law.[523] [...] In case of substantial disagreement within the network, the Commission retains the power to withdraw a case from a national competition authority by itself initiating proceedings in the case."[524]

However, as Stockenhuber/Stillfried rightly observe, the wording of Art 11 par 6 Reg 17 is not bound by such conditions.[525]
An elementary part of the network entails the exchange of information. Art 12 of the new regulation considers investigations, which are to be held in more than one Member State, and reflects the necessity to enable an authority to pass the case to the authority that is in the best position to deal with it.[526] As requested after the publication of the White Paper, the forwarded documents can now be used as evidence and the necessary confidentiality of business secrets seems to be respected.[527] In fact, Art 12 Reg 1 prohibits the use of this information for purposes other than the "purpose of applying Art 81 or Art 82 of the Treaty and in respect of the subject-matter for which it was

---

[521] In this respect, Ehlermann clarifies that this right of evocation does interfere less with the autonomy of national competition authorities than a requirement that asks for the Commission's consent, or the possibility for the Commission to annul a national decision. Such devices would introduce elements of administrative hierarchy, which is absent in the EC Treaty and secondary legislation. See *Ehlermann*, CMLR 2000, 578.

[522] See Art 11 par 6 Reg 1.

[523] See Proposal 21.

[524] See Proposal 10.

[525] See *Stillfried/Stockenhuber*, Zeitschrift für österreichisches und europäisches Wirtschaftsrecht 2001, fn 20.

[526] Art 12 par 1 Reg 1 states that "for the purpose of applying Art 81 and Art 82 of the Treaty the Commission and the competition authorities of the Member States shall have the power to provide one another with [...] any matter of fact or of law, including confidential information."

[527] See *Wißmann*, Journal of World Competition 2000, 144.
Art 20 Reg 17 impedes the use of information forwarded by the Commission. Also see in this respect ECJ case C-67/91 (Asociación Española de Bance Privada).

collected by the transmitting authority."[528] However, as

> "several national laws do not allow the forwarding of confidential information to any other body [...] a harmonisation of the national and Community legislation concerned is needed in order to make satisfactory co-operation possible, at the same time safeguarding the necessary confidentiality of business secrets."[529]

Next, to strengthen the network, it was requested that the Advisory Committee on restrictive practices and dominant positions becomes a full-scale forum to discuss relevant issues[530] and to act as a consultant on Commission-decisions,[531] on individual cases, other competition issues and on national proceedings.[532] Even though the decisions adopted by the Advisory Committee are not binding, the Commission has to "take the utmost account of the opinion delivered by the Advisory Committee [and] it shall inform the Committee of the manner in which its opinion has been taken into account."[533] Moreover, consultations may take place by written procedure,[534] which can be made public,[535] and also may regard cases dealt with by

---

528 See Art 12 par 2 and par 3 Reg 1, which add the following:
"However, where national competition law is applied in the same case and in parallel to Community competition law and does not lead to a different outcome, information exchanged under this Article may also be used for the application of national competition law." Moreover, the information exchanged can "only be used in evidence to impose sanctions on natural persons where:
– the law of the transmitting authority foresees sanctions of a similar kind in relation to an infringement of Art 81 or Art 82 of the Treaty or, in the absence thereof,
– the information has been collected in a way which respects the same level of protection of the rights of defence of natural persons as provided for under the national rules of the receiving authority. However, in this case, the information exchanged cannot be used by the receiving authority to impose custodial sanctions."

529 See *Wißmann*, Journal of World Competition 2000, 144.

530 See *Ehlermann*, CMLR 2000, 579; also see *Todino*, ECLR 2000, 352.
In this respect, Siragusa outlines that the advisory committee would become a forum of discussion in which all national competition authorities' planned decisions would be discussed to ensure that the competition authorities, which might potentially adopt a conflicting decision, can reach a common agreement. See *Siragusa*, The modernisation of EC competition law: risks of cohabitation, private enforcement and other issues, in Ehlermann/Atanasiu, European Competition Law Annual 2000 (2001), 443 (448).

531 See Art 14 par 1 Reg 1.

532 See Art 14 par 2 and 7 Reg 1.

533 See Art 14 par 5 Reg 1.

534 See Art 14 par 4 Reg 1.

535 See Art 14 par 6 Reg 1.
However, in such case the Commission has to take "into account the legitimate interest of undertakings in the protection of their business secrets."

national authorities.[536] Lastly, the Advisory Committee has to be heard in respect of the implementing provisions for Reg 1.[537]
Lastly, whereas the Proposal was rather vague in respect of guarantees for the uniform application of Community competition law,[538] the actual regulation is definitely more pushing - at least in respect of the vertical relationship between the Commission and national authorities - as it prohibits national authorities from making decisions that "run counter to the decision adopted by the Commission".[539]
Taken together, it is welcomed that the relationship between national authorities and the Commission is formalised, with the role of the latter as first among equals. This is particularly stressed by the obligation on authorities to inform the Commission of all decisions they are going to take.[540] However, it still does not seem satisfactory that the Commission has not bound its discretion in respect of its intervention-mechanisms. As a matter of fact, it is not clear under which circumstances the Commission will use its right of evocation or consider a case before a national authority.[541] The same is true for cases that have been decided by national authorities already. Hence, one can criticise that private parties might prefer the security of a Commission decision, and hence direct their complaints to the Commission instead of authorities.[542] Anyhow, the Commission clarifies that a notice on co-operation and an implementing Commission regulation will lay

536 See Art 14 par 7 Reg 1.
In this context, Ehlermann at an earlier stage of the reform process observed that the reform "is mainly concerned with the vertical relationship between the Commission and the national competition authorities. However, it is also highly desirable to promote the co-operation and co-ordination among such authorities. The horizontal relationship between national competition authorities is, of course, in the first place, a matter for themselves." See *Ehlermann*, CMLR 2000, 579.

537 See Art 33 par 2 Reg 1.

538 In fact, according to Art 16 Proposal, national competition authorities and also national courts in adopting their decisions should have been 'only' requested to use every effort to avoid any decision that might oppose decisions adopted by the Commission. This request was linked to Art 10 ECT, imposing on Member States the obligation to make sure that the obligations arising out of the EC Treaty are fulfilled and to abstain from any measure, which could endanger the realization of the objectives of the Treaty. Lenaerts/Van Nuffel have defined this obligation as 'federal good faith'. See *Mavroidis/Neven*, Legal Issues of Economic Integration 2001, 164.

539 See Art 16 par 2 Reg 1.

540 See *Mavroidis/Neven*, Legal Issues of Economic Integration 2001, 166; also see *Schaub*, European Competition Law Annual 2000 (2001), 255; also see *Bogdandy*, European integration and international co-operation 2000, 17.

541 Schaub assumes that "disputes will be satisfactorily solved by intensive consultation and discussion and [the power of evocation] will only be applied in exceptional cases." See Schaub, European Competition Law Annual 2000 (2001), 255.

542 See *Mavroidis/Neven*, Legal Issues of Economic Integration 2001, 166.

down detailed rules.[543] Such a possibility is also scheduled for by Art 33 Reg 1.[544]

3.4.6 Decentralisation to national courts

In the Delimits case,[545] the EJC stressed that national courts can apply 81 par 1 ECT only on the condition that par 3 is not applicable. It was argued that that the lack of jurisdiction over par 3 of national courts under Reg 17 is particularly problematic when private enforcement is being sought, as undertakings can bring court proceedings to a halt by submitting a notification to the Commission.[546] The reform has abolished this principle. This fact is contained in Art 6 Reg 1, which states that national courts "shall have the power to apply Art 81 par 3." Consequently, a national court, which finds that the settings of Art 81 par 3 ECT are met, has to hold that the agreement is valid *ab initio*. As a result, the agreement has to be enforced and any claims for damages, which are based on an alleged violation of Art 81 ECT, have to be rejected.[547] As judges can fully assess whether agreements can be enforced, the responsibilities of the national courts will consequently be increased considerably.[548] Whether it is wise to adopt an approach, which ultimately aims at fostering the readiness to litigate in court is - in my opinion - another question, though.

On the other hand, it has been criticised that the new system simply shifts the work overload from the Commission to national courts.[549] In my opinion, such criticism is rather simplistic though, as it does not consider the fact that

---

[543] See Proposal 19. Also see in this context fn 416 of this dissertation.

[544] In fact, Art 33 Reg 1 authorises the Commission to take "such measures as may be appropriate in order to apply this Regulation. The measures may concern, inter alia :
(a) the form, content and other details of complaints lodged pursuant to Art 7 and the procedure for rejecting complaints;
(b) the practical arrangements for the exchange of information and consultations provided for in Art 11;
(c) the practical arrangements for the hearings provided for in Art 27."

[545] See ECJ case 234/89 (Delimitis).

[546] See White Paper par 100.
It is questioned whether the lack of jurisdiction over par 3 of Art 81 ECT is really the main cause for the limited role of the national judges' role in the application of EC competition law. According to Bourgeois/Humpe, it might be a matter of the limited fact-finding powers, which are available to domestic judges. See *Bourgeois/Humpe*, ECLR 2002, 46.

[547] See Proposal 17.

[548] See *Ehlermann*, CMLR 2000, 584.

[549] See *German Monopolies Commission* par 45.

decentralisation to national courts also implies an increase in work-capacities as more persons are involved in the enforcement process.
Next, the Commission outlines that with the new system, parties will now also be allowed to use Art 81 par 3 ECT to their defence[550] and furthermore, it facilitates the procurement of immediate civil enforcement of those agreements that are in line with EC competition law. Therefore, legal certainty is strengthened and complainants can obtain damages more quickly.[551] Nevertheless, other disadvantages[552] of private enforcement as

550 *Ehlermann/Atanasiu* illustrate in this context, that "in the course of private litigation, the infringement of Articles 81 and 82 ECT can be invoked either as a 'shield' or as a 'sword'. It is invoked as a 'shield' when the defendant who is party to an agreement invokes the nullity of the agreement according to Art 81 par 2 ECT. It is invoked, instead, as a 'sword', when the plaintiff bases a claim for damages or restitution on the illegality of the agreement. In the latter case, the plaintiff can either be party to the allegedly illegal agreement or an outsider (for example, a competitor or a consumer)." See *Ehlermann/Atansiu*, The Modernisation of EC Antitrust Law: Consequences for the Future Role and Function of the EC Courts, ECLR 2002, 72 (78).

551 See White Paper par 100. On the other hand, Siragusa in this context emphasises that "it is, however, unlikely that Art 81 proceedings before national courts would become quicker or would increase in number, merely because national courts had the power to apply Art 81 par 3. Most national courts might not feel at ease in applying a provision whose interpretation focuses on mere policy and economic considerations rather than general principles of law and might prefer to seek advice from the Commission, to refer the matter to the Court of Justice pursuant to Art 234 EC, or - if the Commission or an NCA have already initiated investigations concerning the same contested practice - to stay the proceedings until the outcome of such investigations." See *Siragusa*, in Ehlermann/Atanasiu, European Competition Law Annual 2000 (2001), 446.

552 Pirie outlines advantages and disadvantages of litigating in a National Court:
Advantages:
"(a) Commission may not take up complaint anyway: It is possible that the complainant may not convince the Commission to take up his complaint and will have to turn to national authorities or to the national court if he wishes to pursue his claim. [...]; (b) Control of the case: [...] when the Commission takes up a complaint the complainant has only limited amount of control [...]. On the other hand, in a national court, the plaintiff is in control of the litigation; (c) Remedies: The Commission's remedy for breaches of Art 85 and Art 86 is nullity. It cannot reward damages or restitution. [...]; (d) Combination of EC and national law claims: A claim under EC law can be combined with a claim under national law, so long as the national law does not impair the effective enforcement of EC law. [...]; (e) Interim Relief: It is generally easier to obtain interim relief from national courts than from the Commission. [...]."
Advantages of complaining to the Commission (which may be seen as the disadvantages of complaining to a national court):
"(a) Cost: Actions before national courts are, as general rule, extremely costly and involve the risk of losing and having to pay the defendant's costs as well as your own. On the other hand, a complaint to the Commission [...] will be far less than the price of proceedings before a national court. (b) Evidence/Powers of Investigation: The Commission has wide powers of investigation, [...], which the complainant and in most

for instance high costs or getting hold of evidence[553] still remain. Moreover, the predictability of outcome of claims in respect of an infringement of Art 81 ECT decreases, due to the more economically based interpretation of the notion of restriction of competition.[554] Taken these points together, one can doubt whether national courts will ever play a significant role in enforcing Art 81 ECT.[555]

Apart from these general observations, concern arose in respect of the ability of national courts to apply Art 81 par 3 ECT. It was further questioned whether the differing national procedural law regimes might bear a risk of inconsistency. Other aspects concern the independence of national courts and similarities between the proposed system and the US model of competition law enforcement. These issues will be analysed in subsequent chapters.

---

cases national courts and authorities do not possess. [...]; (c) Jurisdiction: [...] there may be difficulties in establishing that a national court has jurisdiction. Such difficulties do not exist if the Commission has taken up the case; (d) No necessity to prove a causal link: [...] an applicant before a national court would have to prove a causal link between the conduct of the competitor and the damage he suffered, whereas the Commission would not; (e) Positive decision persuasive in national courts and competition authorities: Commission decisions must be taken into consideration by national courts and are extremely persuasive; (f) Increased likelihood of private settlement: [...] it is clear that a favourable private settlement is more likely to be achieved if the complainant has a favourable decision from the Commission; (g) Specialised knowledge: The Commission has more specialised knowledge of European competition law than the national courts. [...] (h) Anonymity: The complainant has a right to remain anonymous in his complaint and in the possible proceedings brought by the Commission. [...] (i) Protection form libel action: Some Member States protect the complainant from libel actions. [...]." See *Pirie*, The complainant in EC competition law, Competition law 2000, 107 (109-111).

553 Generally, the burden of proof lies on the party that is invoking this proof. See *Wißmann*, Journal of World Competition 2000, 132.
In this sense, Art 2 Reg 1 determines that:
"In any national or Community proceedings for the application of Art 81 and Art 82 of the Treaty, the burden of proving an infringement of Art 81 (1) or of Art 82 of the Treaty shall rest on the party or the authority alleging the infringement. The undertaking or association of undertakings claiming the benefit of Art 81 (3) of the Treaty shall bear the burden of proving that the conditions of that paragraph are fulfilled."
In this respect, Mestmäcker indicates the problem that "the facts that are relevant for Art 81 par 3 and that the plaintiff would have to prove to challenge a cartel are, by their very nature, known only by cartel members." See *Mestmäcker*, European Competition Law Annual 2000 (2001), 233.

554 See *Ehlermann/Atanasiu*, ECLR 2002, 78-79; also see White Paper par 75 and fn 23 of this dissertation.

555 See *Wißmann*, Journal of World Competition, 145; also see *Ehlermann/Atanasiu*, ECLR 2002, 78-79; also see *Todino*, ECLR 2000, 350.

3.4.6.1 Ability of national courts to apply Art 81 par 3 ECT

As mentioned, the application of Art 81 par 3 ECT is not easy, but difficulties are no greater than those posed in respect of the application of the Art 82 and Art 86 par 2 ECT: Both articles are directly applicable and at least as 'imprecise' and difficult to apply as Art 81 par 3 ECT.[556] Moreover, it has correctly been highlighted that other law areas, for instance corporate or tax law, require difficult economic evaluations as well.[557] The problems arise from the fact that up to now there has been no guidance from the Commission for the decentralised application of Art 81 par 3 ECT, formal Commission decision are rather scarce and no authorative interpretations have been provided by the Court of Justice. Hence, these problems should be of transitional nature only.[558]

The efficient application of Art 81 par 3 ECT depends on the wording and systematic of the law, but one also has to focus on whether judges are able to perform this task. Indeed, doubts emerged as to whether they are equipped to handle the complex economic and legal questions of fact and law required under Art 81 par 3 ECT.[559] National courts have no profound experience with the application of Art 81 par 3 ECT and as Ehlermann/Atanasiu accurately observe,

> "at least in the beginning national courts will face an additional difficulty deriving from the application of Art 81 par 3 because its interpretation is largely unknown territory for everybody."[560]

---

556 See chapter 3.4.1.3.

557 See *Ehlermann*, CMLR 2000, 585; of this opinion is also *Edward*, The Modernisation of EC Antitrust Policy: Issues for Courts and Judges, European Competition Law Annual 2000 (2001), 565 (568).
In this respect, quite sceptical is Goyder, who observes the following: "I have however grave doubts as to whether national judges would be sensibly employed under present arrangements in seeking in their own to resolve Art 81 par 3 cases, trying to balance the degree to which the agreement or practice at issue actually restricts competition against the four conditions for exemption. Under the adversarial system at least the court would be highly dependent on the resources of the parties to present a full set of arguments and the likely imbalance of resources in a case between, say, a large multinational and a sole trader, may make this difficult. Even if the judge is able to obtain a full picture of the issues, is it a sensible use of judicial manpower, which is scarce, expensive and required for many other public policy tasks? As to the latter, society might rightly regard them as having a higher priority than resolving arguments between commercial undertakings about whether a particular restraint justifies an exemption." See *Goyder*, Providing support for national judges in dealing with competition issues, European Competition Law Annual 2000 (2001), 571 (573).

558 See *Ehlermann*, CMLR 2000, 585.

559 See *Ehlermann*, CMLR 2000, 585.

560 See *Ehlermann/Atansiu*, ECLR 2002, 76; also see *Burrichter*, European Competition Law Annual 2000 (2001), 540.

It was considered, which measures could improve enforcement of community competition law by national courts. Gustafsson in referring to Temple Lang outlines different means in this respect:

> "they may sit with economic advisers or have training in antitrust economics; specialised courts could be established; [...] each Member State could have an independent 'Community Law Advisor' or 'National Advocate General' who would render non-binding opinions as to the correct interpretation of Community law. Other options could be to give the competition authority some form of standing (such as intervention and right to appeal), or to provide for a preliminary reference procedure to a specialised administrative competition body (preferably a court)."[561]

As competition law generally tends to be both complex and lengthy, Goyder convincingly favours judges and courts specialised in competition matters.[562] On the other hand, Ehlermann acknowledges that Art 81 ECT issues include such a wide range of cases that the generalised requirement of specialised judges might be to impracticable and unrealistic.[563] In any case, national courts will

> "need anti-trust training, as, although jurisdictionally competent, they might feel less confident in dealing with a competition case and subsequently utilise referral proceedings for preliminary rulings from the European Court of Justice.[564]"

3.4.6.2 Appropriateness of national procedural law

As the reform obliges national judges to apply EC-competition law, one should consider whether discrepancies between the various national procedural rules might bear a risk of inconsistency. In fact, it has been criticised that due to existing discrepancies between the various national

561 See *Gustafsson*, Some legal implications facing the realisation of the Commission White Paper on modernisation of EC antitrust procedure and the role of national courts in a post-White Paper era, Legal Issues of Economic Integration 2000, 159 (174).

562 See *Goyder*, European Competition Law Annual 2000 (2001), 576; also see *Ehlermann*, CMLR 2000, 557; and *Edward*, European Competition Law Annual 2000 (2001), 565-566.

563 See *Ehlermann*, CMLR 2000, 585.

564 See *Bovis*, Transforming the application of EC competition laws: the case of decentralisation, European Business Law 2001, 98 (101). In this context, also see *Burrichter*, European Competition Law Annual 2000 (2001), 540; and *Edward*, European Competition Law Annual 2000 (2001), 567.

procedural rules, no consistent application of EC law on national level can be guaranteed resulting thus in diverging decisions.[565]

In this context, the Automec II case[566] rules that the Commission is not allowed to direct complaints to national authorities without the existence of certain guarantees at national level. Therefore, wider-reaching suggestions by the Commission concentrating on decentralisation shall focus on the structure, powers, procedures, resources and judicial control of national judges. Anyhow, in respect of such suggestions one can admittedly oppose that EU institutions are not asked to assume responsibilities, simply because an unsatisfactory situation at the national level exists.[567]

Moreover, the new system, by establishing different levels and different bodies, is in need for mechanisms that ensure a division of power, but which also clarify which body has the last word. In this sense, Wißmann criticises that

> "the White Paper does not [nor does Reg 1] address this question to a satisfying extent, arguably because it feels that the political landscape is not yet prepared for the establishment of a hierarchical administrative structure with the Commission or a European Cartel Office on top."[568]

A remedy to the outlined problems could be given by further harmonisation of EC and national competition laws, which eventually lessens the difficulties such a system of double control contains.[569] Nevertheless, such harmonisation of laws might be politically problematic. As a matter of fact,

> "the different procedures in each Member State create an uneven system, which at the moment cannot be harmonised, since in these matters Member States retain their sovereignty with the exception

565 Gustafsson reveals that "one may question whether national civil court proceedings are actually feasible for competition law enforcement in the sense that the outcome of specific cases may vastly vary depending on the procedural law of the Member States. Accordingly, there can be no doubt that the handling of competition issues in national courts vary, eg, as to the conditions for, if at all, *ex officio* investigation and application of the relevant provisions to such issues. Thus forum shopping may not only occur due to (potential) divergent Member State appraisal of Community competition policy, but also because of procedural aspects. Companies, which litigate, and when doing so wish to conceal their potentially or clearly anti-competitive agreement, may thus choose to litigate in a forum not likely to conduct *ex officio* investigations (provided, of course, that the forum in question accepts jurisdiction). See *Gustafsson*, Legal Issues of Economic Integration 2000, 176; also see *Bovis*, European Business Law 2001, 102; and *Weitbrecht*, EuZW 2003, 76.

566 See CFI case T-24/90 (Automec).

567 See *Ehlermann*, CMLR 2000, 582.

568 See *Wißmann*, Journal of World Competition 2000, 148.

569 See *Wißmann*, Journal of World Competition 2000, 147.

of the co-operation contemplated by the third pillar of the EU Treaty."[570]

Consequently, Ehlermann wisely suggests considering problems of disparities and deficiencies of the Member States' courts and authorities at a later stage. The practical experience with this new system shall provide for the necessity of further reforms, which might also include the harmonisation of laws.[571]

3.4.6.3 Co-operation between the Commission and national courts

Intrinsically, the abolition of the exemption monopoly held by the Commission, bears the risk of divergent decisions. This shall be avoided through enhanced co-operation between Commission, national authorities and courts. Mechanisms for co-operation[572] between the Commission and national courts shall foster consistency of interpretation of the competition rules, once its application is decentralised.[573] The foundations for a co-operation with national courts are laid in Art 15 of the new regulation.

First, an information-sharing tool in proceedings for the proper application of Art 81 or Art 82 ECT enables national courts to ask the Commission to transmit necessary information and opinions.[574] Besides, national courts have to forward any written judgement deciding on the application of Art 81 or Art 82 ECT to the Commission.[575]

Next, Reg 1 grants the Commission the power to put forward, on its own initiative (in the role as *amicus curiae*[576]) written observations to courts of the Member States. This competence is granted only on the condition that

570 See *Todino*, ECLR 2000, 351.

571 See *Ehlermann*, CMLR 2000, 582-583.
Burrichter agrees with the fact that harmonisation is not a precondition for allowing direct application of Art 81 par 3 ECT. Indeed, "by subscribing to the Conventions of Brussels and Lugano, the Member States have shown that they do not regard the differences and disparities of their legal systems as being so important; otherwise they would not have agreed to mutually acknowledge the decisions of the Courts of the Member States." See *Burrichter*, European Competition Law Annual 2000 (2001), 544; in this sense also see *Gröning*, National judges in a modernised Community law system. A special view to procedural aspects, European Competition Law Annual 2000 (2001), 579 (583).

572 Such mechanisms are already contained in the 1993 Notice of co-operation between the Commission and national courts, they are not binding though. See chapter 2.4.4.

573 See *Ehlermann*, CMLR 2000, 577

574 See Art 15 par 1 Reg 1.

575 See Art 15 par 2 Reg 1.

576 See Proposal, 23.

the coherent application of Art 81 or Art 82 ECT requires so. Oral observations are only possible by way of the permission of the court in question.[577] Moreover, written and oral observations can also be submitted by national authorities to the national courts of their Member States.[578] The proper-functioning of these intervention-instruments has to be shown by reality, though. In fact, it will probably,

> "absorb a lot of the Commission's resources to be continuously informed on the competitive conditions of a huge variety of different (national/regional) relevant markets and send representatives to judgements dealing with all kinds of restrictions in 15 to 20 Member States. The aim of the [reform], to improve the conditions for the Commission to act rather than react, [could] be immediately undermined."[579]

Furthermore, it was criticised that a mandatory information requirement seems hardly reconcilable with the principle of independency of the courts.[580] Also, the possibility for the Commission to act as *amicus curiae* could create some legal problems.[581] According to Ehlermann, this criticisms

---

[577] See Art 15 par 3 Reg 1.
In this context, Edward recognises that "the courts of all the Member States, as well as the ECJ and the CFI, are already suffering from severe overload, and that this situation is unlikely to change in the near future, if at all. If the proposed new system is to depend on the Commission providing national courts and Community courts with advice and assistance, the Commission cannot be allowed to plead lack of time, resources or manpower as a reason for not doing so. In that connection, it is disturbing that the Commission has already suggested, in a different context, that it should no longer submit observations in all Art 234 references." See *Edward*, European Competition Law Annual 2000 (2001), 567.
More optimistic, Burrichter observes that by this means national authorities and the Commission have the "possibility of avoiding the outcome that national courts take decisions without at least having been informed about the relevant competition aspects." See *Burrichter*, European Competition Law Annual 2000 (2001), 541.

[578] In respect, Art 15 par 3 Reg 1 stresses that oral observations need the previous permission of the court in question. Moreover, "for the purpose of the preparation of their observations only, the competition authorities of the Member States and the Commission may request the relevant court of the Member State to transmit or ensure the transmission to them of any documents necessary for the assessment of the case."

[579] See *Gröning*, European Competition Law Annual 2000 (2001), 582.

[580] See *Ehlermann*, CMLR 2000, 580.

[581] See *Todino*, ECLR 2000, 351.
Meli in this context quite critical states: "Nella proposta di regolamento si ipotizza [...] l'intervento dell'autorità di controllo (communitaria o addirittura nazionale) nei procedimenti ed anche senza sollecitazione. Il che rischia di far definitivamente saltare dei capisaldi che appaiono invero già vacillare: il fenomeno delle autorità indipendenti rappresenta già un indiscutabile mutamento o, per meglio dire, una regressione nel sistema di differenziazione dei poteri su cui si basa la nascita del

might be mitigated by the fact that such obligations do already exist in certain national laws.[582] On the other hand, if compulsory co-operation is not reconcilable with independency of the courts and hence, not adoptable, the envisaged consistency in the adoption of EC competition law might be hindered or at least weakened. What is more, although the *amicus curiae* opinion is not binding on the national judge, it definitely will carry great weight on the decision-finding of the latter. It is correctly feared that an opinion forwarded by the Commission might determine the outcome of the case and thus, the rights of defence of the parties could be bypassed.[583]

As far as consistency is concerned, ultimately even compulsory co-operation cannot guarantee consistent application of the law. Indeed,

> "inconsistency is to some extent the inevitable price of effective decentralisation and the division of power."[584]

This however does not automatically mean that a judge's ruling in Vienna for example, should be less correct than a decision adopted by the Commission.[585] In my opinion, it is more problematic that the regulation does not contain any provisions aiming at avoiding disputes whereby the same issues are heard by different judges. In this respect, it is highlighted that the judgements of national courts have the force of *res judicata* and are recognised by the Courts of the Member States due to the Brussels Convention.[586] Art 21 of the Brussels Convention, which deals with related actions brought in the courts of different Member States is defined rather narrowly though. In fact, it requires any court, other than the court first seized, to stay its proceedings only on the condition that the same cause of action and the same parties are involved in proceedings brought before the courts of different contracting states.[587] A case though, involving a dispute

---

diritto moderno. Oggi se ne ipotizza una intromissione nello svolgimento dell'attività processuale: il che rischia di determinare (o di acuire) una crisi di legittimità del potere giurisdizionale." See *Meli*, Il progetto di modernizzazione del sistema di controllo delle intese anticoncorrenziali ed il ruolo del giudice ordinario, Europa e diritto privato 2001, 117 (131).

582 See *Ehlermann*, CMLR 2000, 580; also see *Todino*, ECLR 2000, 351.

583 See *Bourgeois/Humpe*, ECLR 2002, 46.

584 See *Wißmann*, Journal of World Competition 2000, 147.

585 See *Wißmann*, Journal of World Competition 2000, 147.

586 See White Paper par 100; also see Brussels Convention on jurisdiction and the enforcement of judgements in civil and commercial matters, last amended by the 1997 Accession Convention.

587 Art 21 of the Brussels Convention reads as follows:
1. Where proceedings involving the same cause of action and between the same parties are brought in the courts of different Contracting States, any court other than the court first seized shall of its own motion stay its proceedings until such time as the jurisdiction of the court first seized is established.

between a manufacturer and distributors that are situated in different Member States, does not fall within the application-sphere of Art 21 Brussels Convention, even though the contractual arrangements between the parties would not differ from each other.[588]

Nor can it be easily said that the actions are related,[589] in order to enable the different judges to suspend their proceedings or decline jurisdiction in favour of the court first seized, as requested by Art 22 of the Convention. What is more, it does not contain an obligation on involved judges to stay the proceeding or even decline jurisdiction, but leaves it at their discretion.[590]

---

2. Where the jurisdiction of the court first seized is established, any court other than the court first seized shall decline jurisdiction in favour of that court.

In this respect, Clarkson/Hill clarify that "Art 21 must be understood to require the parallel proceedings to involve three elements: the action must have the same subject-matter (or the same object), as well as the same cause of action and the same parties. [...] Parallel proceedings have the same subject-matter (or object) where, for example, the question whether a contract is binding lies at the heart of two actions or where the issue of liability is central to both actions; parallel proceedings are to be regarded as involving the same cause of action where they are both based on the same contractual relationship or where the same facts and the same rule of law are relied on as the basis of each action." See *Clarkson/Hill*, Jaffey 109.

588 See *Bourgeois/Humpe*, ECLR 2002, 46-47; also see *Bovis*, European Business Law 2001, 102.

Edward emphasises that "at least one of the parties before the courts of the countries concerned (eg the local distributor) would be different [...]. Art 21 and Art 22 of the Brussels Convention (*lis pendens*) would not assist, since the parties to the actions would not be the same, the cause of action would not necessarily be the same and it is very doubtful whether the actions could be said to be 'related'." See *Edward*, European Competition Law Annual 2000 (2001), 570.

589 See *Edward*, European Competition Law Annual 2000 (2001), 570.

Anyhow, the concept of related actions is a broad one. In fact, Art 22 par 3 of the Brussels Convention states that "actions are deemed to be related where they are so closely connected that it is expedient to hear and determine them together to avoid the risk of irreconcilable judgments resulting from separate proceedings." Accordingly, "two actions may be related – on the basis that there is a risk of irreconcilable judgments – even if it would be perfectly possible for the judgments resulting from the two actions to be separately enforced." See *Clarkson/Hill*, Jaffey 112-113.

590 Art 22 par 1 and par 2 of the Brussels Convention read as follows:

1. Where related actions are brought in the courts of different Contracting States, any court other than the court first seized may, while the actions are pending at first instance, stay its proceedings.

2. A court other than the court first seized may also, on the application of one of the parties, decline jurisdiction if the law of that court permits the consolidation of related actions and the court first seized has jurisdiction over both actions.

As Clarkson/Hill emphasise, "it should also be noted that Art 22 is not effective to confer jurisdiction. It is a negative rule, which enables a court other than the court first seized to stay proceedings in a situation in which it has *prima facie* jurisdiction; the

Lastly, the Regulation prohibits a single national judge from making decisions running counter to a decision, which was adopted by the Commission. The same is true of a decision, which the Commission is contemplating in proceedings it has initiated.[591] In other words, a national court has to avoid decisions that could conflict with looming Commission decisions. One may doubt whether these provisions can be reconciled with the principle of independence of courts.[592] Anyhow, this approach seems to be in line with ECJ's case law. In fact, the ECJ held that

> "in order not to breach the general principle of legal certainty, national courts must, when ruling on agreements or practices which may subsequently be the subject of a decision by the Commission, avoid giving decisions which would conflict with a decision contemplated by the Commission in the implementation of Art 85 par 1 and Art 86 and Art 85 par 3 of the Treaty. It is even more important that when national courts rule on agreements or practices which are already the subject of a Commission decision they cannot take decisions running counter to that of the Commission, even if the latter's decision conflicts with a decision given by a national court of first instance.' So the national court hierarchy must look to avoid reaching decisions which conflict with Commission measures in gestation or in the public domain." [593]

effect of Art 22 is not to expand the jurisdiction of the court first seized." See *Clarkson/Hill*, Jaffey 113.

[591] Art 16 par 1 Reg 1 reads as follows:
1.When national courts rule on agreements, decisions or practices under Art 81 or Art 82 of the Treaty which are already the subject of a Commission decision, they cannot take decisions running counter to the decision adopted by the Commission. They must also avoid giving decisions, which would conflict with a decision contemplated by the Commission in proceedings it has initiated. To that effect, the national court may assess whether it is necessary to stay its proceedings. This obligation is without prejudice to the rights and obligations under Art 234 of the Treaty.

[592] See *Schaub* in Baudenbacher, Entwicklungen 13.

[593] See ECJ case C-344/98 (Masterfoods).
This is true only in respect of decisions of the Commission. Hence, one might wonder whether national courts would be bound by a national competition authority's decision declaring that an agreement or practice fulfils the conditions of Art 81 par 3." In fact, there is no indication, that this might be the case. See *Siragusa*, in Ehlermann/Atanasiu, European Competition Law Annual 2000 (2001), 450.

3.4.6.4 Inspiration by US competition law concepts?

Since the publication of the White Paper, the reform has been compared to the US model of competition law enforcement.[594] Generally, it was said that the proposed reform brings EC competition law closer to the US model as the former puts greater weight on enforcement by national courts and hence, implicitly on private action.[595] Compared to the notification system of the EC law, the US-model depends to a much higher extent on an *ex post* control of restrictive practices, even though one can also find elements of *ex ante* control.[596] Moreover, US authorities have a more prosecutorial function than their European counterpart.

Concerning the judiciary, one can observe that US courts have a bigger role in enforcement of competition matters than European courts.[597] Furthermore, the American public administrative enforcement is

---

[594] The substantive rules of US Antitrust law are set out in three statutes: the Sherman Act, the Clayton Act and the Federal Trade Commission (FTC) Act. Apart from these general laws, there is an increasing number of specialised laws (ie: the Newspaper Preservation Act).

The Sherman Act contains two major prohibitions: Section 1 deals with agreements among two or more independent actors, which are directed toward conduct that interferes with trade. More precisely, contracts, combinations or conspiracy in restraint of trade, where US commerce is affected, is illegal. Most types of agreements are judged under a rule of reason, which requires balancing business justifications and any pro-competitive effects of the arrangement against any perceived anticompetitive effects. Section 2 regards single firm activities like monopolisation, attempts to monopolise and combinations or conspiracies to monopolise referring to trade among the US-states or with foreign nations.

The violation of these 2 prohibitions constitutes a criminal offence.

The Clayton Act prohibits four specific kinds of conduct:

- price discrimination subject to cost justification and meeting competition defences
- exclusive dealing and tying arrangements
- interlocking directors
- certain mergers and acquisitions, which lessen competition substantially or create a monopoly.

The Federal Trade Act prohibits all unfair methods of competition, which in substance contain infringements of the Sherman Act and of the Clayton Act.

These laws are enforced by the US Department of Justice, the FTC, private individuals and entities and for certain suits by state attorney generals. See *Paulweber*, Journal of World Competition 2000, 19-21.

[595] See *Ehlermann*, CMLR 2000, 587.

[596] Interestingly, this refers to conduct, which is very risky for US competition (export cartels or merger control) or to politically desirable transactions, whose legal certainty shall be strengthened. See *Paulweber*, Journal of World Competition 2000, 29.

[597] In fact, enforcement in court also happens when administrative authorities are involved. See Hack, Handlungsmöglichkeiten Einzelner bei Kartellrechtsverletzungen, ecolex 2003, 311 (313).

accompanied by a powerful private regime. Indeed, the US law not only provides for strong incentives for private action (treble damages, contingency fees) but also procedural means, such as the compulsory pre-trial discovery procedure.[598] About 80 % of the proceedings are instituted by private persons, whereas officially initiated criminal and civil proceedings amount only to a small proportion and benefit from an easing of the burden of finding proof. Moreover, as antitrust authorities take into account the probability and chances of success of private action, they are enabled to focus their resources on the prosecution of selected companies.[599] This regime is further supplemented by severe civil and criminal sanctions against individual corporate officers, including prison sentences.[600]

Compared to the EU, the economic frame of the USA can be characterised as being more open and having less market regulations. Moreover, personnel-based and financial links between major undertakings and undertakings and banks in the EU, encourage cartelisation. The European environment also accepts co-operations between industry and the state to a much greater extent than in the USA.[601]

Accordingly,

> "in order to successfully pursue the intended shift to an *ex post* control with all its negative impacts on the effectiveness of administrative control, the incentives for private enforcement would have to be improved as well as deterrent elements. A system relying on deterrence requires more severe punishment than the European Member States' laws currently provide. However, the instruments that are essential to the success of the US system, such as contingency fees, punitive damages, and pre-trial discovery, are at present not only inconsistent with the Community's and the Member States' laws, they are realistically not achievable either."[602]

---

598 See *Paulweber*, Journal of World Competition 2000, 29; also see *Mestmäcker*, European Competition Law Annual 2000 (2001) 235; and *Edward*, European Competition Law Annual 2000 (2001), 565; and *Hack*, ecolex 2003, 313.

599 See *German Monopolies Commission* par 36.

600 See *Paulweber*, Journal of World Competition 2000, 29; also see *Hack*, ecolex 2003, 313.

601 See *German Monopolies Commission* par 38; and *Paulweber*, Journal of World Competition 2000, 48; and *Edward*, European Competition Law Annual 2000 (2001), 565.

602 See *Paulweber*, Journal of World Competition 2000, 46.

3.4.7 The situation of undertakings

3.4.7.1 Self assessment pursued by undertakings

The new regime also establishes a completely new situation for undertakings, who 'maintain business practices' that might contravene to EC competition law. Undertakings can no longer rely on decisions of the Commission, which gives legal certainty, but are forced to take on added responsibility, as they will be obliged to autonomously assess the compatibility of their restrictive practices with EC law.[603]

> "With the *ex post* control, the Commission intends to pass the compliance onus to the market place, in an attempt to introduce a sort of self-regulation in anti-trust, where undertakings should themselves judge the potential adverse effects of their restrictive agreements."[604]

This will involve costly legal advice. Such advice will not have legal constitutive power and hence, one can doubt whether a satisfying degree of legal certainty can ultimately be achieved.[605] Whether this is in the interest of undertakings is questionable.[606]

Of particular concern might be the definition of the relevant market.[607] It will be particularly difficult determining the product-related market, as undertakings have not the necessary means to pursue such an investigation and clarification.[608]

Moreover, it should be questioned whether it is justified to impose fines on an undertaking that, acting in good faith and after having conducted the self-assessment, comes to the conclusion that the exemption as provided for by par 3 of Art 81 ECT is applicable, but a competition authority declares the

---

603 See White Paper par 77.

604 See *Bovis*, European Business Law 2001, 101.

605 In this context, Bishop accurately observes that "while business will be able to conduct their own legal and economic analysis prior to entering into agreements, and thereby reduce legal uncertainty somewhat, only in rare instances will such analysis provide unambiguous answers as to the outcome of any potential Commission investigation." See *Bishop*, European Competition Law Annual 2000, 63; also see *Klocker*, WuW 2002, 1151; also see *Immenga*, EuZW 1999, 609.

606 See *Wißmann*, Journal of World Competition 2000, 145; also see *Bovis*, European Business Law 2001, 101.
In this context, Bogdandy stresses that "corporations will [...] only be guaranteed an appropriate level of legal certainty after the system changes to the legal exemption rule if there is a simultaneous concretisation of Art 81 through secondary law. [...]." See *Bogdandy*, European integration and international co-ordination 2001, 20.

607 See *Bishop*, European Competition Law Annual 2000, 60.

608 See *German Monopolies Commission* par 34.

opposite at a later stage.[609] On the other hand, if an authority's decision should not be considered as 'justified', the deterrent effect of fines will decrease.[610]

Lastly, as it would run counter to the new regime, the new regulation does not contain any provision that grants a right for undertakings to get assistance in their assessment by administrative bodies. In fact, such a mechanism would create a new flood of requests, again hindering the Commission or national competition authorities from fulfilling their duties. Nevertheless, the Commission leaves the possibility of voluntarily answering questions relating to cases presenting new or unresolved questions for the application of EC competition law open.[611]

3.4.7.2 Commitments of undertakings

Reg 1 also focuses on the possibility for undertakings, whose agreements might be declared prohibited due to Art 81 par 2 ECT, to amend the agreements concerned in a way that overcomes the objections raised by the Commission or a national authority against the agreement.[612] Such commitments are binding on the undertakings concerned, but as herewith a proceeding is simply concluded by a decision acknowledging that there are no longer grounds for action, such decisions do not bind national authorities or courts.[613]

Moreover, the proceedings may also be reopened by the Commission, in case one of the following facts materialise:

- there has been a material change in any of the facts on which the decision was based;
- the undertakings concerned act contrary to their commitments;
- the decision was based on incomplete, incorrect or misleading information provided by the parties.[614]

Regarding these commitments it is argued that the Commission would be enabled to establish a constant control over the conduct of undertakings,

609 See *Burrichter*, European Competition Law Annual 2000 (2001), 549.

610 See *Wißmann*, Journal of World Competition 2000, 149.

611 See recital 38 Reg 1; particularly see in this context chapter 3.4.3.2.

612 See Art 5 and Art 9 par 1 Reg 1.

613 See *Hossenfelder/Lutz*, WuW 2003, 122.
The explanatory memorandum of the Proposal stated furthermore that commitments may be invoked by third parties before national courts. This option has been dropped by Reg 1 and hence a binding effect for third parties is regulated by national laws. See *Hossenfelder/Lutz*, WuW 2003, 122; also see Proposal 18.

614 See Art 9 par 2 Reg 1; also see chapter 3.4.10, where the significance of commitments for co-operation between authorities and undertakings is stressed.

which eventually could possibly create some "kind of constitutive economic supervision".[615] Whatever the German Monopolies Commission means by this, it seems to neglect that the regime under Reg 17 with its approval procedure had already established strict control over an undertaking's behaviour.

3.4.8 Effects on the European Court of Justice and Court of First Instance

The buffering of risks for coherence and consistency of Communities policies are handled by the infringement procedure with respect to Member States and requests by national courts for preliminary rulings of the ECJ. Through these means, uniform interpretation of EC law is guaranteed.[616] Indeed, whereas Art 226 ECT grants the Commission the power to refer to the Court violations of Community law by Member States, Art 234 ECT[617] forces national courts of last instance to submit questions of interpretation of EC law to the Court of Justice who can then adopt a preliminary ruling. It is at the mere discretion of other national courts to exercise this power.
Even though decisions adopted by national competition authorities may not be appealed directly at the ECJ, such review is possible indirectly through an appeal brought before a national court with the following request from the latter for a preliminary ruling from the ECJ. In fact, national courts do not have much experience with competition issues and as a result, it is suggested that they might increasingly ask the ECJ for its opinion.[618] Problematic in this respect might be that preliminary rulings give answer only

---

[615] See *German Monopolies Commission* par 53.

[616] However, even the ECJ is not able to assure coherent and consistent application in individual cases. See *Ehlermann*, CMLR 2000, 576.

[617] Art 234 ECT reads as follows .
The Court of Justice shall have jurisdiction to give preliminary rulings concerning:
(a) the interpretation of this Treaty;
(b) the validity and interpretation of acts of the institutions of the Community and of the ECB;
(c) the interpretation of the statutes of bodies established by an act of the Council, where those statutes so provide.
Where such a question is raised before any court or tribunal of a Member State, that court or tribunal may, if it considers that a decision on the question is necessary to enable it to give judgment, request the Court of Justice to give a ruling thereon.
Where any such question is raised in a case pending before a court or tribunal of a Member State against whose decisions there is no judicial remedy under national law, that court or tribunal shall bring the matter before the Court of Justice.

[618] See *Ehlermann/Atanasiu*, ECLR 2002, 75-76.

to questions on the interpretation of the law[619] and are often highly abstract in nature. Consequently, they do not apply the law to a certain case but rather have an advisory function and leave the application of the law to the national court. It has correctly been emphasised that preliminary rulings are therefore not sufficient to guarantee consistency in respect of the application of Art 81 ECT. Furthermore, it has been criticised that national courts can only address their request for preliminary ruling to the ECJ and not also to the CFI, nor should the delays in the processing of preliminary rulings be forgotten in this context.[620]

Various alternative solutions to deal with these problems have been discussed. For instance, allowing judicial review of decisions of national authorities by the Court of First Instance and, on appeal, by the European Court of Justice, has been proposed. However, such a mechanism would require a major change of the institutional architecture of the EU Treaty and accordingly, seems to be excessive.[621] In fact, on the one hand there are the new co-operation tools between the involved institutions to guarantee consistency. On the other hand, as mentioned, national authorities' decisions can be reviewed by national courts and their decisions at a further step by the European courts. In this context, it is proposed to enable the Commission not only to take part as *amicus curiae* in national proceedings, but also to exercise a right to initiate actions and/or appeals against decisions of national competition authorities before national courts. Again, such a solution seems to be excessive, as it requires unnecessary amendments of the Treaty of Rome.[622]

Moreover, extending the scope of preliminary rulings to the facts of the case that has given rise to the request, is under consideration. However, this solution should also be rejected on the grounds that it introduces an element of hierarchy between the EC courts and national courts hardly compatible with the principle of co-operation that governs the relationship between the European Courts and national courts.[623] Lastly, it also would bear problems in relation to factual evidence (ie does the ECJ have to assess the facts as presented by the national court?).[624] Taken together, even though the

619 See Art 234 par 1 subpar a.

620 See *Ehlermann/Atanasiu*, ECLR 2002, 76.

621 See *Ehlermann*, CMLR 2000, 583.

622 See *Ehlermann/Atanasiu*, ECLR 2002, 77.

623 In this respect, *Ehlermann/Atanasiu* stress that "the outstanding success of the rule of law in the European Community, more precisely the success of the EC judicial system, and in particular the success of the ECJ, all rest on the loyal, continuous and efficient co-operation between the ECJ and national courts. Nothing should be done at the risk of jeopardising this extraordinarily successful co-operation." See *Ehlermann/Atanasiu*, ECLR 2002, 77.

624 See *Ehlermann/Atanasiu*, ECLR 2002, 77-78.

number of request for preliminary rulings might increase, this correctly shall not be enough ground to change the existing preliminary ruling provision. Ultimately the need for more advise from the ECJ will be of transitional nature only, as national courts should be able to increase significantly their abilities to handle the task at the end.[625] Instead, it seems appropriate to give to the Court of First Instance the primary responsibility for preliminary rulings with regard to the interpretation of EC competition law, which - due to its great experience in competition matters - would definitely enhance the rapidity of proceeding and therefore grant greater legal certainty.[626]
Lastly, one can affirm that as the reform aims to enable the Commission to concentrate its resources on issuing more decisions upon finding that Art 81 or Art 82 ECT had been infringed, more Commission decisions might in turn also lead to an increase in actions for their annulment. This is the natural corollary of the Commission's increased productivity.[627] What is more, it is assumed, that the direct applicability of Art 81 par 3 ECT and the resulting greater need for guidance on the application of the law, will urge the European Courts to give up the self-imposed limited control[628] in favour of a normal-standard type of judicial review, accompanied by the consequent evaluation of complex economic circumstances.[629] As Ehlermann/Atanasiu highlight,

[625] See chapter 3.4.6.1.

[626] *Ehlermann/Atanasiu*, ECLR 2002, 79.

[627] See *Ehlermann/Atanasiu*, ECLR 2002, 74; also see *Gröning*, European Competition Law Annual 2000 (2001), 590.

[628] Ehlermann/Atanasiu, in referring to Judge Cooke, outline that this self-limitation rather expresses the courts' desire not to override the policy-making functions of the Commission than difficulties concerning the economic evaluation of Art 81 par 3 ECT. See *Ehlermann/Atanasiu*, ECLR 2002, fn 12.

[629] Also see chapter 3.4.1.3.
Marenco in this context, stresses, that "in any event, even on the basis that the Courts actually exercise a limited review on the implementation of paragraph 3, a legitimate question seems to be whether this is the result of the text of the Treaty, or rather of the system set up by Reg 17. In such a system, where the implementation of the provision in question is entrusted to the executive (as opposed to the judiciary) it is a logical consequence that the judicial review is one of administrative nature and therefore more limited than the control that ordinary courts would exercise, if they had jurisdiction. The review might tend to be even more limited if, in addition, the task is entrusted to a single administration - the Commission - to the exclusion of national authorities, for such a monopoly can be understood as the wish of the legislator that a consistent policy be developed. If these remarks are correct, nothing prevents the legislator from to triggering a new, more pervasive type of judicial involvement by opting for another system." See *Marenco*, European Competition Law Annual 2000 (2001), 167; also see *Burrichter*, European Competition Law Annual 2000 (2001), 540.

> "the difficulties arising for the EC courts from this novelty should not be overestimated. The quality of the judicial review exercised thus far by the EC courts over the Commission decisions applying Art 81 par 1 or Art 82 is ample proof that the courts will be perfectly able to review by normal standards Commission decisions applying Art 81 par 3."[630]

3.4.9 The Eastern Enlargement of the European Union

In the introduction of the White Paper, the Commission highlights that enlargement of the Union makes the strengthening of competition policy unavoidable and underlines that the administrative structures of the candidates for accession are still not very familiar with the concepts of market and free enterprise.[631] At a first glance, one could argue that it seems more advisable to pursue centralised application of the law, rather than decentralised.[632] This issue was discussed only briefly during the modernisation process.

Basically, the Commission will devote particular attention to the development of competition in the candidate countries and assist the competition authorities concerned, in order to hinder the possibility that the direct effect of Art 81 par 3 ECT might undermine the consistent application of EC competition rules.[633]

More concrete, to tackle the problem one could think about the adoption of a transitional regime, which confers special responsibilities for the Commission in respect of the new territories.[634] On the other hand, it was accurately observed that so-called Europe Agreements between the EU and the accession candidates already force candidates to apply the principles of Art 81 and Art 82 ECT and oblige them to harmonise their competition law with

---

630 See *Ehlermann/Atanasiu*, ECLR 2002, 75.

631 See White Paper par 7.

632 As explained in the foregoing chapters, the pursued decentralisation also bears, to a certain extent, risks for consistency and uniformity.

633 See White Paper par 106.
In this respect, the German Monopolies Commission outlines, that the interpretation of Art 81 par 3 ECT still causes considerable problems. In its opinion, this situation will aggravate as after the eastward enlargement of the European Union, new Member States lacking practical experience in dealing with European competition rules and having weak competition culture will be part of the Union. See *German Monopolies Commission* par 34.

634 See *Ehlermann*, CMLR 2000, 584.

the existing EC competition law:[635] these obligations go far beyond those assumed by the existing Member States.[636]
In this respect, Forrester accurately observes, that

> "the commonest method of implementation of these Treaty obligations has been for the third country to reproduce more or less faithfully the language of Art 81 and Art 82 of the Treaty."[637]

The here-mentioned problems are solvable, but indeed call "for the energetic involvement of the European Commission."[638]

3.4.10 Further critical remarks

Contrary to the old system, the legal exemption system is based on *ex-post* control, which means that it focuses on the scrutinising of agreements, which are - at least from a contractual point of view - already in force. As a result, is was found necessary to strengthen the Commission's powers of enquiry to guarantee that undisclosed restrictions of competition are detected.[639].
Generally, the powers of enquiry have a much broader sphere of application than in the old system. For instance, they include the adoption of interim measures,[640] inquiries into sectors of the economy,[641] requests for all necessary information from owners of undertakings, their representatives and from authorised lawyers.[642] However, undertakings are still responsible

---

635 See *Ehlermann*, CMLR 2000, 584, who refers to Art 63 and Art 69 of the Europe Agreement between the European Communities and their Member States, on the one hand, and the Republic of Poland, on the other hand.

636 See *Ehlermann*, CMLR 2000, 584.

637 See *Forrester*, Legal Issues of Economic Integration 2001, 33.

638 See *Forrester*, Legal Issues of Economic Integration 2001, 34.

639 See White Paper par 109.

640 According to Art 8 Reg 1, interim measures can be adopted on the basis of a *prima facie* finding of infringement in cases of urgency due to the risk of serious and irreparable damage. They are limited in time though and can be adopted in so far this is necessary and appropriate.

641 In fact, where the trend of trade between Member States, the rigidity of prices or other circumstances suggest that competition may be restricted or distorted within the common market, Art 17 Reg 1 empowers the Commission to conduct its inquiries into a particular economic sector or into a particular type of agreements across various sectors and to request that the relevant undertakings supply the information necessary for giving effect to Art 81 and Art 82 ECT of the Treaty. Moreover, the Commission may carry out any inspections necessary for that purpose.

642 See Art 18 par 4 Reg 1.
Under Reg 17, this power was limited to the books and business records which are being examined by the officials conducting an on-site investigation. Under the new regime, such requests for information from the Commission can be made by sending a simple request for information or by decision. See Art 18 par 2 and par 3 Reg 1.

for the accuracy of the information provided by them.[643] Moreover, national governments and competition authorities have to provide the Commission with all the necessary information in order that it is enabled to carry out its duties.[644]

Art 19 of Reg 1 deals with the interrogation of any natural or legal person.[645] In this respect, one can criticise that no fines have to be paid for refusal to comply or submission of false information due to such interrogations. In fact, the imposition of fines is only possible in respect of interrogations according to Art 18 or Art 20 Reg 1.[646] This is especially unsatisfactory when false information is given during a hearing, for which the person invited had the possibility to prepare.[647]

New is also the provision regarding the finding and termination of an infringement, where it explicitly states that such decisions may impose on the undertakings concerned not only any behavioural remedy but furthermore also any "structural remedies which are proportionate to the infringement committed and necessary to bring the infringement effectively to an end."[648] Such structural remedies can even reach the extent of decartelisation.[649]

Finally, the proposal contains specific powers of inspection for the Commission[650] and holds members of associations of undertakings both jointly and separately liable for the payment of the fine.[651]

As the new system abolishes the obligation of notification, the investigating authorities rely exclusively on their own investigative resources and on

---

Also in line with enhanced co-operation within the network, "the Commission shall without delay forward a copy of the simple request or of the decision to the competition authority of the Member State in whose territory the seat of the undertaking or association of undertakings is situated and the competition authority of the Member State whose territory is affected." Moreover, "at the request of the Commission the governments and competition authorities of the Member States shall provide the Commission with all necessary information to carry out the duties assigned to it by this Regulation." See Art 18 par 5 and par 6 Reg 1.

643 See Art 18 par 4 Reg 1.

644 See Art 18 par 6 Reg 1.

645 According to Art 19 par 1 Reg 1, such interviews by the Commission have to be based on the consent of the persons to be interrogated.

646 In fact, Art 19 Reg 1 does not provide for this possibility. Also see Art 23 par 1 Reg 1, which concedes the power to fine only in respect of interrogations made pursuant to Art 18 par 4 (owners of the undertakings, their representatives, authorised lawyers) and Art 20 par 2 subpar 3 Reg 1 (representative of an undertaking or member of the staff).

647 See *Bourgeois/Humpe*, ECLR 2002, 45; also see *Weitbrecht*, WuW 2003, 71; also see *Petsche*, ecolex 2003, 306.

648 See Art 7 Reg 1.

649 See *Weitbrecht*, EuZW 2003, 71; and *Hossenfelder/Lutz*, WuW 2003, 121.

650 See Art 20 Reg 1.

651 See Art 23 par 4 Reg 1.

complaints. Accordingly, it has arguably been criticised that the new regime hinders close *ex-ante* co-operation between undertakings and anti-trust authorities and hence does not foster the co-operation between businesses and the authorities. According to Wißmann, this kind of

> "informal co-operation [...] has proven to be useful in order to prevent restrictive agreements taking effect in those cases in which the undertakings are indeed willing to co-operate with the competition authorities."[652]

Of course, the old regime necessarily supported co-operation between businesses and the Commission. Anyhow, in my opinion the possibility of commitments provides eventually for a similar result as it offers the possibility for undertakings to co-operate even at a moment when it has been discovered that the law had been assessed in a wrong manner.

A further criticised point of *ex-post* control regards horizontal agreements, which have a much more damaging effect to competition than vertical agreements. It has been questioned as to whether own-initiative investigations and complaints are sufficient in providing the necessary information in detecting horizontal agreements.[653]

In this respect, Wißmann states that

> "the new policy, [...] sends a message to operators of horizontal agreements which is in contrast to the view taken by just recently reformed national laws on cartels that recognise the qualitative difference of horizontal and vertical restraints."[654]

However, as national authorities are closer to the markets and hence ultimately to businesses, it has to be seen whether such criticisms will be supported in reality or remain theoretical hair-splitting. Moreover, the powers of enquiry of the Commission have been widened considerably, which ultimately should help to accomplish the task effectively. Besides, complaints also gain importance in discovering collusive behaviour of undertakings. It results, that channels exist to accrue information about business practices.

3.5 Alternatives

In addition to the legal exemption system as a means for modernising the procedural rules of EC competition law, other approaches to get rid of the known problems were discussed. Indeed, the White Paper outlined 4 alternatives to improve the inefficient current situation, without deepening the discussion in this regard though. Nor did the Commission consider

---

[652] See *Wißmann*, Journal of World Competition 2000, 148-149.
[653] See *Wißmann*, Journal of World Competition 2000, 149.
[654] See *Wißmann*, Journal of World Competition 2000, 149.

combining certain aspects of these options, but rather followed an "all or nothing" approach.[655]

3.5.1 Interpretation of Art 81 ECT

The first solution focused on a new manner of interpreting Art 81 ECT insofar as the assessment of an agreement under Art 81 par 1 ECT should also embrace both the harmful and beneficial effects of such an agreement. The Commission argued that this approach would circumscribe the application of par 3 to

> "cases in which the need to ensure consistency between competition policy and other Community policies took precedence over the results of the competition analysis."[656]

As a consequence, par 1 of Art 81 ECT would be interpreted as a 'rule of reason' with its necessity to balance pro-competitive aspects against anti-competitive aspects.[657] Moreover, undertakings would not be urged to submit a notification in respect of their agreements to obtain negative clearance.[658]

The Commission stressed that it has already followed this approach to a certain extent.[659] Nevertheless, in its view the design of Art 81 par 1 ECT does not allow its interpretation as rule of reason to a greater extent. In such a case, par 3 would be eliminated, and this would eventually require a change in the EC Treaty. This is a quite paradoxical situation as par 3 enshrines all the criteria for a 'rule of reason'.[660] It has correctly been observed that by following this approach the modernisation of the EC competition law would finally depend on the cases submitted and therefore, might endure throughout the ages. But that is not enough: according to the White Paper this approach might also divert par 3, which is intended to constitute a legal framework for an economic assessment of restrictive practices and shall not be used to introduce political considerations aimed at circumventing competition rules.[661]

---

[655] See *Wißmann*, Journal of World Competition 2000, 150.

[656] See White Paper par 56.

[657] See White Paper fn 46.

[658] See White Paper par 56

[659] See also ECJ case 258/78 (Nungesses) and ECJ case 161/84 (Pronuptia).

[660] See *Wißmann*, Journal of World Competition 2000, 150.

[661] See White Paper par 57.
In this opinion is also Ehlermann, who observes that the Commission's opinion is a "clear indication that non-competition-oriented political considerations should not determine the assessment under Art 81 par 3." See Ehlermann, CMLR 2000, 549.

This approach would eventually decrease the cases to be dealt with under par 3, as a full competitive balance would be accomplished under par 1. However, one has to bear in mind that such a reading of Art 81 ECT can be achieved solely by the means of a Treaty amendment; this power lies exclusively with the Member States. Wißmann doubts, that such a shift can be achieved quickly as

> "it would take many years until such a disguised amendment of Art 81 par 1 ECT would be accomplished. [...] The backlog of cases, however, is not primarily due to the broad application of Art 81 ECT as such, but due to the limitation of authorities who may apply Art 81 par 3 ECT."[662]

3.5.2 Decentralisation of the application of Art 81 par 3 ECT

The second alternative envisaged the decentralisation of the application of Art 81 par 3 ECT by maintaining the authorisation system. This would have required the abolition of Art 9 par 3 Reg 17 and decentralisation would have necessitated a clear delimitation of responsibilities between the authorities involved. Such could have been based on qualitative criteria (economic and competition focus of activity[663]) or quantitative criteria (turnover figures, market shares).[664]
However, the Commission argued that this approach did not provide for a decrease in the numbers of notifications, but merely would have redistributed the cases between the authorities of the Member States and

---

[662] See *Wißmann*, Journal of World Competition 2000, 150.
Ehlermann acknowledges that the adoption of a new regulation "has the advantage of speed, clarity and certainty, provided, of course, that the judges in Luxembourg do not consider the regulation to be incompatible with the EC Treaty, if its legality is challenged either directly or indirectly." See *Ehlermann*, CMLR 2000, 549.
Moreover, in respect of a possible restrictive interpretation of Art 81 par 1 ECT, Ehlermann correctly stresses that "the competition rules of the EC Treaty are part of the fundamental legal structure underlying the internal market. This structure would be weakened if their scope of application were reduced, and if, as a consequence, national competition statutes, which differ among themselves, were to fill the resulting gap." See *Ehlermann*, CMLR 2000, 550.

[663] In this respect one is referred to the theory of the centre of gravity, according to which the cases can be allocated between the Commission and the national authorities. This theory was elaborated by the German Competition Authority and focuses on the effects of the agreement and on the need to safeguard competition. Cases of Community relevance should be reserved to the Commission, though. See White Paper par 59; also see *Holmes*, Journal of World Competition 2000, 55.

[664] See White Paper, par 59 – par 62.

the Commission.[665] Why such redistribution may be seen as disadvantage in terms of an easing of the work burden is not quite comprehensible, though.[666]

Next, the Commission affirmed that herewith focusing on the most serious of infringements, which hardly ever are notified, would not be achieved.[667] In my opinion, this statement does not seem quite logical, as under Reg 17 the Commission already had the possibility to initiate own investigation, which first of all should concentrate on detecting the most serious infringements.

A further critical remark in this context regarded the fact that decisions adopted by a national authority are enforceable only within its territory, and hence, cases that involve more than one Member State can hardly be dealt with.[668] Again, such an argument did not necessarily call for a directly applicable exemption system, but rather for co-operation between institutions and for corresponding recognition procedures.[669]

Lastly, the Commission highlighted, that this option implied that all national authorities would have to institute notification systems, which could have been rather burdensome not just for the current Member States, but especially for the new ones.[670]

However, Wißmann correctly affirmed, that

> "it seems somewhat inconsistent to reject this approach on the grounds that the question of the allocation of cases may not easily be solved and that it could particularly prove to be difficult for the new Member States' authorities to introduce notification systems."[671]

---

665 Also see *Wißmann*, Journal of World Competition 2000, 150.

666 Also see *Stillfried/Stockenhuber*, Zeitschrift für österreichisches und europäisches Wirtschaftsrecht 2001, 152 fn 52.

667 See White Paper par 60.

668 See White Paper par 60.

669 See *German Monopolies Commission* par 68; also see *Ehlermann*, CMLR 2000, 551.

670 See White Paper par 62.

671 See *Wißmann*, Journal of World Competition 2000, 151; also see *Ehlermann*, CMLR 2000, 551.
Of this opinion is also Holmes, but adds that "the feelings amongst Member States is that the central problems of the current system would remain unchanged; the Commission would still retain a monopoly over a notification and exemption system. Any freeing-up of resources would not, it is considered, be sufficient to lead to a fundamental re-targeting of resources towards investigation of cartels." See *Holmes*, Journal of World Competition 2000, 56.

3.5.3 Broadening the scope of application of Art 4 par 2 Reg 17

A third alternative approach to improve the current authorisation system focused on the scope of application of Art 4 par 2 Reg 17, which could have been widened in order to contain further types of agreements. As known, Art 4 par 2 waived the prior notification requirement for certain types of agreements. Consequently, Art 6 par 1 Reg 17 was not applicable.[672] This alternative also provided for the possibility of encompassing cases of late notification.
According to the Commission, this option had to be rejected on the grounds that it did not make the Commission's supervision-task easier,[673] nor did it allow the addressing of the most serious restrictions, since the monopoly of application of Art 81 par 3 ECT granted to the Commission was still upheld.[674] This argumentation is not satisfactory, as the

> "monopoly of the Commission as set forth in Art 9 par 1 of Regulation 17 is an entirely independent issue, and there are no reasons apparent why a lessening of the notification requirement may not come along with a decentralised jurisdiction as to Art 81 par 3 ECT."[675]

3.5.4 Procedural simplification

The last alternative put forward by the Commission concentrated on the simplification of the procedure of handling cases by formal decisions, in order to guarantee that formal decisions were issued more rapidly and undertakings could gain legal certainty more easily. It provided for the abolition of the translation-criteria both for the notice and the decision, which, according to Reg 17, have to be published in the Official Journal. This option furthermore envisaged a simplification of the consultation procedure to be held with the Advisory Committee.[676]
A variant then followed to introduce a general application of the opposition procedure, which stems from block exemptions. This procedure rules that in cases where an agreement is neither expressly exempted nor expressly prohibited, it can be notified to the Commission. The Commission has the possibility to oppose it within six months. The consequence of the time

[672] See White Paper par 63.
[673] See White Paper par 64.
[674] See White Paper par 65.
[675] See *Wißmann*, Journal of World Competition 2000, 151.
[676] See White Paper par 66.

lapsed without formal decision is the exemption of the agreement.[677] However, I doubt that such a provision would have been wise, as a time-limit also bears the risk that serious restraints of competition might not be scrutinised within the defined period at all.

Furthermore, the Commission criticised that this option would not have lead to a reduction in the number of notification with the result that the Commission's workforce would have been still impeded in considering the most serious restrictions. Especially the fact that all notifications would be handled through formal decisions, implies that undertakings might be encouraged to notify their agreements.[678] Moreover,

> "a large number of agreements, which would still need an exemption, are not notified. Every Enlargement will increase this number. Purely administrative, procedural reforms will not be able to handle these notifications efficiently."[679]

3.5.5 Combination of decentralisation with a reform of the authorisation system

Apart from the Commission's alternatives, further possible methods of tackling the current problems were discussed. Basically, they requested the adjusting of the current system in order to make it workable. These alternatives focused on the need to enable competition authorities to apply vertical agreements to a higher degree on *ex post* control, whereas hard-core vertical and horizontal restraints should have been kept under a pre-screening mechanism. Additionally, national cartel offices could have helped to decrease the Commission's workload and promote a widespread application of the EC competition rules.[680]

The majority of notifications submitted to the Commission concern vertical agreements: hence it has correctly been argued that the new-styled block exemptions by exempting a large bulk of vertical agreements assure that the Commission's resources can focus their attention on the remaining

[677] See White Paper par 67.

[678] See White Paper par 66.
Wißmann criticises, that this comment "blatantly reveals the Commission's reservation concerning notifications as such and any pre-screening of restrictive agreements." See *Wißmann*, Journal of World Competition 2000, 151.

[679] See *Ehlermann*, CMLR 2000, 546; also see *Holmes*, Journal of World Competition 2000, 56.

[680] See *Wißmann*, Journal of World Competition 2000, 152; also see *Deringer*, EuZW 2000, 9-10.

agreements: especially hard-core vertical agreements and horizontal agreements.[681]

The remaining work could have been distributed between the Commission and national authorities, by empowering the latter to apply par 3 of Art 81 ECT and by granting them the power to withdraw the benefit of a block exemption.[682] Truly, a general decentralisation and the simplification of the administrative procedures would have helped the Commission in decreasing the burdensome workload.[683]

Furthermore, Deringer proposed voluntary notification rather than mandatory, with the effect that notified agreements become interim valid until a court or authority declares by a constitutive decision otherwise. Conversely, agreements not notified are deemed to be in breach of the law. The burden of self assessment would still rely on undertakings. Especially agreements in the grey area could be notified, as this approach gives a higher level of legal certainty and protection, than a legal exemption system does.[684]

Quite interesting was the proposal of the German Monopolies Commission to supplement the staff of the cartel unit in the DG IV, through assigning national authorities to Brussels.[685]

---

681 See *Wißmann*, Journal of World Competition 2000, 153.
682 See *Wißmann*, Journal of World Competition 2000, 153.
683 See *Wißmann*, Journal of World Competition 2000, 153.
684 See *Deringer*, EuZW 2000, 10.
685 See *German Monopolies Commission* par 67.

4 The impact of the reform on the Italian competition system

Until now, the dissertation has considered decentralisation without analysing the concrete possible impact on a Member State of the EC or indeed on its legal system. In fact, particularly chapter 3.4.5 and chapter 3.4.6 outlined the different issues, which were raised during the reform process, albeit from a rather general perspective. Obviously, not all of these issues may be of great importance in respect of the Italian competition system. Hence, the following subchapters analyse those, which directly influence the functioning of the Italian antitrust system. However, before starting the analysis it is necessary to briefly illustrate how the rather young Italian competition regime is structured, especially in correlation to EC competition law.[686]

---

686 Wise, in concisely sketching the historical circumstances of the drafting-process of the Italian competition law regime, emphasises that "central influence has historically been treated as more important than competition in Italy's large-scale industries. Government policy encouraged investment in selected 'high-tech' growth industries early in the last century, and when conditions shifted, banks helped industries organise cartels, in steel, chemicals, paper, and machinery to protect those investments. [...] Before World War II, cartels and protection prevented competition and discouraged innovation, and major industries, such as vehicles, tires, steel, and shipbuilding, were virtually monopolies. After the war, political structures were completely transformed. During the reconstruction, there were signs of reform in economic policy too, in decisions to end price controls and open up to foreign trade. But a large state-enterprise sector remained, and it became increasingly inefficient in the 1960s and 1970s, as firms were managed for political as well as business objectives. [...] Concerns about the competitive incentives and performance of the state-owned firms were matched by problems in the private sector. The largest privately owned industrial firms in Italy have traditionally had ownership structures, such as family control through cross-shareholdings magnifying minority positions, which have been linked in other countries to problems with corporate governance, financial stability, and competition. At the other end of the size scale, Italy has become well known for its flourishing small and medium-sized, family-owned firms, in manufacturing as well as services. In this characteristic form of successful Italian industry, flexible firms deal with suppliers and competitors in complex networks of mutually reinforcing, geographically specialised systems. Although risks exist that co-operative relationships and protective regulation can constrain competition unnecessarily even at that scale, there has been little need for intervention by central government laws and institutions in promoting or controlling competition. [...] Membership of the European Communities, and particularly the European single market programme, strongly influenced Italy's approach to competition policies. Increasing competition in the larger market exposed inefficiencies in Italian industry. [...] EU rules about state aids have forced Italy to re-examine and ultimately dismantle its structures of central support and control." See *Wise*, Review of competition law and policy in Italy, OECD Journal of competition law and policy 2001, 66 (68-69).

4.1 Competition law in Italy

Italy Competition law is governed by three sets of rules: firstly, by provisions contained in the Italian Civil Code,[687] secondly, by the specific 'Competition and Fair Trading Act' and last but not least by the EC provisions in competition matters. It is the 'Competition and Fair Trading Act',[688] which may be considered as the national counterpart to Art 81 and Art 82 ECT, also instituting and determining the competences of the national competition authority, which is one of the main-addressees of Reg 1. Accordingly, only the latter two sets of rules are of relevance for my dissertation. However, more important is, at this point, the question, which are the legal foundations that empower the Italian bodies to apply EC competition law.

4.1.1 Application of Art 81 and 82 ECT by the Italian Competition Authority

National authorities are not allowed to apply EC competition law, without being explicitly empowered to do so by a national provision.[689] Law 287 did not empower the Italian Authority to apply EC competition law. However, following the Commission's shift to decentralised application of EC competition law, the Italian legislator conferred the Authority to directly apply Art 81 par 1 and Art 82 ECT by means of the procedures provided by Art 12 to Art 15 of law 287. This competence is limited by the obligation to suspend the proceedings, in case the Commission starts a procedure referring to the same case though.
The substantial competence in granting the Authority the ability to directly apply Art 81 par 1 and Art 82 ECT is contained in Art 54 par 5 law 52/96,[690]

[687] See for instance Art 2557 or Art 2596 Italian Civil Code.

[688] Law 287/90 of 10 October 1990, hereinafter referred to as law 287 or Competition Act.

[689] See *Pizzicaroli*, L'applicazione della disciplina comunitaria della concorrenza da parte dell'autorità garante del mercato in Italia, Diritto Comunitario e degli scambi internazionali 2001, 601 (606).

[690] See *Tizzano*, L'applicazione decentrata degli art 85 e 86 Ce in Italia, Foro italiano 1997, 35 (45); and Art 54 par 5 law 52 of 6 February 1996, which reads as follows: "The Competition Authority, in its capacity as the national authority responsible for competition and fair trading, shall, save where otherwise provided by section 20 of law 287 of 10 October 1990, enforce Art 85 (1) and Art 86 of the Treaty instituting the European Community, exercising the powers and acting in conformity with the procedures provided by Title II, Chapter II, of law 287 of 1990. The Authority shall inform the European Commission and suspend the proceedings in the event that the Commission commences a procedure under Community legislation relating to the same case."

which mirrors the Commission's shift from centralisation to decentralisation.[691] In fact, Art 54 par 1 to par 4 law 52 contain provisions that make the Authority an executive branch of the Commission in respect of the application of EC competition law by carrying out investigations and by assisting the officials of the Commission. In addition, the Authority may request the assistance and use the service of the Customs and Excise policy (Guardia di Finanza) to carry out the necessary investigations.[692]
Quite interestingly, the Commission emphasises that the Authority did not apply Art 81 and Art 82 ECT very ambitiously.[693] A possible reason might be the similarities between Italian competition law and EC competition law. Consequently, national law is applied even in cases that also regard EC law. Moreover, under Reg 17, national authorities, when applying Art 81 par 1 ECT, would have to refer the evaluation of the conditions as established in par 3 to the Commission. This might also be a reason, why national authorities tend to apply their own national rules, especially when they are drafted similarly to EC law.[694] Quite interesting to mention in this context is the fact that Art 54 law 52,[695] which enabled the Authority to apply both, national competition rules and Art 81 and Art 82 ECT in cases having their centre of gravity in Italy, offered a more effective means of hindering undertakings from applying the obstruction mechanism contained in Art 9 par 3 Reg 17.[696]

4.1.2 Application of Art 81 and 82 ECT by Italian courts

In respect of Italian competition law, Art 33 law 287 determines that the competence for nullity proceedings, claims for damages and emergency

According to the Commission though, in the absence of such a provision, the necessary competence to apply Art 81 and Art 82 ECT could have been based on the fact, that domestic law contains a corresponding provision concerning infringements of competition on the national territory. See *Europäische Kommission*, Die Anwendung der Artikel 85 und 86 des EG-Vertrags durch die Gerichte der Mitgliedstaaten (1997), 324.

691 See *Tizzano*, Il Foro Italiano 1997, 40.

692 See Art 54 par 1 and par 2 law 52. In this respect, Art 54 par 3 law 52 determines that "the results of the investigations performed [...] are submitted exclusively to the European Commission and may not be used for any other purposes." Also this provision has to be brought in line with Art 12 Reg 1.

693 See *Europäische Kommission*, Anwendung 325. Also see fn 748.

694 See *Pace*, L'evoluzione della tutela amministrativa della concorrenza nel diritto antitrust comunitario e nazionale, Il diritto dell'Unione Europea 1999, 356 (374-375); also see *Pizzicaroli*, Diritto comunitario e degli scambi internazionali 2001, 614.

695 Law 52 of 6 February 1996.

696 See *Pizzicaroli*, Diritto comunitario e degli scambi internazionali 2001, 607.

measures is with the court of appeal, thereby bypassing the competence of the 'tribunale' (court of first instance).[697] Such an exclusive jurisdiction, which runs counter to the principle of a two-step-jurisdiction is quite seldom and can be applied only if explicitly provided for.[698] Hence, this limitation is only applicable to national competition law and the question concerning the jurisdiction over the application of Art 81 and Art 82 ECT has to be determined according to the Italian Civil Procedural Law Code (CPC).[699]
In fact, even before the Competition Act had been enacted, Italian courts enforced Art 81 par 1 and Art 82 ECT and national legal provisions contained in the Civil Code. Concerning the categories of disputes left in the competence of the Italian courts of first instance, one can identify:

- cases concerning breaches of antitrust legislation other than nullity actions and claims for damages
- cases involving the competition rules of EC Treaty
- cases arising from the Italian Civil Code (CC).[700]

These cases are not dealt with by 'enlarged courts' or specialised courts, but by generalist judges, who rule over the broad field of private law. At the end of the day, "antitrust cases are a tiny percentage of every one of those judges' dockets,"[701] though.

---

[697] See *Auletta/Salanitro*, Diritto commerciale[10] (1996), 98.
See Art 33 par 2 law 287, which reads as follows:
"Annulment proceedings and claims for damages, and petitions of emergency measures to be adopted in respect of infringements of the provisions of Titles I to IV, must be filed before the Court of Appeal having jurisdiction over the place."
Law 287 empowers the Court of appeal - as court of both first and last instance - to deal with nullity actions and claims for damages. Judicial review in respect of the decisions adopted by this Court lies with the Cassation Court (Supreme Court), but only for questions of law. See *Tavassi*, Towards the application of Article 81 (3) by national courts in Italy, Rivista italiana di diritto pubblico comunitario 2001, 123 (125); also see *Wise*, OECD Journal of competition law and policy 2001, 89.

[698] See *Europäische Kommission*, Anwendung 331.

[699] It follows, that a case involving an infringement of EC-competition law, which is dealt with by a court of first instance and in which questions are raised in respect of law 287, the judge should derogate the relevant aspects to the court of appeal. However, this mechanism bears the risk that two divergent verdicts of different courts may be adopted. See *Europäische Kommission*, Anwendung 331; also see *Mangini/Olivieri*, Diritto Antitrust (2000), 124.

[700] See Art 2598 (unfair competition behaviour) and Art 2597 CC (enterprises in a position of legal monopoly). Also see *Tavassi*, Rivista italiana di diritto pubblico comunitario 2001, 125. Among the kinds of conduct treated under these rules are for instance acts that are likely to confuse the costumer about the origin of a product or service (similar names or logos) and disparagement (discrediting a competitor's products). See Wise, OECD Journal of Competition law and policy 2001, 85; also see Trabucchi, Istituzioni di diritto civille[5], 1994, 333.

[701] See *Tavassi*, Rivista italiana di diritto pubblico comunitario 2001, 124.

Lastly, as enforcement of the law is accomplished on the one hand by the Competition Authority and on the other hand by the Italian judiciary, it might also prove useful to briefly consider the relations between these two bodies. In this respect, it has been highlighted that even though the antitrust law was emanated in 1990, there are still areas, which are not clearly distinguishable in respect of the different competencies of the Italian courts and the Antitrust Authority and more precisely, between the decisions adopted by the 2 bodies. It can be observed that the examination of the economic aspects of competition cases lies generally within the competence of the Competition Authority, rather than with the courts. On the other hand, this does not imply that a complainant - before initiating proceedings in the ordinary courts - has to lodge a suit with the Authority as a prerequisite.[702] Even though the Authority's decisions are not binding on the courts, its decisions often constitute "supplementary elements of evaluation or presumption of the existence of specific infringements and behaviour.[703]" However,

> "it is not possible to deny that the decisions of the Competition Authority and those of the courts are linked, nor to deny the possibility that they may conflict with one another. The risk of conflicting decisions is inherent in the system devised by the legislator. It is partly ascribable to the diversity of functions which each authority must perform, but the possibilities of conflict are real."[704]

To sum up, one can observe that whereas the judges are primarily responsible for dealing with litigation between enterprises, the competition authority's duties are comprised of the supervision, consultation and protection of competition. In other words, it aims at safeguarding the general interest.[705] Generally, one can say that the role of the ordinary judge is to support and balance the powers allotted to the Authority.[706]

Having given a short overview of the norms that empower the Italian bodies to apply EC competition rules, I want to address now those points in question that might give rise to discussion when adapting the national regime to the

---

[702] See *Tavassi*, Rivista italiana di diritto pubblico comunitario 2001, 129.
Moreover, Tavassi clarifies that such a conditionality would definitely be against Art 24 par 1 of the Italian Constitution, which determines that anybody may go to court to protect his rights. See *Tavassi*, Rivista italiana di diritto pubblico comunitario 2001, 130.

[703] See *Tavassi*, Rivista italiana di diritto pubblico comunitario 2001, 131.

[704] See *Tavassi*, Rivista italiana di diritto pubblico comunitario 2001, 131.

[705] As Tavassi clarifies in this context, the role of Italian judges is not to safeguard the general interest or the consumer interest, but the ordinary judge is empowered to rule on 'subjective rights'. See *Tavassi*, Rivista italiano di diritto pubblico comunitario 2001, 124.

[706] See *Tavasssi*, Rivista italiano di diritto pubblico comunitario 2001, 126.

new European reality. To begin with, I will consider the Italian Competition Act in the light of the changed and new reality. Then I will draw the attention to specific issues relating to decentralisation to the Competition Authority on the one hand, and to the Italian courts on the other.

4.2 Specific issues

4.2.1 Law 278 – the Italian 'Competition and Fair Trading Act': an assessment in the light of the modernisation process

In Italian law, responsibility for dealing with competition matters is divided between the judicial authority and the Competition Authority, which was set up by the Italian Competition Act. This was enacted on the 10 October 1990.[707] Until then, competition-distorting agreements had to be prosecuted by the judiciary according to EC Competition law[708] and the provisions of the Civil Code.[709]

The new provisions followed Art 81 and Art 82 ECT and the Merger directive and acknowledge the primacy of EC law. In fact, Art 1 par 1 law 287 states that

> "the provisions of this Act [...] apply to agreements, abuse of a dominant position and concentration outside the scope of Articles 65 and/or 66 of the Treaty establishing the European Coal and Steel Community, Articles 85 and/or 86 of the Treaty establishing the European Economic Community, EEC Regulations or Community acts having an equivalent statutory effect."

It becomes clear, that law 287 has a residual function and applies only when Art 81 and Art 82 ECT do not apply, and accordingly when trade between

---

707 Law 278/90 was published in the 'Gazzetta Ufficiale', n 240 on the 13 October 1990 and entered into force the following day. It was based on two draft laws from 1988: namely draft law 1012 of senator Rossi and the draft government law 1240 of minister Battaglia. The final draft was highly influenced by the debate in the Industrial Committee of the Senate concerning the two draft laws and is strongly based on the draft of minister Battaglia. The final draft was proposed to the upper house in July 1990, which approved it with slight modifications. See *Siragusa/Sforzolini*, Il diritto della concorrenza italiano e comunitario: un nuovo rapporto, Foro Italiano 1992, 249 (250).

708 See *Europäische Kommission*, Anwendung 319.

709 In respect of other industrialised nations, Italy was quite late in adopting an own competition act. Instead, the provisions of the Civil Code applied. See *Benedettelli*, Sul rapporto fra diritto comunitario e diritto italiano della concorrenza, Foro italiano 1990, 235; also see *Corsi*, Diritto dell'impresa (2001), 367.

Member States is not affected.[710] It results, that Art 3 Reg 1 would not have been necessary for the Italian reality. Moreover, the whole structure of the law outlines a new model for the relationship between EC law and national competition law, which solely at a last step focuses on the question whether trade between Member States is distorted.[711]

As drafted similar to Art 81 ECT, law 287 states that agreements between undertakings

> "which have as their object or effect appreciable prevention, restriction or distortion of competition within the national market or a substantial part of it,"[712]

---

[710] As seen, national competence applies only if Community competence does not. In this respect the Authority does not function as the Italian branch of the Commission but has to be considered as independent in respect of this latter. The functions of the Authority are complementary to the Commission. See *Tizzano*, Foro italiano 1997, 39; also see *Fiale*, Diritto comerciale[14] (2002), 169.

[711] See *Europäische Kommission*, Anwendung 322.

The approach adopted by law 278 is also described as a system of 'reciprocal exclusivity', which is based on the assumption that Community and State mutually accept each other's jurisdiction. As a consequence, the law specifically limits its application-sphere to agreements, abuses and concentrations that are not within the sphere of application of EC law. The Italian legislator imposed self-limitation, which was rather unusual and which went beyond the obligations as requested by the then Art 5 par 2 ECT and the principle of primacy of EC law. See *Siragusa/Sforzolini*, Il Foro Italiano 1992, 252-253

This restriction of competences established by the Italian legislator was variously commentated upon. On the one hand it was said that the law eliminates beforehand the danger of contrasting competition law practice on the national and on Community level. On the other hand, it was emphasised that the application-sphere of the national law was severely restricted and the relationship between national and EC Law focused upon new and in respect of the other Member States contrasting criteria. The new model excludes beforehand the application of national competition law from facts, which fall within the application-sphere of EC-competition law. Hence, it has been criticised that collusive behaviour of undertakings, which hampers interstate trade but also and particularly national trade, is exclusively regulated by EC law. As a result, a controlling-gap might arise. See *Europäische Kommission*, Anwendung 322-323.

Moreover, one shall bear in mind, that Italian competition law – as every other national regime does – does not consider competition law as a method of eventually establishing the common market, which already exists within the national territory, but rather aims to guarantee that the parties respect the principles of a system of undistorted competition. Consequently, different goals require different action. Also see in this sense *Europäische Kommission*, Anwendung 321.

[712] See Art 2 par 2 law 287, which specifically mentions agreements, which:

- directly or indirectly fix purchase or selling prices or other contractual conditions
- limit or restrict competition, market outlets or market access, investment, technical development or technological progress
- share markets or sources of supply

are prohibited and consequently null and void[713].

The task to ascertain any infringement of this law is conferred to a five-headed independent body - the Competition Authority[714] -, whose members are elected for seven years by the presidents of the two chambers of the Italian Parliament.[715] The Authority takes fully part of the public administration, but acts "with total autonomy and independence of judgment and assessment" in respect of the Executive or other institutions of the state.[716]

In line with Reg 17, requests for exemption from the cartel-prohibition have to be submitted to the Authority, thus a prior notification system with its constitutive effect is instituted.[717] It is deemed that - in line with Reg 17 - no sanction may be applied, once a request for exemption is filed.[718] However, unlike the Commission under the old regime, the Authority has to "decide within a period of 120 days of the date on which the application is filed." An authorisation also may regard categories of agreements.[719] Similar to Art 81 par 3 ECT, Art 4 par 3 law 287 allows an authorisation of collusive behaviour - upon mandatory notification by the undertaking concerned - on the condition that the conditions of supply in the market are improved with a substantial benefit to the consumers.[720] Besides, it also lists non-competitive

- apply to other trading partners objectively dissimilar conditions for equivalent transactions, thereby placing them at an unjustifiable competitive disadvantage
- make the conclusion of contracts subject to acceptance by the other parties of supplementary obligations, which, by their nature or according to commercial usage, have no connection with the subject of such contracts.

713 See Art 2 par 2 law 287.

714 Hereinafter referred to as the Authority

715 See Art 10 par 1 and par 2 law 287; also see *Fiale*, Diritto commerciale, 167-168.

716 It has in common this characteristic with other independent institutions, such as the CONSOB (national stock exchange commission). See *Mangini/Olivieri*, Antitrust 113. Moreover, as being part of the public administration, it is consequently also governed by the relevant norms of the Italian Constitution (ie Art 97) and by those norms that regulate administrative proceedings. Furthermore, the Authority is also bound on the administrative principle of 'tipicità degli atti', what means that it can only adopt those acts explicitly provided for by law, excluding thus *a priori* the adoption of comfort letters. See *Mangini/Olivieri*, Antitrust 115; also see *Mazzarolli/Pericu/Romano/Roversi Monaco/Scoca*, Diritto amministrativo II/V^2 (1998), 1413.

717 See *Pardolesi*, Deroghe al divieto di intese restrittive della libertà di concorrenza, in Frignani, Diritto Antitrust Italiano 1993, 400 (401).

718 See *Pardolesi*, Antitrust 401.

719 See Art 4 law 287.

720 See *Corsi*, Diritto dell'impresa 368.
The onus of proof is on those who request the exemption. See *Zambrano*, Principi ed orientamenti dell'Autorità Garante in materia di intese nel corso del 1999, Concorrenza e mercato - rassegna degli orientamenti dell'Autorità Garante 2000, 3 (15).

matters.[721] From a systematical point of view though, one can observe that the authorization procedure is contained under a different norm[722] than the prohibition.[723] For agreements for which no exemption-authorisation is compulsory, voluntary notification allows to get clarification in respect of the possible illegal nature of an agreement, helping thus to foster legal certainty. Also in this case a time-limit of 120 days applies. After that, no investigation may take place, with the sole exception that the notification was untrue or incomplete.[724]

Norms dealing with the abuse of a dominant position and with concentrations are contained in Art 3[725] and Art 5 to Art 7 law 287[726] respectively.

Next, the Competition Act also regulates the hierarchy and the allocation of cases between Commission and Authority. In fact, Art 1 par 2 states that

---

[721] More precisely, according to Art 4 par 1 law 287, such improvements shall:
- "take into account the need to guarantee the undertakings the necessary level of international competitiveness
- be related, with increases of production, improvements in the quality of production or distribution, or with technical and technological progress".
Moreover, Art 4 law 287 provides for the possibility to revoke the exemption in case of abuse or the conditions upon which the exemption was granted do no longer exist.

[722] See Art 4 law 287.

[723] See Art 2 law 287; also see *Meli*, Il progetto di modernizzazione del sistema di controllo delle intese anticoncorrenziali ed il ruolo del giudice ordinario, Europa e diritto privato, 117 (122-123).

[724] See Art 13 law 287.

[725] Similar to Art 82 ECT, Art 3 law 287, mentions examples for the abuse of a dominant position:
- "directly or indirectly to impose unfair purchase or selling prices of other unfair contractual conditions
- to limit or restrict production, market outlets or market access, investment, technical development or technological progress
- to apply to other trading partners objectively dissimilar conditions for equivalent transactions, thereby placing them at an unjustifiable competitive disadvantage
- to make the conclusion of contracts subject to acceptance by the other parties of supplementary obligations which, by their nature or according to commercial usage, have no connection with the subject of such contracts."
As Frignani/Rossi outline, also "with reference to abuses of dominant positions, there are no sharp discordances between EC and Italian Law." See *Frignani/Rossi*, EU and Italian antitrust rules: concordances and discordances, Diritto del commercio italiano 2001, 811 (821).

[726] See Art 5 to Art 7 law 287; such concentrations are subject to notification to determine whether a dominant position on the domestic market is created or strengthened and by which competition is eliminated or appreciably restricted. Consequently, the authority may prohibit the concentration or define the necessary remedies in order to prevent the unlawful consequences.

> "where the Competition Authority [...] considers that a case does not fall within the scope of this Act, [...], it shall inform the Commission of the European Communities and forward to it any relevant information at its disposal."

Accordingly, Tavassi concludes that under law 287 the national competition authority shall primarily deal with cases whose effects are above all felt in the national territory.[727] Of course, such an approach is in strict contrast to the new philosophy of decentralisation as pursued by the reform and has to be amended.

Moreover, similar to Reg 17, the Authority has to "suspend any investigation into cases in respect of which the Commission [...] has opened a formal procedure [...] save for any aspects entirely of domestic relevance."[728] However, as we have seen, under Reg 1 the opening of a formal procedure by the Commission does not automatically lead to a suspension of the national investigation, but requires consultation with the national authority.[729] Accordingly, the Italian law should be amended in this respect.

Further provisions[730] regard banks, insurance companies and the broadcasting and publishing undertakings. Moreover, the Authority has wide-ranging consultative powers on existing and on draft legislation in respect of the Italian Parliament and of the Italian government.[731] In fact, Art 21 par 1 law 287 states that "in order to contribute to more effective protection of competition and the market, the Authority shall identify cases of particular relevance in which the provisions of law or regulations or general administrative provisions are creating distortions to competition to the sound operation of the market which are not justified by the requirements of general interest." If distortions are created in respect of EC competition law, the Authority is empowered – in case of inactivity of the national legislator – to simply disapply the contrasting national law.[732]

---

[727] See *Tavassi*, Rivista italiana di diritto pubblico comunitario 2001, 126; also see *Fiale*, Diritto commerciale, 169.

[728] See Art 1 par 3 law 287.
The Commission stresses that Art 1 par 2 and par 3 law 287 have never been applied due to the continuous co-operation between the Commission and Authority. See *Europäische Kommission*, Anwendung 323.

[729] See chapter 3.4.5.4.

[730] See Art 20 law 287.

[731] See Art 21 law 287.
Moreover, Art 22 law 287 outlines that "the Authority may express opinions on draft legislation or regulations and on problems relating to competition and the market whenever it deems this appropriate or whenever requested to do so by the government departments and agencies concerned."

[732] In this case, the Authority acts as *longa manus* of the European Commission. See *Negri*, Ruolo più forte all'Antitrust, Il sole - 24 ore, 249 (2003) 26.

Art 14 law 287 deals with the Authority's possibility to request information and to conduct inspections.[733] Interestingly, Art 14 par 1 lists attorneys among those who may submit representations, submissions and opinions during the course of investigations. However, it does not explicitly provide for the possibility of supplying 'all necessary' information, as Art 18 par 4 Reg 1 does. Moreover, inspections of the authority are limited to books and records and do not contain the possibility - as Reg 1 does in favour of the Commission - to enter premises, land and means of transport. As under the new regime, both the Commission and National authorities have to enforce Art 81 and Art 82 ECT fully, it seems advisable, in order to guarantee efficient enforcement of the law at European as well as at national level, to widen the powers of inspection of the Italian authority to reach the same extent as of the Commission.[734]

Next, the "information and data regarding the undertakings under investigation by the Authority are wholly confidential and may not be divulged [...]."[735] As requested by Art 12 Reg 1, this provision has to be amended in order to allow the proper functioning of the co-operation mechanisms within the network of authorities.[736] In respect of fines, the Authority can adopt them regarding "anyone who refuses or fails to provide the information."[737] It seems that by this means also those natural and legal person can be fined, who are out of the reach of the Commission according to Art 19 and Art 23 Reg 1.[738]

Furthermore, the Authority may order the remedy of the infringements. As explained, the Commission may, under the new regime, also impose remedies of structural nature.[739] Such a device is not provided for by the

---

733 See Art 14 par 2 law 287, which reads as follows:
"The Authority may, at any stage of the investigation, request undertakings, entities and individuals to supply any information in their possession and exhibit any documents of relevance to the investigation; it may conduct inspections of the undertaking's books and records and make copies of them, availing itself of the co-operation of other government agencies where necessary; it may produce expert reports and economic and statistical analyses, and consult experts on any matter of relevance to the investigation."

734 On the other hand, under the current national regime, the Italian authority can already make use of the Guardia di Finanza (Customs and Excise Police), who are vested with the powers and the authority given by tax legislation, to carry out investigations in respect of infringements of European competition law. See chapter 4.1.2.1.

735 See Art 14 par 3 law 287.

736 Also see in this context *Mangini/Olivieri*, Antitrust 115.

737 In fact, Art 14 par 5 law 287 reveals that "the Authority may fine anyone who refuses or fails to provide the information or exhibit the documents referred to in subsection (2) without justification [...]."

738 See chapter 3.4.10. In this context, also see chapter 4.2.2.2.

739 See chapter 3.4.10.

Italian Authority, which can impose fines, also in case of non-compliance with the order of remedy, and additionally, order the law-infringing undertaking to suspend activities for up to 30 days.[740] As the consequences of structural remedy can be rather wide-ranging,[741] I would suggest to reserve this means for the most serious infringements, which shall be dealt with, under the new regime, by the Commission.[742]
Besides, law 287 also contains provisions regarding the judiciary. First of all, it provides for the appeal against the decisions adopted by the authority. In fact, administrative measures taken by the authority fall within the exclusive jurisdiction of the administrative courts and more precisely, as the law states, the appeals have to be filed exclusively before the Latium Regional Administrative Tribunal (TAR). Secondly, annulment proceedings, claims for damages and petitions for emergency measures in respect of cartels, abuse of dominant positions and mergers, fall within the exclusive competence of the Court of Appeal having jurisdiction over the place and having hence jurisdiction in the first and last instance.[743] Accordingly, the Authority is precluded - contrary to the Commission and its enhanced powers – from adopting interim measures, which are in the exclusive competence of the Court of Appeal.[744]

---

740 See Art 15 law 287.

741 See chapter 3.4.10.

742 In fact, the necessity to apply a structural remedy should, in my opinion, also be grounds for taking a case out of the jurisdiction of a national authority.

743 See Art 33 law 287, which reads as follows:
1. Appeals against administrative measures adopted under the provisions of Titles I to IV of this Act fall within the exclusive jurisdiction of the administrative courts. They must be filed before the Latium Regional Administrative Tribunal.
2. Annulment proceedings and claims for damages, and petitions for emergency measures to be adopted in respect of infringements of the provisions of Titles I to IV, must be filed before the Court of Appeal having jurisdiction over the place.
Also see in this context *Fiale*, Diritto commerciale 175.
Moreover, it is criticised that the criteria to establish the competences between the administrative and the civil judges should be clarified as the current criteria has given raise to interference and contrasts. See *Tizzano*, Il Foro Italiano 1997, 47.

744 See Art 33 law 287.
Of course, apart from these circumstances, courts can adopt interim measures according to standard rules. See *Tavassi*, Rivista italiano di diritto pubblico comunitario 2001, 126-127. Particularly see in this context chapter 4.2.2.2 of this dissertation.

4.2.2 Decentralisation to the Italian Competition Authority

In respect of this group of issues, one has to consider three significant points in question: firstly, whether the authority has enough experience to fully and wholly apply Art 81 ECT, and secondly, whether the investigative powers of the authority are such as to guarantee consistent enforcement of the law. Finally, it should be asked whether the notification system as contained in law 287 necessarily has to be substituted by a legal exemption system in order to make the national system compatible with the new Reg 1.

4.2.2.1 Experience in applying EC competition law

One issue in the whole debate surrounding decentralised application of EC law concerns the capacity of national authorities to apply EC law. As seen in chapter 3.4.5.1, in order that NCAs can apply EC law efficiently, it is helpful that their own national law is similar to EC laws, as through this, experience can be gained. Law 287 is indeed very similar to EC competition law, at least from a procedural law point of view. Even though law 287 does not further regulate the substantial law as for instance the definition of significant terms like 'agreements', 'undertakings', or 'appreciable', this gap is filled by a direct link to EC law. Indeed, Art 1 par 4 law 287 explicitly states that "the provisions [...] shall be interpreted in accordance with the principles of the European Community competition law."[745] With this solution, doubts at national level in respect of these concepts were challenged. Indeed,

> "Italian law, by opting to invoke Community principles, has enabled [...] the Competition Authority in Italy to refer directly to the European Community's more than forty years of accumulated experience in the realm of competition. [...] As a result, legislative developments in Italy would seem consistent with the intention of making laws uniform throughout the Community – above all with a view towards creating a network of institutions able to deal with the implementation of competition rules."[746]

---

[745] This principle is valid in respect of Community regulations as well as interpretative ruling of the ECJ. See *Tavassi*, Rivista italiana di diritto pubblico comunitario 2001, 133.
For a concise overview of the definitions and handling of these terms, see *Zambrano*, Concorrenza e mercato – rassegna degli orientamenti dell'Autorità Garante 2000, 4-6.

[746] See *Tavassi*, Rivista italiana di diritto pubblico comunitario 2001, 135.

Hence, there should be no real problem for the Authority to apply par 3 of Art 81 ECT.[747]
The Authority however, has directly applied EC competition law in a rather sporadic way. In fact, under EC law it has considered only eight cases, concerning among others, the market for air-transport, restrictive practices in respect of the production and retailing of lighters and pay-TV.[748]

4.2.2.2 Investigative powers: dissimilarities to the powers of the Commission

Next, it has to be considered whether one can find procedural differences to such an extent that might inhibit that EC law can be applied consistently and effectively at national level. As seen in chapter 4.2.1, significant differences are recognisable in respect of investigations, and, in this context, in respect of the application of interim measures, which the Authority is not empowered to adopt.[749] This limitation stems from Art 54 law 52, which states that the

[747] Considering the system as installed in 1990, it seems efficient enough to guarantee equivalent application of the Art 81 and Art 82 ECT. See *Tizzano*, Il Foro Italiano 1997, 46.
In this context, Todino stresses that "this referral has proved over time to be a strong harmonising factor with respect to EC practice, as the Italian authority has systematically incorporated, in its enforcement activity, Community principles in the field of antitrust. To date, the integration between these two domains is such that in most decisions applying Italian competition law, EC case law is commonly quoted. In fact, the Italian experience is not unique as other countries have moved in the same direction, thus adapting their legislation to EC rules and practice." See *Todino*, ECLR 2000, 353.

[748] Regarding Art 81 ECT the Authority adopted 2 decisions, both in 2000:
Case A274 (Stream/Telepiù, non violation of Art 81 ECT)
Case I318 (Consorzio industrie fiammiferi, violation of Art 81 ECT)
Regarding Art 82 ECT, it adopted 7 decisions:
Case A263 (Unapace/Enel, violation of Art 82 ECT)
Case I318 (Consorzio industrie fiammiferi, non violation of Art 82 ECT)
Case A274 (Stream/Telepiù, violation of Art 82 ECT)
Case A247 (Aeroporti di Roma, violation of Art 82 ECT)
Case A291 (Assoviaggi/Alitalia, violation of Art 82 ECT)
Case A329 (Blugas/SNAM, violation of Art 82)
Case A299 (International Mail Express Italy/Poste Italiane, violation of Art 82 ECT)
Current proceeding concerning Art 82 ECT:
Case A333 (ENEL Trade clienti idonei)

[749] See in this context, *Mastroianni*, Osservazioni in merito alla effettività del sistema italiano di tutela "decentrata" del diritto comunitario della concorrenza, Il diritto dell'Unione Europea 2001, 78 (88).

Competition Authority shall exercise the powers and act "in conformity with the procedures provided by Title II, Chapter II, of law 287 of 1990."[750]

As the effectiveness of intervention by the national authority depends to a large extent on the power to adopt interim or emergency measures, doubts have correctly been expressed as to whether the Italian Authority may adopt decisions and open proceedings with the same efficiency as the Commission is enabled to.[751] Interestingly, under the old regime such powers were not even expressingly conferred to the Commission by any legislative act. With the verdict adopted in the Camera care case, the ECJ filled this gap in favour of the Commission.[752]

In this sense, the capacity for national authorities to apply interim-measures has apparently been granted by the new regulation. In fact, Art 5 Reg 1 by indicating the decisions national authorities may apply expressly cites interim measure.

In this context, the Commission explicitly states that competition authorities have to act in accordance not only with the new regulation but also with the applicable national procedural rules.[753] Thus, a dilemma is created as one regime allows certain measures another denies. Therefore, it seems imperative to adjust law 287 in order to empower the Authority to adopt interim measures as well,[754] also reflecting thus the principle according to which national rules "may not be so framed to render virtually impossible the execercise of rights conferred by Community law."[755]

Contrary to this, Mastroianni[756] - in citing the Court of Appeal of Milan - points out that such a mechanism could hardly be incorporated into the national legal order, as these are reserved to the judiciary. However, he correctly acknowledges, that there could be a necessity in order to readapt the Italian competition system to the EC-regime.[757]

---

750 See *Pizzicaroli*, Diritto comunitario e degli scambi internazionali 2001, 617.

751 See *Pizzicaroli*, Diritto comunitario e degli scambi internazionali 2001, 616.

752 See chapter 3.1.2.

753 See Proposal 16.

754 See in this context also Weitbrecht, who observes in referring to German competition law, that due to the reform it seems necessary to adjust the national competition regime. See *Weitbrecht*, EuZW 2003, 73.

755 See ECJ case 199/82 (San Giorgio); also see in this context *Todino*, L'autorità e l'applicazione decentrata degli articoli 85 e 86 del trattato CE, Temi e problemi 1997, 1 (28-29).

756 See *Mastroianni*, Il diritto dell'Unione Europea 2001, 88.

757 See *Mastroianni*, Il diritto dell'Unione Europea 2001, 89.
In this tenor also see *European Commission*, Notices of co-operation between the Commission and national, par 45, which states that "[...] the effectiveness of the national authority's action depends notably on whether that authority is able to take interim measures if it deems it necessary, without prejudice to the possibility, found in

On the other hand, one might argue that undertakings are allowed to call for emergency measures from ordinary courts, as Art 33 par 2 law 287 states. Such a power in favour of national courts has been recognised by the ECJ especially in situations in which neither national law nor Community law do provide for such measures. This power is based on the principle of the effectiveness of EC law.[758] However, the effectiveness of this option can be criticised on several grounds: Firstly, in contrast to an interim measure adopted by the Authority, the involvement of an ordinary judge seems to be rather burdensome and what is more, rather time wasting. Secondly, the ordinary judge is directed towards the protection of single interests and not towards the protection of a general interest like the safeguarding of the undistorted functioning of markets.[759] As Todino correctly observes, this interest has to be protected independently of any subjective interest. [760] Lastly, it is argued that an ordinary judge when adopting an emergency measure still has to verify whether the preconditions for the measure exist, hence making the whole procedure even more complex and time-consuming. Taken together, one can rightly criticise that denying the Italian authority to apply interim-measures, may frustrate the effective application of the Community law.[761]

A further difference between the investigating powers of the Commission and the Authority is constituted by the faculty of the former to grant immunity of fines.[762] Such an instrument definitely helps to foster the flow of information to detect forbidden cartels. The Authority currently cannot adopt such means.[763] Hence, one can correctly argue that their investigations are kept under more difficult circumstances than those of the Commission and ultimately its duty to detect restrictive practices is thereby hindered. In order to make decentralisation as most effective as possible it seems wise to provide such an instrument also at national level.[764]

---

the law of certain Member States, that such measures may be taken with the requisite degree of effectiveness by a court."

758 See ECJ case C-465/93 (Atlanta); also see *Pizzicaroli*, Diritto comunitario e degli scambi internazionali 2001, 617.

759 See *Pizzicaroli*, Diritto comunitario e degli scambi internazionali 2001, 617.

760 See *Todino*, Temi e problemi 1997, 30.

761 In this sense see *Todino*, Temi e problemi 1997, 30-31.

762 See chapter 2.4.4. In this respect also see *Pizzicaroli*, Diritto comunitario e degli scambi internazionali 2001, 617.

763 Anyhow, as being part of the public administration, the Authority also has to consider the principle of proportionality of the sanctions it considers to impose. This implies that it shall take account of the collaboration of the parties involved. See *Mangini/Olivieri*, Antitrust 116.

764 See *Pizzicaroli*, Diritto comunitario e degli scambi internazionali 2001, 619.

4.2.2.3 Two different regimes?

In respect of enforcement of Art 81 and Art 82 ECT, the Commission stresses that

> "the competition authorities of the Member States are to take effective action against the conduct in question, acting in accordance with the [...] Regulation and applicable national procedural rules"[765]

As we know, law 278 is shaped along the pattern of Reg 17 and accordingly incorporates a notification procedure. Hence, as at Community level a legal exemption system is installed, one might question, whether it is necessary to change the national regime in order to adopt a legal exemption system as well.

Of course, applicable national rules in this context are those, which determine the investigative powers or the powers of remedy.[766] Hence, agreements that - at a first glance - relate to inter-state trade, will be ruled by the Authority according to the legal exemption system as provided for by EC law in combination with the applicable national procedural rules. Quite interesting that under these Italian rules, undertakings will still have the possibility to notify their agreements, on a voluntary basis, to get clarification from the Authority in respect of the legal validity of their businesses. Indeed, Art 54 par 5 law 52 in referring to Art 13 law 278 expressingly provides for this possibility.

However, what if an undertaking by assessing its restrictive practice under European law determines the exemption based on Art 81 par 3 ECT, discovers or better still the national authority discovers at a later stage, that the agreement does not have to comply with EC law but with national law? As we know, the national regime requests a notification for a valid exemption, which in this case would not have been asked for due to the incorrect assessment of the undertaking. As a result of the non existing notification with its possible consequent earlier exemption, the agreement could be declared void and prohibited under national law, at least until a notification for request of exemption according to Art 4 par 3 law 287 is filed. In order to guarantee legal certainty and especially to ensure effective business-conducting, the current procedural rules as adopted by the Italian legislator, should be amended to incorporate the legal exemption system.

However, one shall bear in mind that these means do not give immunity in respect of the norms contained in the Civil Code. See *Pizzicaroli*, Diritto comunitario e degli scambi internazionali 2001, 618.

765 See Proposal 16.

766 See Art 54 par 5 law 52.

4.2.3 Decentralisation to Italian courts

This subchapter deals, to begin with, with the experience of Italian courts in the field of EC competition law also posing the question of whether Italian courts will face considerable problems when applying Art 81 par 3 ECT. Then, it will be analysed which points in question obligatory co-operation might bear and last but not least, it will draw its attention to some procedural matters.

4.2.3.1 Experience in applying EC competition law

Art 1 par 4 law 278 does not only apply to the Authority, but also to Italian courts.[767] Before the Italian Competition Act was enacted, Italian courts had scarce if any previous experience of competition matters, nor did they have sufficient experience with EC law as a whole.[768] Nevertheless, even if the Authority has admittedly gathered sufficient skills and knowledge in this field, it has to be outlined that the activity of courts in this field was rather humble.[769] Accurately,

> "while Art 1 par 4 of the competition act has immediately worked quite well with reference to antitrust Authority, which, as an 'absolute beginner', has taken the Commission as an example to follow, it has not been the same for the courts, which have been more reluctant to depart from deeply-rooted national traditions and move towards the 'new' trails of competition law, under the guide of EC rules and enforcement experience."[770]

This opinion is supported by the fact that courts have not been very keen in using the power to grant interlocutory measures like preliminary injunctions as provided for by Art 33 par 2 law 287 either. A reason might be that such powers may interfere rather heavily with contractual relationships between for instance a dominant undertaking and its business partners: this is not very customary to Italian private law. More generally, one can observe that

---

[767] Initially it was feared that Italian courts might not take favourably to this limitation. On the contrary, lots of rulings drew upon the principles established in Art 1 to Art 8 ECT, and also on case-law of the ECJ, the Court of First Instance and the Commission. Moreover, national judges act as 'Community judges' and therefore must comply with Community provisions. Conflicting national provisions have to be disregarded, without giving any importance as to whether these rules were adopted prior to or subsequent to the EC rule. See *Tavassi*, Rivista italiana di diritto pubblico comunitario 2001, 133.

[768] See *Frignani/Rossi*, Diritto del commercio italiano 2001, 813.

[769] See *Wise*, Journal of competition law and policy 2001, 91; also see *Mangini/Olivieri*, Antitrust 114.

[770] See *Frignani/Rossi*, Diritto del commercio italiano 2001, 813.

> "the protection of individuals against harmful consequences of antitrust violations, through judicial action, is not satisfactorily developed yet."[771]

Doubts can also be raised in respect of the economic foundations of antitrust judgments, which are not always clearly expressed. Courts (TAR, Consiglio di Stato and ordinary courts) are not very accustomed to economic analysis and refrain from embracing economic theories in legal reasonings.[772] As a matter of fact,

> "the link between the application of antitrust law and the economic analysis, in Italy, is not yet as deep and transparent as it is in the United States, and as it will be more and more in the EU."[773]

In respect of the ability of judges to effectively apply EC law, one has to consider moreover the standard of proof in the Italian law system as this indicates how courts can get evidence about competition infringements and help in the economic assessment of competition issues.

The rules on the matter of proof for antitrust cases are dictated by the Italian civil procedural rules, which provide for the principle of 'allegation by the parties'.[774] This means that courts primarily find the evidence from the litigations.[775] However, the judges are not free in investigating the facts: what evidence is admissible, its form and manner of presentation and acceptance is strictly regulated by the law.[776] Therefore, the question is posed as to how a judge can deepen his knowledge of the economic aspects of a case. As explained, such an understanding is particularly important when applying Art 81 par 3 ECT. Moreover, it is questioned whether the principle of allegation of the parties, which means that judges examine only those aspects which parties have chosen to present, might enable a full and complete pursuance of the economic analysis.[777]

Remedies in this context might be given by the fact that, in addition to the motion by the litigants, Italian courts also have the possibility of special

---

771 Interestingly, Fringnani/Rossi highlight, that "the national tradition of contract law has influenced the judicial application of Italian antitrust law, while EC law has been much more resistant to influences from national private laws." See *Fringnani/Rossi*, Diritto del commercio italiano 2001, 813.

772 See *Frignani/Rossi*, Diritto del commercio italiano 2001, 814; also see *Wise*, Journal of competition law and policy 2001, 91.

773 See *Frignani/Rossi*, Diritto del commercio italiano 2001, 814.

774 See Art 2697 CC.

775 For instance, claims have been rejected due to the plaintiff's failure to demonstrate competing firms' market power and competition distorting effects of agreements. See *Tavassi*, Rivista italiana di diritto pubblico comunitario 2001, 131.

776 See section III CPC; also see *Tavassi*, Rivista italiana di diritto pubblico comunitario 2001, 132.

777 See *Tavassi*, Rivista italiana di diritto pubblico comunitario 2001, 135-136; also see *Todino*, ECLR 2000, 350.

investigative measures or instruments. First, there is the possibility to refer to the investigations carried out by the Authority. However, as it is not mandatory to bring a case before the Authority before jurisdictional proceedings are initiated, the Authority's decisions are often simply not available.[778] Secondly, Art 213 CPC empowers judges to seek information from a government department.[779] If requested by one of the parties to the proceeding, obtaining external advice or better yet from a third party, can be based on Art 210 CPC.[780] Of course, experts can also be called upon to provide the necessary economic aspects of a dispute to help appraise the main facts of the case.[781] These experts can be nominated solely in situations where the parties are able to illustrate the market context to the case.[782] Moreover, in the Italian legal system, such an expert's view does not constitute proof but rather it shall supplement the judge's knowledge in case he does not have the necessary technical familiarity, which is needed in order to appraise the evidence. This expert opinion is not binding on the judge.[783]

Anyhow, I would not overestimate the fear that clear and sufficient evidence could not be produced. In fact, one shall bear in mind, that because of the adversarial system parties will definitively look for the necessary evidence. Ultimately it is in the judge's competence to decide whether enough evidence

778 At this point one shall bear in mind that a judge is not bound on the decision reached by the Authority. See chapter 4.1.2.

779 Art 213 CPC reads as follows:
"Fuori dei casi previsti negli articoli 210 e 211, il giudice può richiedere d'ufficio alla pubblica amministrazione le informazioni scritte relative ad atti e documenti dell'amministrazione stessa, che è necessario acquisire al processo."

780 Art 210 par 1 CPC reads as follows:
"[...] il giudice istruttore, su istanza di parte, può ordinare all'altra parte o a un terzo di esibire in giudizio un documento o altra cosa di cui ritenga necessaria l'acquisizione al processo."
Moreover, one shall be aware that in the Italian legal system, judges are not allowed to receive or use private information about the case before them. See Art 97 of 'decree of the king' n 1368 of 18 December 1941 (regulation implementing the CPC), which states:
"Il giudice non può ricevere private informazioni sulle cause pendenti davanti a sé, né può ricevere memorie se non per mezzo della cancelleria."

781 See Art 191 par 1 CPC, which reads as follows:
"Nei casi di cui agli articoli 61 e seguenti il giudice istruttore, con l'ordinanza prevista, nomina un consulente tecnico e fissa l'udienza nella quale questi deve comparire."

782 See Satta/Punzi, Diritto processuale civile[12] (1996), 380-381.

783 See Satta/Punzi, Diritto Processuale 101;
Tavassi clarifies, that "the judge must explain his reasons for rejecting the conclusions of the expert whom he has chosen." See *Tavassi*, Rivista italiana di diritto pubblico comunitario 2001, 137.

has been produced or not.[784] In addition, as we have seen, the Italian legal system provides for tools that help to gain information in respect of a case. However, it seems recommendable to give judges and lawyers special training to foster their economic understanding, which is necessary to correctly apply competition law. As seen in chapter 3.4.6.1, there are solutions that help to cope with the problem.[785] Mastroianni pleads for specialised sections within ordinary courts that would deal exclusively with matters concerning national as well as Community competition law, also involving, if possible, external experts.[786]. In my opinion, this seems quite a practical solution, even though it will surely not be necessary to institute special sections at every ordinary court. Perceivable are special sections in the larger economic areas, where it seems more likely that a dispute concerning EC competition law might arise.

4.2.3.2 Co-operation between the Commission and Italian courts

A second point in question focuses on co-operation. As explained,[787] the trend of involving national judges in the enforcement of EC competition law initiated before the White Paper was published. Indeed, the Notice on co-operation between the Commission and national judges pursued the idea of harmonising the various concerns and obliged the judges to take account of the Commission's competence in order to make sure that no incompatible decisions are enacted.[788] This goal was supported by such means as for instance, the request for the suspension of proceedings or by the prerogative to issue decisions in line with the Commission's decisions. However, all these suggestions have not been incorporated into Italian procedural law and therefore remained 'dead letter'.[789]

---

[784] As Art 209 CPC states:
Il giudice istruttore dichiara chiusa l'assunzione quando sono eseguiti i mezzi ammessi o quando, dichiarata la decadenza di cui all'articolo [208 CPC], non vi sono altri mezzi da assumere, oppure quando egli ravvisa superflua, per i risultati già raggiunti, la ulteriore assunzione."

[785] According to Tavassi, the choice of the legislator to refer competition disputes to the Court of Appeal indicates that they have a certain degree of specialisation in economic cases as "they have the opportunity to acquire a sound knowledge of economic matters since they handle cases brought by firms". See *Tavassi*, Rivista italiana di diritto pubblico comunitario 2001, 138,

[786] See *Mastroianni*, Il diritto dell'Unione Europea 2001, 92.

[787] See chapter 3.2, consider the Notices on co-operation; also see chapter 2.4.4.

[788] Also see chapter 2.4.4.

[789] See *Meli*, Europa e diritto privato 2001, 129.

On the other hand, the new regulation departs from mere suggestions and strengthens and enhances co-operation.[790] The homogeneity called for by the new policy to work properly necessitates the introduction of appropriate mechanisms in order to ensure uniformity. As we have seen, such is provided for by Art 15 Reg 1. The question is, how such an instrument shall be implemented in national procedural law. A part-solution to the dilemma could be found by applying Art 213 CPC,[791] which allows national judges to be informed by the public administration. However, it is clear that this norm does refer to information rather than real and proper opinions, which, although not binding, in the end-effect assist in eventually determining the verdict.[792] On the other hand, no solution without the adjustment of Italian procedural law seems to be possible in respect of the judicial duty to inform the Commission. In fact, whereas § 90 of the German GWB orders judges to inform the authority of all causes dealt with, no such mechanism is provided for by the Italian procedural system.[793]

4.2.3.3 Some specific observations in respect of the court of appeal and the TAR

As illustrated, the exclusive competence of the court of appeal as provided for by Art 33 par 2 law 287 is definitely exceptional as it runs counter to one of the essential principles of modern legal systems. It is therefore impossible to interpret this rule by analogy to Community law. In other words, Community law, when applied by national judges follows the ordinary pattern with its two-step judiciary.

It is argued, that this fact might become a problem due to the fact that the dividing line between EC competition law and national competition law is rather vague. Even though eventually a decision adopted according to law 287 cannot differ from a decision adopted under EC law - provided of course that Art 3 Reg 1 applies - the parties will get robbed of a further step of appeal, when Italian competition law is applied. This seems rather irrational. Moreover, it will also be quite complicated to gather investigations of national competition law as well as Community competition law. According to

[790] See chapter 3.4.6.3.

[791] For Art 213 CPC see fn 779.

[792] See in this context chapter 4.2.3.1.

[793] See *Meli*, Europa e diritto privato 2001, 131.
See also Todino, who observes that "as for the obligation for national courts to keep the Commission informed, no legal impediments exist to this arrangement, as long as it concerns the communication of the judgment rendered by national courts. By contrast, it may prove too heavy a task for national courts if implied an obligation to send the whole file." See *Todino*, ECLR 2000, 351.

the Commission, such accumulation should be one of the advantages of judicial enforcement of the law, as opposed to enforcement by the Commission.[794] I agree with Mastorianni when he observes that all in all the solution as adopted by the national legislator seems to keep judicial enforcement of competition law too complex. As a consequence it seems advisable to abrogate Art 33 par 2 law 287, where it gives exclusive competence to the Court of appeal.[795]

Next, in respect of appeals before the administrative courts in Rome,[796] it is observed that their case law is intrinsically linked to national administrative law, both under a substantial as well as a procedural point of view.[797] In this sense, Frignani/Rossi underpin that

> "the TAR and the Consiglio di Stato apply very restrictively the traditional principles of Italian administrative law in order to determine who has cause of action (standing) against illegal acts of the antitrust Authority; as a consequence, many decisions of such Authority, particularly regarding the control of concentrations between undertakings, may be deprived of any judicial control."[798]

Indeed, generally only those persons, who have a recognised and law-protected interest negatively affected by an act of the public administration, are subjected to a cause of action against such an act.[799] In this tenor, the case law[800] of the TAR determines that only the undertakings that are the addressees of the decisions of the Authority have a standing in court. As a result, those parties, who are beneficiaries of antitrust regulations, namely competitors and consumers, are denied any standing, even though they have intervened in the proceeding in front of the Authority. As a reason it is indicated that the Authority aims at protecting the general interest of guaranteeing free competition and not the interest of a single person.

In this regard, it is correctly criticised denying an appeal to third parties, who have - according to Art 33 law 287 - the possibility to file a civil action for recovering damages as a consequence of antitrust violation, as such

---

794 *European Commission*, Notice on the co-operation between national judges and the Commission.

795 See *Mastroianni*, Il diritto dell'Unione Europea 2001, 89-91.

796 The 'Tribunale Amministrativo Regionale per il Lazio' (TAR); and the 'Consiglio di Stato' as the court competent for appeals from decisions of TAR Lazio.

797 See *Frignani/Rossi*, Diritto del commercio italiano 2001, 814.

798 See *Frignani/Rossi*, Diritto del commercio italiano 2001, 814.

799 See *Frignani/Rossi*, Diritto del commercio italiano 2001, 827; also see *Mazzarolli/Pericu/Romano/Roversi Monaco/Scoca*, Diritto amministrativo 1860.

800 See decision of TAR Lazio, September 2001, Codacons/Autorità Garante della Concorrenza e del Mercato.

damages refer to the same alleged violations which are the object of the authority's decisions.[801]
Moreover, under this traditional approach adopted by the TAR in respect of appeals, it is no wonder that the control over acts of the public administration does not embrace the entering into the merits of the Authority's decision.[802] On the other hand, one can observe that it is advocated that a control into the merits shall progressively be given to the CFI in respect of the Commission's acts.[803] Such an approach should be observed when amending law 287. In fact, it is correctly highlighted that there is a risk that the Authority might violate rights of individuals: such violations should be part of full judicial review.[804]

801 See *Frignani/Rossi*, Diritto del commercio italiano 2001, 827-828.

802 but concentrates on the traditional control of administrative acts, like lack of competence or error of law; also see *Mangini/Olivieri*, Antitrust 120.

803 Also see chapter 3.4.8.

804 See *Frignani/Rossi*, Diritto del commercio italiano 2001, 828

5 Conclusions

This dissertation has dealt with the procedural rules of European Competition law and analysed the switch from centralised enforcement of Art 81 and Art 82 ECT towards decentralised enforcement involving, in addition to the Commission, also national authorities and courts. This reform is combined with the introduction of a system that institutes a regime of control over the correct and coherent application of these articles using an *ex-post* approach, which also provides a stronger role to private litigation. The consequences for national bodies were then illustrated in the example of the Italian judiciary and Italian competition authority.
In the first part (chapter 2), I briefly touched the core-concepts and ideas that are the backbone of competition theory, I explained the concept of competition within the framework of the European Community and stressed its importance for the core-project of the EC, which is the common market. Then I outlined the substantive law, which has to be applied according to the new procedural rules.
The second part (chapter 3) of my dissertation centred on the process of modernisation. To begin with, I focused on Reg 17, which was the first regulation implementing Art 81 and Art 82 ECT, indicating also the path that led to its adoption in 1962. Then I focused on the various motives that made the whole process of modernisation necessary. It turned out that the notification system, with the monopoly hold by the Commission, was rather useful in establishing a common competition culture within the Community, especially considering the fact that Europe in general did not have much, if indeed any, experience in applying these concepts. Anyhow, what was useful at that time has turned out to be outdated in modern times as the notification regime as applied under Reg 17 was at the end inefficient. Reasons for it were found in the fact that the mandatory notification created an enormous administrative burden on the Commission, which, due to its limited resources, was no longer able to concentrate on the most serious infringements of the law. Even though the Commission tried to solve the problems by various means (especially by issuing block exemptions, informal comfort letters and notices), these initiatives did not prove to have sustained success. Also the fact that the Eastern-enlargement of the EU would intensify the work of the Commission was a further reason for abandoning the original regime. Next, the decentralised application of EC law will ultimately converge national and Community law and hence, ease the adopting of commercial strategies by undertakings. Moreover, the initial reason for introducing a centralised system, the non existent competition culture, was outdated as well, as during the roughly 40 years of EC competition law, a solid foundation especially in terms of case-law of the European judiciary, further guidelines

and clarifying notices of the Commission was created. On the other hand, the Commission is still aware that guidance may still be needed for the just and coherent application of the law. Hence, the reform also brings with it a means to ensure that uniform and consistent enforcement may be guaranteed. This is necessary also under the prerogative that the newly installed legal exemption system does not contain, with exemptions, the possibility to adopt decisions clarifying whether an agreement does conform with the law.

Then, I commented on the various issues that were raised during the modernisation process. To begin with I concentrated on the question of whether the new regime is compatible with the Treaty of Rome or whether the Treaty has to be amended in order that the new enforcement system can be embedded within this framework. Several arguments were put forward to show the necessity of a Treaty amendment. Most of them were not convincing though. For instance, it was demonstrated that Art 81 par 3 ECT can be applied directly and hence by national bodies. Moreover, the argument that the new regime establishes a system of control of abuse, which is inherent in Art 82 ECT and not in Art 81 ECT, also had to be disregarded. The same is true for the arguments based on the wording of Art 83 par 2 subpar b and Art 84 ECT. Anyhow, no valid argument was found in order to prove the argument that the wording of Art 81 par 3 ECT was wrong. On the contrary, severe doubts were raised emphasising that the new regime, which does not require any authoritative act to exempt an agreement from the prohibition of Art 81 ECT, cannot be brought in line with the stringent phrasing of the Treaty. As a result, one can correctly argue that the new regime runs counter to the concepts as enshrined in the Treaty.

Then I considered the argument that notifications actually were rather successful in providing the Commission with relevant information about business practices. Hence, it was argued that the notification system should not be abolished. Contrary to this, I emphasised the fact that even though notifications were abolished other means can be procured to guarantee that the necessary market-data is provided. In this context, I focused on the enhanced co-operation of the Commission and national bodies and on the incentives of private litigation.

Next, I considered block exemptions and individual exemptions in the context of the new regime. It was clarified that under the new regime they will not have constitutive but declaratory power and that their importance has to be seen primarily in the task of clarifying the application of Art 81 par 3 ECT. The same is true for guidelines and notices. These means are part of the mechanisms that shall guarantee the uniform and consistent application of EC competition law.

Afterwards, I concentrated on the new relationship between EC competition law and national competition law and concluded that the primacy of EC competition law over national rules was further fostered. Moreover, it was reasoned that the enhanced supremacy of EC law primarily represses those national laws, which differ form EC rules. Indeed, this is an important step in order to create a level playing field for businesses within the common market.

Then, the analysis drew its attention to specific issues regarding decentralisation to national authorities on the one hand and decentralisation to national courts on the other. In respect of the former, I clarified that even though divergences among the Member States in the quality of law-enforcement by the various national authorities might still exist, Reg 1 impels Member States to guarantee a certain minimum standard. Moreover, some divergences in the application of the law are permissible in reflecting also the cultural diversity of Europe. In this context, it was further correctly criticised that national decisions have territorially limited effect bearing the risk of multiple jurisdiction. Hence, the reform process cannot be deemed to have been completed to a satisfying extent. This is further true for an effective mechanism of case allocation between the various national bodies and the Commission. The risk of forum shopping can hence not be neglected. As a result, the new regulation should be amended to incorporate one of the described allocation mechanisms. Moreover, to limit inconsistent decision-making by the various competition authorities involved, a network is installed to enhance co-operation between them. Whereas the means for information sharing seem to be quite effective, harmonisation of national laws seems to be necessary in order to allow that the shared documents can be used as evidence in all proceedings. To further strengthen the network, the Advisory Committee on restrictive practices and dominant positions has acquired an enhanced role not only as a discussion forum in respect European Competition law, but also in respect of various national competition matters. Uniformity of the law is furthermore fostered through a provision prohibiting national authorities from adopting decisions that run counter to Commission decisions. Herewith the important role of the Commission as a vest of guidance for the correct application of the law is once more underpinned.

An important factor of the success of the legal exemption system stems from private litigation, which shall be achieved through decentralisation to national courts. Anyhow, especially due to the described disadvantages of private enforcement, one can doubt whether national courts will ever play a significant role in enforcing EC competition law. Nevertheless, in respect of national courts it was highlighted that possible initial problems in applying the law will not hinder the effective application of Art 81 par 3 ECT eventually, as there are several means to improve enforcement. Definitely more problematic is the fact that the various national judges apply the law according to their own national procedural law. As a result, diverging decisions might follow. This risk can only be avoided through harmonisation of the national procedural law regimes. On the other hand, diverging decisions shall be limited through enhanced co-operation with the Commission and national courts themselves. In respect of the duty of national judges in transmitting information and opinions to the Commission and other courts, as well as in respect of a possible intervention in a court-proceeding by the Commission and national authorities, the question of reconcilability with the principle of independency of courts was raised. However, under the premise of the necessary consistency in the enforcement of EC competition law, doubts in relation to this, seem to be neglectable. Next, it was correctly criticised that no effective means exists of hindering the fact that disputes on the same issue are heard by different judges, due to the Brussels Convention being only partially helpful in this context. On the other hand, consistent application is fostered through the provision urging national courts to avoid decisions that conflict with Commission decisions. Lastly, I considered whether the quite successful American antitrust law, which is also based on a legal exemption system, might be a helpful guidance for an efficient smoothing off of the European modernisation process. As a result, it was shown that those instruments that guarantee the success of the American regime are not consistent with the Community's and Member States' laws.

Having finished the discussion concentrating on decentralisation to national institutions, I considered the situation of undertakings as the ultimate addressees of the new regime. I criticised the fact that, as they have to autonomously assess the compatibility of their restrictive practices, the new regime cannot guarantee the same degree of legal certainty as the former regime with the notification procedure and the consequent clarifying Commission decision.

Then I considered the reform and its possible indirect effects on the duties of the European Court of Justice and the Court of First Instance. In this regard, I stressed that due to the lack of experience of national courts, the European judiciary will have to handle more preliminary rulings called upon by guide-seeking national courts. Anyhow, this shall be no ground to change the existing preliminary ruling system. Rather it seems to be useful to give the Court of First Instance the primary responsibility for preliminary rulings on the interpretation of EC competition law, as it has gained deep knowledge in this matter. What is more, it would also be welcomed if the European courts gave up their self-imposed limited control over the application of EC competition rules, so that better guidance on the application of the law will result.

Afterwards, I analysed whether the fact of the accession to the Union of states whose experience with concepts of competition policy is rather novice, might bear a risk of non-consistent and non-uniform application of the law. However, it was argued that such fear should not be overvalued, as the accession-states are obliged to harmonise their competition rules with the existing EC competition law. However, strong commitment by the Commission is requested to offer help in the correct application of the competition rules.
As the Commission is deemed to detect the most serious infringements, it was furthermore requested to update its investigative powers. In fact, the new regime officially introduced the possibility of adopting interim measures and also considerably enhanced the possibilities of requesting information not only from owners of undertakings and their representatives, but also from authorised lawyers and any other natural or legal person. A further innovation is the possibility of adopting structural remedies. Moreover, it was questioned whether *ex-post* control based on own-initiative investigations and on complaints may suffice in providing the necessary information. Anyhow, one can oppose that not only the powers of enquiry have been amplified considerably, also the fact that national authorities, which are deemed to be closer to markets, will help to gain significant insight into business practices. Indeed, one should not neglect the fact, that information-sharing within the network will create an important data-pool reflecting business practices.
The final issue of the second part of my dissertation focused briefly on possible alternatives to the legal exemption system. These concentrate on the interpretation of Art 81 par 1 ECT as a rule of reason, on mere decentralised application of Art 81 par 3 ECT without the introduction of *ex-post* control, on the broadening of the scope of the application of Art 4 par 2 Reg 17, in order to make sure that fewer agreements have to be notified and on procedural simplification when issuing a formal decision due to a notification. Neither of these alternatives seemed to be satisfying, although admittedly a combination of the various elements of these alternatives could prove to constitute a successful alternative. However, the discussion regarding the reform did not go so far as to consider such an alternative solution in depth.
The last part of my dissertation (chapter 4) considered the possible consequences for the Italian Antitrust Authority and Italian courts and especially for the rules that govern these bodies' functioning. After having illustrated the legal foundations for the application of EC competition law by the Authority and national courts, I commented upon the various issues that can be raised. To begin with, I considered the Italian Competition Act by comparing it with Reg 1. It was found, among others, that the Italian law

already contains a hierarchical order between EC law and national competition law, which anticipates the solution as introduced by Art 3 Reg 1. Then I commented upon those issues, which specifically regard decentralisation to the Italian Authority and courts. I considered the aspect of the ability of the Italian Authority to apply Art 81 par 3 ECT. It was clarified that as Italian competition law is strongly linked to EC competition law, there should be no severe problems in this respect. On the other hand, the national regime has to be adjusted to provide for the possibility of adopting interim measures, as this is *expressis verbis* requested by Art 5 Reg 1. Moreover, in order to make decentralisation most effective it seems to be wise to grant the Authority the power to grant immunity of fines, a power the Commission already possesses and which helps to foster the flow of information in detecting forbidden cartels. Then I argued that it seems necessary to also install a legal exemption system at national level and to adjust the existing procedural rules to that extent.
The last batch of issues regarded decentralisation to Italian courts. In this respect, I outlined that Italian judges do not have vast experience in the application of EC competition law. Moreover, I looked at various means in order that national judges can obtain external advice in respect of economic matters. Several options were outlined. Ultimately, one should consider whether to institute specialised sections within ordinary courts (although not every ordinary court would require one) that shall deal exclusively with matters concerning national as well as Community competition law. Next, I analysed how co-operation with the Commission, national authorities and courts can best be achieved. Currently, no valid provision exists, which allows such enhanced co-operation, and the procedural rules have to be adjusted in this respect, for instance along the lines of the German § 90 GWB. Lastly, some observations were made regarding the exclusive competence of the court of appeal in respect of nullity proceedings, claims for damages and emergency measures. Such an exclusive competence, which runs counter to the principle of a two-step judiciary, cannot be applied to Community law. This has to follow the normal pattern. As the dividing line between national and Community competition law is rather vague, it has appropriately been proposed to abrogate Art 33 par 2 law 287 in this respect in order to allow a two-step judiciary system also in the context of Italian competition law. Moreover, in respect of the administrative courts, before which decisions of the Authority may be appealed, it is observed that due to the fact of a rather limited possibility of cause of action, many decisions of the Authority may be deprived of any judicial control. Hence, an amendment to law 287 should be taken into consideration to rectify this situation.

Taking into account the issues raised in respect of the modernised procedural rules, one can observe that the main concern in respect of the reform, which are constituted by a lack of consistency and uniformity in the application of EC law, can be rejected, whilst not perfect the new regime does offer quite effective instruments in guaranteeing consistent and uniform enforcement. Nevertheless, still-to-dos can be found, among others, in respect of effective case allocation, the territorially limited effect of Authorities' decisions and regarding harmonisation of national procedural rules. Questionable is the reform however from the point of view of undertakings, whose interest in gaining as much legal certainty as possible has not been considered to a satisfying extent. From an Italian perspective, one can say that the national institutions seem to be prepared to a satisfying extent. Adaptation to the new regime is nevertheless required.

Nevertheless, how ever good and efficient the reform may be, one shall not forget the Damocles-sword that is pending over the question of compatibility of the whole reform with the Treaty.

6 Appendix

6.1 Reg 17/62

Article 1 Basic provision
Without prejudice to Articles 6, 7 and 23 of this Regulation, agreements, decisions and concerted practices of the kind described in Article 85 (1) of the Treaty and the abuse of a dominant position in the market, within the meaning of Article 86 of the Treaty, shall be prohibited, no prior decision to that effect being required.

Article 2 Negative clearance
Upon application by the undertakings or associations of undertakings concerned, the Commission may certify that, on the basis of the facts in its possession, there are no grounds under Article 85 (1) or Article 86 of the Treaty for action on its part in respect of an agreement, decision or practice.

Article 3 Termination of infringements
1. Where the Commission, upon application or upon its own initiative, finds that there is infringement of Article 85 or Article 86 of the Treaty, it may by decision require the undertakings or associations of undertakings concerned to bring such infringement to an end.
2. Those entitled to make application are:
(a) Member States;
(b) natural or legal persons who claim a legitimate interest.
3. Without prejudice to the other provisions of this Regulation, the Commission may, before taking a decision under paragraph 1, address to the undertakings or associations of undertakings concerned recommendations for termination of the infringement.

Article 4 Notification of new agreements, decisions and practices
1. Agreements, decisions and concerted practices of the kind described in Article 85 (1) of the Treaty, which come into existence after the entry into force of this Regulation, and in respect of which the parties seek application of Article 85 (3) must be notified to the Commission. Until they have been notified, no decision in application of Article 85 (3) may be taken.
2. Paragraph 1 shall not apply to agreements, decisions and concerted practices where:
(1) the only parties thereto are undertakings from one Member State and the agreements, decisions or practices do not relate either to imports or to exports between Member States;
(2) (a) the agreements or concerted practices are entered into by two or more

undertakings, each operating, for the purposes of the agreement, at a different level of the production or distribution chain, and relate to the conditions under which the parties may purchase, sell or resell certain goods or services;

(b) not more than two undertakings are party thereto, and the agreements only impose restrictions on the exercise of the rights of the assignee or user of industrial property rights, in particular patents, utility models, designs or trade marks, or of the person entitled under a contract to the assignment, or grant, of the right to use a method of manufacture or knowledge relating to the use and to the application of industrial processes;

(3) they have as their sole object:

(a) the development or uniform application of standards or types; or

(b) joint research and development;

(c) specialisation in the manufacture of products, including agreements necessary for achieving this:

– where the products which are the subject of specialisation do not, in a substantial part of the common market, represent more than 15% of the volume of business done in identical products or those considered by consumers to be similar by reason of their characteristics, price and use, and

– where the total annual turnover of the participating undertakings does not exceed 200 million unit of account.

These agreements, decisions and practices may be notified to the Commission.

Article 5 Notification of existing agreements, decisions and practices

1. Agreements, decisions and concerted practices of the kind described in Article 85 (1) of the Treaty, which are in existence at the date of entry into force of this Regulation, and in respect of which the parties seek application of Article 85 (3) shall be notified to the Commission before 1 November 1962. However, notwithstanding the foregoing provisions, any agreements, decisions and concerted practices to which not more than two undertakings are party shall be notified before 1 February 1963.

2. Paragraph 1 shall not apply to agreements, decisions or concerted practices falling within Article 4 (2); these may be notified to the Commission.

Article 6 Decisions pursuant to Article 85 (3)

1. Whenever the Commission takes a decision pursuant to Article 85 (3) of the Treaty, it shall specify therein the date from which the decision shall take effect. Such a date shall not be earlier than the date of notification.

2. The second sentence of paragraph 1 shall not apply to agreements, decisions or concerted practices falling within Article 4 (2) and Article 5 (2),

nor to those falling within Article 5 (1), which have been notified within the time limit specified in Article 5 (1).

Article 7 Special provisions for existing agreements, decisions and practices
1. Where agreements, decisions and concerted practices in existence at the date of entry into force of this Regulation and notified within the time limits specified in Article 5 (1) do not satisfy the requirements of Article 85 (3) of the Treaty and the undertakings or associations of undertakings concerned cease to give effect to them or modify them in such a manner that they no longer fall within the prohibition contained in Article 85 (1) or that they satisfy the requirements of Article 85 (3), the prohibition contained in Article 85 (1) shall apply only for a period fixed by the Commission. A decision by the Commission pursuant to the foregoing sentence shall not apply as against undertakings and associations of undertakings, which did not expressly consent to the notification.
2. Paragraph 1 shall apply to agreements, decisions and concerted practices falling within Article 4 (2), which are in existence at the date of entry into force of this Regulation if they are notified before 1 January 1967.

Article 8 Duration and revocation of decisions under Article 85 (3)
1. A decision in application of Article 85 (3) of the Treaty shall be issued for a specified period and conditions and obligations may be attached thereto.
2. A decision may on application be renewed if the requirements of Article 85 (3) of the Treaty continue to be satisfied.
3. The Commission may revoke or amend its decision or prohibit specified acts by the parties:
(a) where there has been a change in any of the facts, which were basic to the making of the decision;
(b) where the parties commit a breach of any obligation attached to the decision;
(c) where the decision is based on incorrect information or was induced by deceit;
(d) where the parties abuse the exemption from the provisions of Article 85 (1) of the Treaty granted to them by the decision.
In cases to which subparagraphs (b), (c) or (d) apply, the decision may be revoked with retroactive effect.

Article 9 Powers
1. Subject to review of its decision by the Court of Justice, the Commission shall have sole power to declare Article 85 (1) inapplicable pursuant to Article 85 (3) of the Treaty.
2. The Commission shall have power to apply Article 85 (1) and Article 86 of

the Treaty; this power may be exercised notwithstanding that the time limits specified in Article 5 (1) and in Article 7 (2) relating to notification have not expired.
3. As long as the Commission has not initiated any procedure under Articles 2, 3 or 6, the authorities of the Member States shall remain competent to apply Article 85 (1) and Article 86 in accordance with Article 88 of the Treaty; they shall remain competent in this respect notwithstanding that the time limits specified in Article 5 (1) and in Article 7 (2) relating to notification have not expired.

Article 10
Liaison with the authorities of the Member States
1. The Commission shall forthwith transmit to the competent authorities of the Member States a copy of the applications and notifications together with copies of the most important documents lodged with the Commission for the purpose of establishing the existence of infringements of Articles 85 or 86 of the Treaty or of obtaining negative clearance or a decision in application of Article 85 (3).
2. The Commission shall carry out the procedure set out in paragraph 1 in close and constant liaison with the competent authorities of the Member States; such authorities shall have the right to express their views upon that procedure.
3. An Advisory Committee on Restrictive Practices and Monopolies shall be consulted prior to the taking of any decision following upon a procedure under paragraph 1, and of any decision concerning the renewal, amendment or revocation of a decision pursuant to Article 85 (3) of the Treaty.
4. The Advisory Committee shall be composed of officials competent in the matter of restrictive practices and monopolies. Each Member State shall appoint an official to represent it who, if prevented from attending, may be replaced by another official.
5. The consultation shall take place at a joint meeting convened by the Commission; such a meeting shall be held not earlier than fourteen days after dispatch of the notice convening it. The notice shall, in respect of each case to be examined, be accompanied by a summary of the case together with an indication of the most important documents, and a preliminary draft decision.
6. The Advisory Committee may deliver an opinion notwithstanding that some of its members or their alternates are not present. A report of the outcome of the consultative proceedings shall be annexed to the draft decision. It shall not be made public.

Article 11 Requests for information

1. In carrying out the duties assigned to it by Article 89 and by provisions adopted under Article 87 of the Treaty, the Commission may obtain all necessary information from the Governments and competent authorities of the Member States and from undertakings and associations of undertakings.

2. When sending a request for information to an undertaking or association of undertakings, the Commission shall at the same time forward a copy of the request to the competent authority of the Member State in whose territory the seat of the undertaking or association of undertakings is situated.

3. In its request the Commission shall state the legal basis and the purpose of the request and also the penalties provided for in Article 15 (1) (b) for supplying incorrect information.

4. The owners of the undertakings or their representatives and, in the case of legal persons, companies or firms, or of associations having no legal personality, the persons authorised to represent them by law or by their constitution shall supply the information requested.

5. Where an undertaking or association of undertakings does not supply the information requested within the time limit fixed by the Commission, or supplies incomplete information, the Commission shall by decision require the information to be supplied. The decision shall specify what information is required, fix an appropriate time limit within which it is to be supplied and indicate the penalties provided for in Article 15 (1) (b) and Article 16 (1) (c) and the right to have the decision reviewed by the Court of Justice.

6. The Commission shall at the same time forward a copy of its decision to the competent authority of the Member State in whose territory the seat of the undertaking or association of undertakings is situated.

Article 12 Inquiry into sectors of the economy

1. If in any sector of the economy the trend of trade between Member States, price movements, inflexibility of prices or other circumstances suggest that in the economic sector concerned competition is being restricted or distorted within the common market, the Commission may decide to conduct a general inquiry into that economic sector and in the course thereof may request undertakings in the sector concerned to supply the information necessary for giving effect to the principles formulated in Articles 85 and 86 of the Treaty and for carrying out the duties entrusted to the Commission.

2. The Commission may in particular request every undertaking or association of undertakings in the economic sector concerned to communicate to it all agreements, decisions and concerted practices which are exempt from notification by virtue of Article 4 (2) and Article 5 (2).

3. When making inquiries pursuant to paragraph 2, the Commission shall

also request undertakings or groups of undertakings whose size suggests that they occupy a dominant position within the common market or a substantial part thereof to supply to the Commission such particulars of the structure of the undertakings and of their behaviour as are requisite to an appraisal of their position in the light of Article 86 of the Treaty.
4. Article 10 (3) to (6) and Articles 11, 13 and 14 shall apply correspondingly.

Article 13 Investigations by the authorities of the Member States
1. At the request of the Commission, the competent authorities of the Member States shall undertake the investigations which the Commission considers to be necessary under Article 14 (1), or which it has ordered by decision pursuant to Article 14 (3). The officials of the competent authorities of the Member States responsible for conducting these investigations shall exercise their powers upon production of an authorisation in writing issued by the competent authority of the Member State in whose territory the investigation is to be made. Such authorisation shall specify the subject matter and purpose of the investigation.
2. If so requested by the Commission or by the competent authority of the Member State in whose territory the investigation is to be made, the officials of the Commission may assist the officials of such authorities in carrying out their duties.

Article 14 Investigating powers of the Commission
1. In carrying out the duties assigned to it by Article 89 and by provisions adopted under Article 87 of the Treaty, the Commission may undertake all necessary investigations into undertakings and associations of undertakings. To this end the officials authorised by the Commission are empowered:
(a) to examine the books and other business records;
(b) to take copies of or extracts from the books and business records;
(c) to ask for oral explanations on the spot;
(d) to enter any premises; land and means of transport of undertakings.
2. The officials of the Commission authorised for the purpose of these investigations shall exercise their powers upon production of an authorisation in writing specifying the subject matter and purpose of the investigation and the penalties provided for in Article 15 (1) (c) in cases where production of the required books or other business records is incomplete. In good time before the investigation, the Commission shall inform the competent authority of the Member State in whose territory the same is to be made of the investigation and of the identity of the authorised officials.
3. Undertakings and associations of undertakings shall submit to investigations ordered by decision of the Commission. The decision shall

specify the subject matter and purpose of the investigation, appoint the date on which it is to begin and indicate the penalties provided for in Article 15 (1) (c) and Article 16 (1) (d) and the right to have the decision reviewed by the Court of Justice.
4. The Commission shall take decisions referred to in paragraph 3 after consultation with the competent authority of the Member State in whose territory the investigation is to be made.
5. Officials of the competent authority of the Member State in whose territory the investigation is to be made may, at the request of such authority or of the Commission, assist the officials of the Commission in carrying out their duties.
6. Where an undertaking opposes an investigation ordered pursuant to this Article, the Member State concerned shall afford the necessary assistance to the officials authorised by the Commission to enable them to make their investigation. Member States shall, after consultation with the Commission, take the necessary measures to this end before 1 October 1962.

Article 15 Fines
1. The Commission may by decision impose on undertakings or associations of undertakings fines of 100 to 5000 units of account where, intentionally or negligently:
(a) they supply incorrect or misleading information in an application pursuant to Article 2 or in a notification pursuant to Articles 4 or 5; or
(b) they supply incorrect information in response to a request made pursuant to Article 11 (3) or (5) or to Article 12, or do not supply information within the time limit fixed by a decision taken under Article 11 (5); or
(c) they produce the required books or other business records in incomplete form during investigations under Article 13 or 14, or refuse to submit to an investigation ordered by decision issued in implementation of Article 14 (3).
2. The Commission may by decision impose on undertakings or associations of undertakings fines of 1,000 to 1,000,000 units of account, or a sum in excess thereof but not exceeding 10% of the turnover in the preceding business year of each of the undertakings participating in the infringement where, either intentionally or negligently:
(a) they infringe Article 85 (1) or Article 86 of the Treaty; or
(b) they commit a breach of any obligation imposed pursuant to Article 8 (1).
In fixing the amount of the fine, regard shall be had both to the gravity and to the duration of the infringement.
3. Article 10 (3) to (6) shall apply.
4. Decisions taken pursuant to paragraphs 1 and 2 shall not be of a criminal law nature.

5. The fines provided for in paragraph 2 (a) shall not be imposed in respect of acts taking place:
(a) after notification to the Commission and before its decision in application of Article 85 (3) of the Treaty, provided they fall within the limits of the activity described in the notification;
(b) before notification and in the course of agreements, decisions or concerted practices in existence at the date of entry into force of this Regulation, provided that notification was effected within the time limits specified in Article 5 (1) and Article 7 (2).
6. Paragraph 5 shall not have effect where the Commission has informed the undertakings concerned that after preliminary examination it is of opinion that Article 85 (1) of the Treaty applies and that application of Article 85 (3) is not justified.

Article 16 Periodic penalty payments
1. The Commission may by decision impose on undertakings or associations of undertakings periodic penalty payments of 50 to 1000 units of account per day, calculated from the date appointed by the decision, in order to compel them:
(a) to put an end to an infringement of Article 85 or 86 of the Treaty, in accordance with a decision taken pursuant to Article 3 of this Regulation;
(b) to refrain from any act prohibited under Article 8 (3);
(c) to supply complete and correct information which it has requested by decision taken pursuant to Article 11 (5);
(d) to submit to an investigation which it has ordered by decision taken pursuant to Article 14 (3).
2. Where the undertakings or associations of undertakings have satisfied the obligation which it was the purpose of the periodic penalty payment to enforce, the Commission may fix the total amount of the periodic penalty payment at a lower figure than that which would arise under the original decision.
3. Article 10 (3) to (6) shall apply.

Article 17 Review by the Court of Justice
The Court of Justice shall have unlimited jurisdiction within the meaning of Article 172 of the Treaty to review decisions whereby the Commission has fixed a fine or periodic penalty payment; it may cancel, reduce or increase the fine or periodic penalty payment imposed.

Article 18 Unit of account
For the purposes of applying Articles 15 to 17 the unit of account shall be

that adopted in drawing up the budget of the Community in accordance with Articles 207 and 209 of the Treaty.

Article 19 Hearing of the parties and of third persons

1. Before taking decisions as provided for in Articles 2, 3, 6, 7, 8, 15 and 16, the Commission shall give the undertakings or associations of undertakings concerned the opportunity of being heard on the matters to which the Commission has taken objection.

2. If the Commission or the competent authorities of the Member States consider it necessary, they may also hear other natural or legal persons. Applications to be heard on the part of such persons shall, where they show a sufficient interest, be granted.

3. Where the Commission intends to give negative clearance pursuant to Article 2 or take a decision in application of Article 85 (3) of the Treaty, it shall publish a summary of the relevant application or notification and invite all interested third parties to submit their observations within a time limit which it shall fix being not less than one month. Publication shall have regard to the legitimate interest of undertakings in the protection of their business secrets.

Article 20 Professional secrecy

1. Information acquired as a result of the application of Articles 11, 12, 13 and 14 shall be used only for the purpose of the relevant request or investigation.

2. Without prejudice to the provisions of Articles 19 and 21, the Commission and the competent authorities of the Member States, their officials and other servants shall not disclose information acquired by them as a result of the application of this Regulation and of the kind covered by the obligation of professional secrecy.

3. The provisions of paragraphs 1 and 2 shall not prevent publication of general information or surveys which do not contain information relating to particular undertakings or associations of undertakings.

Article 21 Publication of decisions

1. The Commission shall publish the decisions, which it takes pursuant to Articles 2, 3, 6, 7 and 8.

2. The publication shall state the names of the parties and the main content of the decision; it shall have regard to the legitimate interest of undertakings in the protection of their business secrets.

Article 22 Special provisions

1. The Commission shall submit to the Council proposals for making certain

categories of agreement, decision and concerted practice falling within Article 4 (2) or Article 5 (2) compulsorily notifiable under Article 4 or 5.
2. Within one year from the date of entry into force of this Regulation, the Council shall examine, on a proposal from the Commission, what special provisions might be made for exempting from the provisions of this Regulation agreements, decisions and concerted practices falling within Article 4 (2) or Article 5 (2).

Article 23 Transitional provisions applicable to decisions of authorities of the Member States
1. Agreements, decisions and concerted practices of the kind described in Article 85 (1) of the Treaty to which, before the entry into force of this Regulation, the competent authority of a Member State has declared Article 85 (1) to be inapplicable pursuant to Article 85 (3) shall not be subject to compulsory notification under Article 5. The decision of the competent authority of the Member State shall be deemed to be a decision within the meaning of Article 6; it shall cease to be valid upon expiration of the period fixed by such authority but in any event not more than three years after the entry into force of this Regulation. Article 8 (3) shall apply.
2. Applications for renewal of decisions of the kind described in paragraph 1 shall be decided upon by the Commission in accordance with Article 8 (2).

Article 24 Implementing provisions
The Commission shall have power to adopt implementing provisions concerning the form, content and other details of applications pursuant to Articles 2 and 3 and of notifications pursuant to Articles 4 and 5, and concerning hearings pursuant to Article 19 (1) and (2).

Article 25
1. As regards agreements, decisions and concerted practices to which Article 85 of the Treaty applies by virtue of accession, the date of accession shall be substituted for the date of entry into force of this Regulation in every place where reference is made in this Regulation to this latter date.
2. Agreements, decisions and concerted practices existing at the date of accession to which Article 85 of the Treaty applies by virtue of accession shall be notified pursuant to Article 5 (1) or Article 7 (1) and (2) within six months from the date of accession.
3. Fines under Article 15 (2) (a) shall not be imposed in respect of any act prior to notification of the agreements, decisions and practices to which paragraph 2 applies and which have been notified within the period therein specified.
4. New Member States shall take the measures referred to in Article 14 (6)

within six months from the date of accession after consulting the Commission.
5. The provisions of paragraphs 1 to 4 above still apply in the same way in the case of the accession of the Hellenic Republic, the Kingdom of Spain and of the Portuguese Republic.
6. The provisions of paragraphs 1 to 4 still apply in the same way in the case of the accession of Austria, Finland and Sweden. However, they do not apply to agreements, decisions and concerted practises, which at the date of accession already fall under Article 53 of the EEA Agreement. This Regulation shall be binding in its entirety and directly applicable in all Member States.

6.2 Reg 1/2003

CHAPTER I PRINCIPLES

Article 1 Application of Articles 81 and 82 of the Treaty
1. Agreements, decisions and concerted practices caught by Article 81(1) of the Treaty, which do not satisfy the conditions of Article 81(3) of the Treaty, shall be prohibited, no prior decision to that effect being required.
2. Agreements, decisions and concerted practices caught by Article 81(1) of the Treaty, which satisfy the conditions of Article 81(3) of the Treaty, shall not be prohibited, no prior decision to that effect being required.
3. The abuse of a dominant position referred to in Article 82 of the Treaty shall be prohibited, no prior decision to that effect being required.

Article 2 Burden of proof
In any national or Community proceedings for the application of Articles 81 and 82 of the Treaty, the burden of proving an infringement of Article 81(1) or of Article 82 of the Treaty shall rest on the party or the authority alleging the infringement. The undertaking or association of undertakings claiming the benefit of Article 81(3) of the Treaty shall bear the burden of proving that the conditions of that paragraph are fulfilled.

Article 3 Relationship between Articles 81 and 82 of the Treaty and national competition laws
1. Where the competition authorities of the Member States or national courts apply national competition law to agreements, decisions by associations of undertakings or concerted practices within the meaning of Article 81(1) of the Treaty which may affect trade between Member States within the meaning of that provision, they shall also apply Article 81 of the Treaty to such agreements, decisions or concerted practices. Where the competition

authorities of the Member States or national courts apply national competition law to any abuse prohibited by Article 82 of the Treaty, they shall also apply Article 82 of the Treaty.
2. The application of national competition law may not lead to the prohibition of agreements, decisions by associations of undertakings or concerted practices which may affect trade between Member States but which do not restrict competition within the meaning of Article 81(1) of the Treaty, or which fulfil the conditions of Article 81(3) of the Treaty or which are covered by a Regulation for the application of Article 81(3) of the Treaty. Member States shall not under this Regulation be precluded from adopting and applying on their territory stricter national laws, which prohibit or sanction unilateral conduct engaged in by undertakings.
3. Without prejudice to general principles and other provisions of Community law, paragraphs 1 and 2 do not apply when the competition authorities and the courts of the Member States apply national merger control laws nor do they preclude the application of provisions of national law that predominantly pursue an objective different from that pursued by Articles 81 and 82 of the Treaty.

CHAPTER II POWERS

Article 4 Powers of the Commission
For the purpose of applying Articles 81 and 82 of the Treaty, the Commission shall have the powers provided for by this Regulation.

Article 5 Powers of the competition authorities of the Member States
The competition authorities of the Member States shall have the power to apply Articles 81 and 82 of the Treaty in individual cases. For this purpose, acting on their own initiative or on a complaint, they may take the following decisions:
— requiring that an infringement be brought to an end,
— ordering interim measures,
— accepting commitments,
— imposing fines, periodic penalty payments or any other penalty provided for in their national law.
Where on the basis of the information in their possession the conditions for prohibition are not met they may likewise decide that there are no grounds for action on their part.

Article 6 Powers of the national courts
National courts shall have the power to apply Articles 81 and 82 of the Treaty.

CHAPTER III COMMISSION DECISIONS

Article 7 Finding and termination of infringement
1. Where the Commission, acting on a complaint or on its own initiative, finds that there is an infringement of Article 81 or of Article 82 of the Treaty, it may by decision require the undertakings and associations of undertakings concerned to bring such infringement to an end. For this purpose, it may impose on them any behavioural or structural remedies, which are proportionate to the infringement committed and necessary to bring the infringement effectively to an end. Structural remedies can only be imposed either where there is no equally effective behavioural remedy or where any equally effective behavioural remedy would be more burdensome for the undertaking concerned than the structural remedy. If the Commission has a legitimate interest in doing so, it may also find that an infringement has been committed in the past.
2. Those entitled to lodge a complaint for the purposes of paragraph 1 are natural or legal persons who can show a legitimate interest and Member States.

Article 8 Interim measures
1. In cases of urgency due to the risk of serious and irreparable damage to competition, the Commission, acting on its own initiative may by decision, on the basis of a *prima facie* finding of infringement, order interim measures.
2. A decision under paragraph 1 shall apply for a specified period of time and may be renewed in so far this is necessary and appropriate.

Article 9 Commitments
1. Where the Commission intends to adopt a decision requiring that an infringement be brought to an end and the undertakings concerned offer commitments to meet the concerns expressed to them by the Commission in its preliminary assessment, the Commission may by decision make those commitments binding on the undertakings. Such a decision may be adopted for a specified period and shall conclude that there are no longer grounds for action by the Commission.
2. The Commission may, upon request or on its own initiative, reopen the proceedings:
(a) where there has been a material change in any of the facts on which the decision was based;
(b) where the undertakings concerned act contrary to their commitments; or
(c) where the decision was based on incomplete, incorrect or misleading information provided by the parties.

Article 10 Finding of inapplicability

Where the Community public interest relating to the application of Articles 81 and 82 of the Treaty so requires, the Commission, acting on its own initiative, may by decision find that Article 81 of the Treaty is not applicable to an agreement, a decision by an association of undertakings or a concerted practice, either because the conditions of Article 81(1) of the Treaty are not fulfilled, or because the conditions of Article 81(3) of the Treaty are satisfied. The Commission may likewise make such a finding with reference to Article 82 of the Treaty.

CHAPTER IV COOPERATION

Article 11 Cooperation between the Commission and the competition authorities of the Member States

1. The Commission and the competition authorities of the Member States shall apply the Community competition rules in close cooperation.

2. The Commission shall transmit to the competition authorities of the Member States copies of the most important documents it has collected with a view to applying Articles 7, 8, 9, 10 and Article 29(1). At the request of the competition authority of a Member State, the Commission shall provide it with a copy of other existing documents necessary for the assessment of the case.

3. The competition authorities of the Member States shall, when acting under Article 81 or Article 82 of the Treaty, inform the Commission in writing before or without delay after commencing the first formal investigative measure. This information may also be made available to the competition authorities of the other Member States.

4. No later than 30 days before the adoption of a decision requiring that an infringement be brought to an end, accepting commitments or withdrawing the benefit of a block exemption Regulation, the competition authorities of the Member States shall inform the Commission. To that effect, they shall provide the Commission with a summary of the case, the envisaged decision or, in the absence thereof, any other document indicating the proposed course of action. This information may also be made available to the competition authorities of the other Member States. At the request of the Commission, the acting competition authority shall make available to the Commission other documents it holds which are necessary for the assessment of the case. The information supplied to the Commission may be made available to the competition authorities of the other Member States. National competition authorities may also exchange between themselves information necessary for the assessment of a case that they are dealing with under Article 81 or Article 82 of the Treaty.

5. The competition authorities of the Member States may consult the Commission on any case involving the application of Community law.
6. The initiation by the Commission of proceedings for the adoption of a decision under Chapter III shall relieve the competition authorities of the Member States of their competence to apply Articles 81 and 82 of the Treaty. If a competition authority of a Member State is already acting on a case, the Commission shall only initiate proceedings after consulting with that national competition authority.

Article 12 Exchange of information
1. For the purpose of applying Articles 81 and 82 of the Treaty the Commission and the competition authorities of the Member States shall have the power to provide one another with and use in evidence any matter of fact or of law, including confidential information.
2. Information exchanged shall only be used in evidence for the purpose of applying Article 81 or Article 82 of the Treaty and in respect of the subject-matter for which it was collected by the transmitting authority. However, where national competition law is applied in the same case and in parallel to Community competition law and does not lead to a different outcome, information exchanged under this Article may also be used for the application of national competition law.
3. Information exchanged pursuant to paragraph 1 can only be used in evidence to impose sanctions on natural persons where:
– the law of the transmitting authority foresees sanctions of a similar kind in relation to an infringement of Article 81 or Article 82 of the Treaty or, in the absence thereof,
– the information has been collected in a way which respects the same level of protection of the rights of defence of natural persons as provided for under the national rules of the receiving authority. However, in this case, the information exchanged cannot be used by the receiving authority to impose custodial sanctions.

Article 13 Suspension or termination of proceedings
1. Where competition authorities of two or more Member States have received a complaint or are acting on their own initiative under Article 81 or Article 82 of the Treaty against the same agreement, decision of an association or practice, the fact that one authority is dealing with the case shall be sufficient grounds for the others to suspend the proceedings before them or to reject the complaint. The Commission may likewise reject a complaint on the ground that a competition authority of a Member State is dealing with the case.
2. Where a competition authority of a Member State or the Commission has

received a complaint against an agreement, decision of an association or practice, which has already been dealt with by another competition authority, it may reject it.

Article 14 Advisory Committee

1. The Commission shall consult an Advisory Committee on Restrictive Practices and Dominant Positions prior to the taking of any decision under Articles 7, 8, 9, 10, 23, Article 24(2) and Article 29(1).

2. For the discussion of individual cases, the Advisory Committee shall be composed of representatives of the competition authorities of the Member States. For meetings in which issues other than individual cases are being discussed, an additional Member State representative competent in competition matters may be appointed. Representatives may, if unable to attend, be replaced by other representatives.

3. The consultation may take place at a meeting convened and chaired by the Commission, held not earlier than 14 days after dispatch of the notice convening it, together with a summary of the case, an indication of the most important documents and a preliminary draft decision. In respect of decisions pursuant to Article 8, the meeting may be held seven days after the dispatch of the operative part of a draft decision. Where the Commission dispatches a notice convening the meeting, which gives a shorter period of notice than those specified above, the meeting may take place on the proposed date in the absence of an objection by any Member State. The Advisory Committee shall deliver a written opinion on the Commission's preliminary draft decision. It may deliver an opinion even if some members are absent and are not represented. At the request of one or several members, the positions stated in the opinion shall be reasoned.

4. Consultation may also take place by written procedure. However, if any Member State so requests, the Commission shall convene a meeting. In case of written procedure, the Commission shall determine a time-limit of not less than 14 days within which the Member States are to put forward their observations for circulation to all other Member States. In case of decisions to be taken pursuant to Article 8, the time limit of 14 days is replaced by seven days. Where the Commission determines a time-limit for the written procedure, which is shorter than those specified above, the proposed time-limit shall be applicable in the absence of an objection by any Member State.

5. The Commission shall take the utmost account of the opinion delivered by the Advisory Committee. It shall inform the Committee of the manner in which its opinion has been taken into account.

6. Where the Advisory Committee delivers a written opinion, this opinion shall be appended to the draft decision. If the Advisory Committee recommends publication of the opinion, the Commission shall carry out such publication

taking into account the legitimate interest of undertakings in the protection of their business secrets.
7. At the request of a competition authority of a Member State, the Commission shall include on the agenda of the Advisory Committee cases that are being dealt with by a competition authority of a Member State under Article 81 or Article 82 of the Treaty. The Commission may also do so on its own initiative. In either case, the Commission shall inform the competition authority concerned. A request may in particular be made by a competition authority of a Member State in respect of a case where the Commission intends to initiate proceedings with the effect of Article 11(6). The Advisory Committee shall not issue opinions on cases dealt with by competition authorities of the Member States. The Advisory Committee may also discuss general issues of Community competition law.

Article 15 Cooperation with national courts
1. In proceedings for the application of Article 81 or Article 82 of the Treaty, courts of the Member States may ask the Commission to transmit to them information in its possession or its opinion on questions concerning the application of the Community competition rules.
2. Member States shall forward to the Commission a copy of any written judgment of national courts deciding on the application of Article 81 or Article 82 of the Treaty. Such copy shall be forwarded without delay after the full written judgment is notified to the parties.
3. Competition authorities of the Member States, acting on their own initiative, may submit written observations to the national courts of their Member State on issues relating to the application of Article 81 or Article 82 of the Treaty. With the permission of the court in question, they may also submit oral observations to the national courts of their Member State. Where the coherent application of Article 81 or Article 82 of the Treaty so requires, the Commission, acting on its own initiative, may submit written observations to courts of the Member States. With the permission of the court in question, it may also make oral observations. For the purpose of the preparation of their observations only, the competition authorities of the Member States and the Commission may request the relevant court of the Member State to transmit or ensure the transmission to them of any documents necessary for the assessment of the case.
4. This Article is without prejudice to wider powers to make observations before courts conferred on competition authorities of the Member States under the law of their Member State.

Article 16 Uniform application of Community competition law
1. When national courts rule on agreements, decisions or practices under

Article 81 or Article 82 of the Treaty which are already the subject of a Commission decision, they cannot take decisions running counter to the decision adopted by the Commission. They must also avoid giving decisions, which would conflict with a decision contemplated by the Commission in proceedings it has initiated. To that effect, the national court may assess whether it is necessary to stay its proceedings. This obligation is without prejudice to the rights and obligations under Article 234 of the Treaty.
2. When competition authorities of the Member States rule on agreements, decisions or practices under Article 81 or Article 82 of the Treaty which are already the subject of a Commission decision, they cannot take decisions which would run counter to the decision adopted by the Commission.

CHAPTER V POWERS OF INVESTIGATION

Article 17 Investigations into sectors of the economy and into types of agreements
1. Where the trend of trade between Member States, the rigidity of prices or other circumstances suggest that competition may be restricted or distorted within the common market, the Commission may conduct its inquiry into a particular sector of the economy or into a particular type of agreements across various sectors. In the course of that inquiry, the Commission may request the undertakings or associations of undertakings concerned to supply the information necessary for giving effect to Articles 81 and 82 of the Treaty and may carry out any inspections necessary for that purpose. The Commission may in particular request the undertakings or associations of undertakings concerned to communicate to it all agreements, decisions and concerted practices. The Commission may publish a report on the results of its inquiry into particular sectors of the economy or particular types of agreements across various sectors and invite comments from interested parties.
2. Articles 14, 18, 19, 20, 22, 23 and 24 shall apply *mutatis mutandis*.

Article 18 Requests for information
1. In order to carry out the duties assigned to it by this Regulation, the Commission may, by simple request or by decision, require undertakings and associations of undertakings to provide all necessary information.
2. When sending a simple request for information to an undertaking or association of undertakings, the Commission shall state the legal basis and the purpose of the request, specify what information is required and fix the time-limit within which the information is to be provided, and the penalties provided for in Article 23 for supplying incorrect or misleading information.
3. Where the Commission requires undertakings and associations of

undertakings to supply information by decision, it shall state the legal basis and the purpose of the request, specify what information is required and fix the time-limit within which it is to be provided. It shall also indicate the penalties provided for in Article 23 and indicate or impose the penalties provided for in Article 24. It shall further indicate the right to have the decision reviewed by the Court of Justice.

4. The owners of the undertakings or their representatives and, in the case of legal persons, companies or firms, or associations having no legal personality, the persons authorised to represent them by law or by their constitution shall supply the information requested on behalf of the undertaking or the association of undertakings concerned. Lawyers duly authorised to act may supply the information on behalf of their clients. The latter shall remain fully responsible if the information supplied is incomplete, incorrect or misleading.

5. The Commission shall without delay forward a copy of the simple request or of the decision to the competition authority of the Member State in whose territory the seat of the undertaking or association of undertakings is situated and the competition authority of the Member State whose territory is affected.

6. At the request of the Commission the governments and competition authorities of the Member States shall provide the Commission with all necessary information to carry out the duties assigned to it by this Regulation.

Article 19 Power to take statements

1. In order to carry out the duties assigned to it by this Regulation, the Commission may interview any natural or legal person who consents to be interviewed for the purpose of collecting information relating to the subject-matter of an investigation.

2. Where an interview pursuant to paragraph 1 is conducted in the premises of an undertaking, the Commission shall inform the competition authority of the Member State in whose territory the interview takes place. If so requested by the competition authority of that Member State, its officials may assist the officials and other accompanying persons authorised by the Commission to conduct the interview.

Article 20 The Commission's powers of inspection

1. In order to carry out the duties assigned to it by this Regulation, the Commission may conduct all necessary inspections of undertakings and associations of undertakings.

2. The officials and other accompanying persons authorised by the Commission to conduct an inspection are empowered:

(a) to enter any premises, land and means of transport of undertakings and associations of undertakings;
(b) to examine the books and other records related to the business, irrespective of the medium on which they are stored;
(c) to take or obtain in any form copies of or extracts from such books or records;
(d) to seal any business premises and books or records for the period and to the extent necessary for the inspection;
(e) to ask any representative or member of staff of the undertaking or association of undertakings for explanations on facts or documents relating to the subject-matter and purpose of the inspection and to record the answers.
3. The officials and other accompanying persons authorised by the Commission to conduct an inspection shall exercise their powers upon production of a written authorisation specifying the subject matter and purpose of the inspection and the penalties provided for in Article 23 in case the production of the required books or other records related to the business is incomplete or where the answers to questions asked under paragraph 2 of the present Article are incorrect or misleading. In good time before the inspection, the Commission shall give notice of the inspection to the competition authority of the Member State in whose territory it is to be conducted.
4. Undertakings and associations of undertakings are required to submit to inspections ordered by decision of the Commission. The decision shall specify the subject matter and purpose of the inspection, appoint the date on which it is to begin and indicate the penalties provided for in Articles 23 and 24 and the right to have the decision reviewed by the Court of Justice. The Commission shall take such decisions after consulting the competition authority of the Member State in whose territory the inspection is to be conducted.
5. Officials of as well as those authorised or appointed by the competition authority of the Member State in whose territory the inspection is to be conducted shall, at the request of that authority or of the Commission, actively assist the officials and other accompanying persons authorised by the Commission. To this end, they shall enjoy the powers specified in paragraph 2.
6. Where the officials and other accompanying persons authorised by the Commission find that an undertaking opposes an inspection ordered pursuant to this Article, the Member State concerned shall afford them the necessary assistance, requesting where appropriate the assistance of the police or of an equivalent enforcement authority, so as to enable them to conduct their inspection.

7. If the assistance provided for in paragraph 6 requires authorisation from a judicial authority according to national rules, such authorisation shall be applied for. Such authorisation may also be applied for as a precautionary measure.
8. Where authorisation as referred to in paragraph 7 is applied for, the national judicial authority shall control that the Commission decision is authentic and that the coercive measures envisaged are neither arbitrary nor excessive having regard to the subject matter of the inspection. In its control of the proportionality of the coercive measures, the national judicial authority may ask the Commission, directly or through the Member State competition authority, for detailed explanations in particular on the grounds the Commission has for suspecting infringement of Articles 81 and 82 of the Treaty, as well as on the seriousness of the suspected infringement and on the nature of the involvement of the undertaking concerned. However, the national judicial authority may not call into question the necessity for the inspection nor demand that it be provided with the information in the Commission's file. The lawfulness of the Commission decision shall be subject to review only by the Court of Justice.

Article 21 Inspection of other premises
1. If a reasonable suspicion exists that books or other records related to the business and to the subject matter of the inspection, which may be relevant to prove a serious violation of Article 81 or Article 82 of the Treaty, are being kept in any other premises, land and means of transport, including the homes of directors, managers and other members of staff of the undertakings and associations of undertakings concerned, the Commission can by decision order an inspection to be conducted in such other premises, land and means of transport.
2. The decision shall specify the subject matter and purpose of the inspection, appoint the date on which it is to begin and indicate the right to have the decision reviewed by the Court of Justice. It shall in particular state the reasons that have led the Commission to conclude that a suspicion in the sense of paragraph 1 exists. The Commission shall take such decisions after consulting the competition authority of the Member State in whose territory the inspection is to be conducted.
3. A decision adopted pursuant to paragraph 1 cannot be executed without prior authorisation from the national judicial authority of the Member State concerned. The national judicial authority shall control that the Commission decision is authentic and that the coercive measures envisaged are neither arbitrary nor excessive having regard in particular to the seriousness of the suspected infringement, to the importance of the evidence sought, to the involvement of the undertaking concerned and to the reasonable likelihood

that business books and records relating to the subject matter of the inspection are kept in the premises for which the authorisation is requested. The national judicial authority may ask the Commission, directly or through the Member State competition authority, for detailed explanations on those elements, which are necessary to allow its control of the proportionality of the coercive measures envisaged. However, the national judicial authority may not call into question the necessity for the inspection nor demand that it be provided with information in the Commission's file. The lawfulness of the Commission decision shall be subject to review only by the Court of Justice.
4. The officials and other accompanying persons authorised by the Commission to conduct an inspection ordered in accordance with paragraph 1 of this Article shall have the powers set out in Article 20(2)(a), (b) and (c). Article 20(5) and (6) shall apply *mutatis mutandis*.

Article 22 Investigations by competition authorities of Member States
1. The competition authority of a Member State may in its own territory carry out any inspection or other fact-finding measure under its national law on behalf and for the account of the competition authority of another Member State in order to establish whether there has been an infringement of Article 81 or Article 82 of the Treaty. Any exchange and use of the information collected shall be carried out in accordance with Article 12.
2. At the request of the Commission, the competition authorities of the Member States shall undertake the inspections which the Commission considers to be necessary under Article 20(1) or which it has ordered by decision pursuant to Article 20(4). The officials of the competition authorities of the Member States who are responsible for conducting these inspections as well as those authorised or appointed by them shall exercise their powers in accordance with their national law. If so requested by the Commission or by the competition authority of the Member State in whose territory the inspection is to be conducted, officials and other accompanying persons authorised by the Commission may assist the officials of the authority concerned.

CHAPTER VI PENALTIES

Article 23 Fines
1. The Commission may by decision impose on undertakings and associations of undertakings fines not exceeding 1 % of the total turnover in the preceding business year where, intentionally or negligently:
(a) they supply incorrect or misleading information in response to a request made pursuant to Article 17 or Article 18(2);
(b) in response to a request made by decision adopted pursuant to Article 17

or Article 18(3), they supply incorrect, incomplete or misleading information or do not supply information within the required time-limit;
(c) they produce the required books or other records related to the business in incomplete form during inspections under Article 20 or refuse to submit to inspections ordered by a decision adopted pursuant to Article 20(4);
(d) in response to a question asked in accordance with Article 20(2)(e),
– they give an incorrect or misleading answer,
– they fail to rectify within a time-limit set by the Commission an incorrect, incomplete or misleading answer given by a member of staff, or
– they fail or refuse to provide a complete answer on facts relating to the subject-matter and purpose of an inspection ordered by a decision adopted pursuant to Article 20(4);
(e) seals affixed in accordance with Article 20(2)(d) by officials or other accompanying persons authorised by the Commission have been broken.
2. The Commission may by decision impose fines on undertakings and associations of undertakings where, either intentionally or negligently:
(a) they infringe Article 81 or Article 82 of the Treaty; or
(b) they contravene a decision ordering interim measures under Article 8; or
(c) they fail to comply with a commitment made binding by a decision pursuant to Article 9.
For each undertaking and association of undertakings participating in the infringement, the fine shall not exceed 10 % of its total turnover in the preceding business year. Where the infringement of an association relates to the activities of its members, the fine shall not exceed 10 % of the sum of the total turnover of each member active on the market affected by the infringement of the association.
3. In fixing the amount of the fine, regard shall be had both to the gravity and to the duration of the infringement.
4. When a fine is imposed on an association of undertakings taking account of the turnover of its members and the association is not solvent, the association is obliged to call for contributions from its members to cover the amount of the fine. Where such contributions have not been made to the association within a time-limit fixed by the Commission, the Commission may require payment of the fine directly by any of the undertakings whose representatives were members of the decision-making bodies concerned of the association. After the Commission has required payment under the second subparagraph, where necessary to ensure full payment of the fine, the Commission may require payment of the balance by any of the members of the association which were active on the market on which the infringement occurred. However, the Commission shall not require payment under the second or the third subparagraph from undertakings which show that they have not implemented the infringing decision of the association

and either were not aware of its existence or have actively distanced themselves from it before the Commission started investigating the case. The financial liability of each undertaking in respect of the payment of the fine shall not exceed 10 % of its total turnover in the preceding business year.
5. Decisions taken pursuant to paragraphs 1 and 2 shall not be of a criminal law nature.

Article 24 Periodic penalty payments

1. The Commission may, by decision, impose on undertakings or associations of undertakings periodic penalty payments not exceeding 5 % of the average daily turnover in the preceding business year per day and calculated from the date appointed by the decision, in order to compel them:
(a) to put an end to an infringement of Article 81 or Article 82 of the Treaty, in accordance with a decision taken pursuant to Article 7;
(b) to comply with a decision ordering interim measures taken pursuant to Article 8;
(c) to comply with a commitment made binding by a decision pursuant to Article 9;
(d) to supply complete and correct information which it has requested by decision taken pursuant to Article 17 or Article 18(3);
(e) to submit to an inspection which it has ordered by decision taken pursuant to Article 20(4).
2. Where the undertakings or associations of undertakings have satisfied the obligation, which the periodic penalty payment was intended to enforce, the Commission may fix the definitive amount of the periodic penalty payment at a figure lower than that which would arise under the original decision. Article 23(4) shall apply correspondingly.

CHAPTER VII LIMITATION PERIODS

Article 25 Limitation periods for the imposition of penalties

1. The powers conferred on the Commission by Articles 23 and 24 shall be subject to the following limitation periods:
(a) three years in the case of infringements of provisions concerning requests for information or the conduct of inspections;
(b) five years in the case of all other infringements.
2. Time shall begin to run on the day on which the infringement is committed. However, in the case of continuing or repeated infringements, time shall begin to run on the day on which the infringement ceases.
3. Any action taken by the Commission or by the competition authority of a Member State for the purpose of the investigation or proceedings in respect of an infringement shall interrupt the limitation period for the imposition of

fines or periodic penalty payments. The limitation period shall be interrupted with effect from the date on which the action is notified to at least one undertaking or association of undertakings, which has participated in the infringement. Actions, which interrupt the running of the period, shall include in particular the following:
(a) written requests for information by the Commission or by the competition authority of a Member State;
(b) written authorisations to conduct inspections issued to its officials by the Commission or by the competition authority of a Member State;
(c) the initiation of proceedings by the Commission or by the competition authority of a Member State;
(d) notification of the statement of objections of the Commission or of the competition authority of a Member State.
4. The interruption of the limitation period shall apply for all the undertakings or associations of undertakings, which have participated in the infringement.
5. Each interruption shall start time running afresh. However, the limitation period shall expire at the latest on the day on which a period equal to twice the limitation period has elapsed without the Commission having imposed a fine or a periodic penalty payment. That period shall be extended by the time during which limitation is suspended pursuant to paragraph 6.
6. The limitation period for the imposition of fines or periodic penalty payments shall be suspended for as long as the decision of the Commission is the subject of proceedings pending before the Court of Justice.

Article 26 Limitation period for the enforcement of penalties
1. The power of the Commission to enforce decisions taken pursuant to Articles 23 and 24 shall be subject to a limitation period of five years.
2. Time shall begin to run on the day on which the decision becomes final.
3. The limitation period for the enforcement of penalties shall be interrupted:
(a) by notification of a decision varying the original amount of the fine or periodic penalty payment or refusing an application for variation;
(b) by any action of the Commission or of a Member State, acting at the request of the Commission, designed to enforce payment of the fine or periodic penalty payment.
4. Each interruption shall start time running afresh.
5. The limitation period for the enforcement of penalties shall be suspended for so long as:
(a) time to pay is allowed;
(b) enforcement of payment is suspended pursuant to a decision of the Court of Justice.

CHAPTER VIII HEARINGS AND PROFESSIONAL SECRECY

Article 27 Hearing of the parties, complainants and others

1. Before taking decisions as provided for in Articles 7, 8, 23 and Article 24(2), the Commission shall give the undertakings or associations of undertakings which are the subject of the proceedings conducted by the Commission the opportunity of being heard on the matters to which the Commission has taken objection. The Commission shall base its decisions only on objections on which the parties concerned have been able to comment. Complainants shall be associated closely with the proceedings.

2. The rights of defence of the parties concerned shall be fully respected in the proceedings. They shall be entitled to have access to the Commission's file, subject to the legitimate interest of undertakings in the protection of their business secrets. The right of access to the file shall not extend to confidential information and internal documents of the Commission or the competition authorities of the Member States. In particular, the right of access shall not extend to correspondence between the Commission and the competition authorities of the Member States, or between the latter, including documents drawn up pursuant to Articles 11 and 14. Nothing in this paragraph shall prevent the Commission from disclosing and using information necessary to prove an infringement.

3. If the Commission considers it necessary, it may also hear other natural or legal persons. Applications to be heard on the part of such persons shall, where they show a sufficient interest, be granted. The competition authorities of the Member States may also ask the Commission to hear other natural or legal persons.

4. Where the Commission intends to adopt a decision pursuant to Article 9 or Article 10, it shall publish a concise summary of the case and the main content of the commitments or of the proposed course of action. Interested third parties may submit their observations within a time limit which is fixed by the Commission in its publication and which may not be less than one month. Publication shall have regard to the legitimate interest of undertakings in the protection of their business secrets.

Article 28 Professional secrecy

1. Without prejudice to Articles 12 and 15, information collected pursuant to Articles 17 to 22 shall be used only for the purpose for which it was acquired.

2. Without prejudice to the exchange and to the use of information foreseen in Articles 11, 12, 14, 15 and 27, the Commission and the competition authorities of the Member States, their officials, servants and other persons working under the supervision of these authorities as well as officials and civil servants of other authorities of the Member States shall not disclose

information acquired or exchanged by them pursuant to this Regulation and of the kind covered by the obligation of professional secrecy. This obligation also applies to all representatives and experts of Member States attending meetings of the Advisory Committee pursuant to Article 14.

CHAPTER IX EXEMPTION REGULATIONS

Article 29 Withdrawal in individual cases

1. Where the Commission, empowered by a Council Regulation, such as Regulations 19/65/EEC, (EEC) No 2821/71, (EEC) No 3976/87, (EEC) No 1534/91 or (EEC) No 479/92, to apply Article 81(3) of the Treaty by regulation, has declared Article 81(1) of the Treaty inapplicable to certain categories of agreements, decisions by associations of undertakings or concerted practices, it may, acting on its own initiative or on a complaint, withdraw the benefit of such an exemption Regulation when it finds that in any particular case an agreement, decision or concerted practice to which the exemption Regulation applies has certain effects which are incompatible with Article 81(3) of the Treaty.

2. Where, in any particular case, agreements, decisions by associations of undertakings or concerted practices to which a Commission Regulation referred to in paragraph 1 applies have effects which are incompatible with Article 81(3) of the Treaty in the territory of a Member State, or in a part thereof, which has all the characteristics of a distinct geographic market, the competition authority of that Member State may withdraw the benefit of the Regulation in question in respect of that territory.

CHAPTER X GENERAL PROVISIONS

Article 30 Publication of decisions

1. The Commission shall publish the decisions, which it takes pursuant to Articles 7 to 10, 23 and 24.

2. The publication shall state the names of the parties and the main content of the decision, including any penalties imposed. It shall have regard to the legitimate interest of undertakings in the protection of their business secrets.

Article 31 Review by the Court of Justice

The Court of Justice shall have unlimited jurisdiction to review decisions whereby the Commission has fixed a fine or periodic penalty payment. It may cancel, reduce or increase the fine or periodic penalty payment imposed.

Article 32 Exclusions

This Regulation shall not apply to:

(a) international tramp vessel services as defined in Article 1(3)(a) of Regulation (EEC) No 4056/86;
(b) a maritime transport service that takes place exclusively between ports in one and the same Member State as foreseen in Article 1(2) of Regulation (EEC) No 4056/86;
(c) air transport between Community airports and third countries.

Article 33 Implementing provisions
1. The Commission shall be authorised to take such measures as may be appropriate in order to apply this Regulation. The measures may concern, *inter alia*:
(a) the form, content and other details of complaints lodged pursuant to Article 7 and the procedure for rejecting complaints;
(b) the practical arrangements for the exchange of information and consultations provided for in Article 11;
(c) the practical arrangements for the hearings provided for in Article 27.
2. Before the adoption of any measures pursuant to paragraph 1, the Commission shall publish a draft thereof and invite all interested parties to submit their comments within the time-limit it lays down, which may not be less than one month. Before publishing a draft measure and before adopting it, the Commission shall consult the Advisory Committee on Restrictive Practices and Dominant Positions.

CHAPTER XI TRANSITIONAL, AMENDING AND FINAL PROVISIONS

Article 34 Transitional provisions
1. Applications made to the Commission under Article 2 of Regulation No 17, notifications made under Articles 4 and 5 of that Regulation and the corresponding applications and notifications made under Regulations (EEC) No 1017/68, (EEC) No 4056/86 and (EEC) No 3975/87 shall lapse as from the date of application of this Regulation.
2. Procedural steps taken under Regulation No 17 and Regulations (EEC) No 1017/68, (EEC) No 4056/ 86 and (EEC) No 3975/87 shall continue to have effect for the purposes of applying this Regulation.

Article 35 Designation of competition authorities of Member States
1. The Member States shall designate the competition authority or authorities responsible for the application of Articles 81 and 82 of the Treaty in such a way that the provisions of this regulation are effectively complied with. The measures necessary to empower those authorities to apply those Articles shall be taken before 1 May 2004. The authorities designated may include courts.

2. When enforcement of Community competition law is entrusted to national administrative and judicial authorities, the Member States may allocate different powers and functions to those different national authorities, whether administrative or judicial.
3. The effects of Article 11(6) apply to the authorities designated by the Member States including courts that exercise functions regarding the preparation and the adoption of the types of decisions foreseen in Article 5. The effects of Article 11(6) do not extend to courts insofar as they act as review courts in respect of the types of decisions foreseen in Article 5.
4. Notwithstanding paragraph 3, in the Member States where, for the adoption of certain types of decisions foreseen in Article 5, an authority brings an action before a judicial authority that is separate and different from the prosecuting authority and provided that the terms of this paragraph are complied with, the effects of Article 11(6) shall be limited to the authority prosecuting the case which shall withdraw its claim before the judicial authority when the Commission opens proceedings and this withdrawal shall bring the national proceedings effectively to an end.

Article 36 Amendment of Regulation (EEC) No 1017/68
Regulation (EEC) No 1017/68 is amended as follows:
1. Article 2 is repealed;
2. in Article 3(1), the words 'The prohibition laid down in Article 2' are replaced by the words 'The prohibition in Article 81(1) of the Treaty';
3. Article 4 is amended as follows:
(a) In paragraph 1, the words 'The agreements, decisions and concerted practices referred to in Article 2' are replaced by the words 'Agreements, decisions and concerted practices pursuant to Article 81(1) of the Treaty';
(b) Paragraph 2 is replaced by the following:
'2. If the implementation of any agreement, decision or concerted practice covered by paragraph 1 has, in a given case, effects which are incompatible with the requirements of Article 81(3) of the Treaty, undertakings or associations of undertakings may be required to make such effects cease.'
4. Articles 5 to 29 are repealed with the exception of Article 13(3) which continues to apply to decisions adopted pursuant to Article 5 of Regulation (EEC) No 1017/68 prior to the date of application of this Regulation until the date of expiration of those decisions;
5. in Article 30, paragraphs 2, 3 and 4 are deleted.

Article 37 Amendment of Regulation (EEC) No 2988/74
In Regulation (EEC) No 2988/74, the following Article is inserted:
'*Article 7a* Exclusion
This Regulation shall not apply to measures taken under Council Regulation

(EC) No 1/2003 of 16 December 2002 on the implementation of the rules on competition laid down in Articles 81 and 82 of the Treaty.

Article 38 Amendment of Regulation (EEC) No 4056/86
Regulation (EEC) No 4056/86 is amended as follows:
1. Article 7 is amended as follows:
(a) Paragraph 1 is replaced by the following:
'1. *Breach of an obligation*
Where the persons concerned are in breach of an obligation which, pursuant to Article 5, attaches to the exemption provided for in Article 3, the Commission may, in order to put an end to such breach and under the conditions laid down in Council Regulation (EC) No 1/2003 of 16 December 2002 on the implementation of the rules on competition laid down in Articles 81 and 82 of the Treaty adopt a decision that either prohibits them from carrying out or requires them to perform certain specific acts, or withdraws the benefit of the block exemption which they enjoyed.
(b) Paragraph 2 is amended as follows:
(i) In point (a), the words 'under the conditions laid down in Section II' are replaced by the words 'under the conditions laid down in Regulation (EC) No 1/2003';
(ii) The second sentence of the second subparagraph of point (c) (i) is replaced by the following: 'At the same time it shall decide, in accordance with Article 9 of Regulation (EC) No 1/2003, whether to accept commitments offered by the undertakings concerned with a view, *inter alia*, to obtaining access to the market for non-conference lines.'
2. Article 8 is amended as follows:
(a) Paragraph 1 is deleted.
(b) In paragraph 2 the words 'pursuant to Article 10' are replaced by the words 'pursuant to Regulation (EC) No 1/2003'.
(c) Paragraph 3 is deleted;
3. Article 9 is amended as follows:
(a) In paragraph 1, the words 'Advisory Committee referred to in Article 15' are replaced by the words 'Advisory Committee referred to in Article 14 of Regulation (EC) No 1/2003';
(b) In paragraph 2, the words 'Advisory Committee as referred to in Article 15' are replaced by the words 'Advisory Committee referred to in Article 14 of Regulation (EC) No 1/2003';
4. Articles 10 to 25 are repealed with the exception of Article 13(3), which continues to apply to decisions adopted pursuant to Article 81(3) of the Treaty prior to the date of application of this Regulation until the date of expiration of those decisions;
5. in Article 26, the words 'the form, content and other details of complaints

pursuant to Article 10, applications pursuant to Article 12 and the hearings provided for in Article 23(1) and (2)' are deleted.

Article 39 Amendment of Regulation (EEC) No 3975/87
Articles 3 to 19 of Regulation (EEC) No 3975/87 are repealed with the exception of Article 6(3) which continues to apply to decisions adopted pursuant to Article 81(3) of the Treaty prior to the date of application of this Regulation until the date of expiration of those decisions.

Article 40 Amendment of Regulations No 19/65/EEC, (EEC) No 2821/71 and (EEC) No 1534/91
Article 7 of Regulation No 19/65/EEC, Article 7 of Regulation (EEC) No 2821/71 and Article 7 of Regulation (EEC) No 1534/91 are repealed.

Article 41 Amendment of Regulation (EEC) No 3976/87
Regulation (EEC) No 3976/87 is amended as follows:
1. Article 6 is replaced by the following:
'Article 6
The Commission shall consult the Advisory Committee referred to in Article 14 of Council Regulation (EC) No 1/2003 of 16 December 2002 on the implementation of the rules on competition laid down in Articles 81 and 82 of the Treaty before publishing a draft Regulation and before adopting a Regulation.
2. Article 7 is repealed.

Article 42 Amendment of Regulation (EEC) No 479/92
Regulation (EEC) No 479/92 is amended as follows:
1. Article 5 is replaced by the following:
'Article 5
Before publishing the draft Regulation and before adopting the Regulation, the Commission shall consult the Advisory Committee referred to in Article 14 of Council Regulation (EC) No 1/2003 of 16 December 2002 on the implementation of the rules on competition laid down in Articles 81 and 82 of the Treaty.
2. Article 6 is repealed.

Article 43 Repeal of Regulations No 17 and No 141
1. Regulation No 17 is repealed with the exception of Article 8(3), which continues to apply to decisions adopted pursuant to Article 81(3) of the Treaty prior to the date of application of this Regulation until the date of expiration of those decisions.
2. Regulation No 141 is repealed.

3. References to the repealed Regulations shall be construed as references to this Regulation.

Article 44 Report on the application of the present Regulation
Five years from the date of application of this Regulation, the Commission shall report to the European Parliament and the Council on the functioning of this Regulation, in particular on the application of Article 11(6) and Article 17. On the basis of this report, the Commission shall assess whether it is appropriate to propose to the Council a revision of this Regulation.

Article 45 Entry into force
This Regulation shall enter into force on the 20th day following that of its publication in the *Official Journal of the European Communities*. It shall apply from 1 May 2004. This Regulation shall be binding in its entirety and directly applicable in all Member States.

6.3 Law 287

TITLE I AGREEMENTS, ABUSE OF DOMINANT POSITION AND CONCENTRATIONS

Article 1 Scope and relationship to Community law
1. The provisions of this Act implementing Article 41 of the Constitution protecting and guaranteeing the right of free enterprise, apply to agreements, abuse of a dominant position and concentrations outside the scope of Articles 65 and/or 66 of the Treaty establishing the European Coal and Steel Community, Articles 85 and/or 86 of the Treaty establishing the European Economic Community (EEC), EEC Regulations or Community acts having an equivalent statutory effect.
2. Where the Competition Authority, within the meaning of article 10, hereinafter referred to as 'the Authority', considers that a case does not fall within the scope of this Act, as defined in subsection (1), it shall inform the Commission of the European Communities and forward to it any relevant information at its disposal.
3. The Authority shall suspend any investigation into cases in respect of which the Commission of the European Communities has opened a formal procedure under the provisions referred to in subsection (1) above, save for any aspects entirely of domestic relevance.
4. The provisions of this Title shall be interpreted in accordance with the principles of the European Community competition law.

Article 2 Agreements restricting freedom of competition

1. The following shall be regarded as agreements: accords and/or concerted practices between undertakings, and any decisions, even if adopted pursuant to their Articles or Bylaws, taken by consortia, associations of undertakings and other similar entities.

2. Agreements are prohibited between undertakings which have as their object or effect appreciable prevention, restriction or distortion of competition within the national market or within a substantial part of it, including those that:

a) directly or indirectly fix purchase or selling prices or other contractual conditions;

b) limit or restrict production, market outlets or market access, investment, technical development or technological progress;

c) share markets or sources of supply;

d) apply to other trading partners objectively dissimilar conditions for equivalent transactions, thereby placing them at an unjustifiable competitive disadvantage;

e) make the conclusion of contracts subject to acceptance by the other parties of supplementary obligations, which, by their nature or according to commercial usage, have no connection with the subject of such contracts.

3. Prohibited agreements are null and void.

Article 3 Abuse of a dominant position

1. The abuse by one or more undertakings of a dominant position within the domestic market or in a substantial part of it is prohibited. It is also prohibited:

a) directly or indirectly to impose unfair purchase or selling prices or other unfair contractual conditions;

b) to limit or restrict production, market outlets or market access, investment, technical development or technological progress;

c) to apply to other trading partners objectively dissimilar conditions for equivalent transactions, thereby placing them at an unjustifiable competitive disadvantage;

d) to make the conclusion of contracts subject to acceptance by the other parties of supplementary obligations which, by their nature or according to commercial usage, have no connection with the subject of such contracts.

Article 4 Exemption from the prohibition of agreements restricting competition

1. The Authority may authorize, for a limited period, agreements or categories of agreements prohibited under article 2 which have the effect of improving the conditions of supply in the market, leading to substantial benefits for

consumers. Such improvements shall be identified taking also into account the need to guarantee the undertakings the necessary level of international competitiveness and shall be related, in particular, with increases of production, improvements in the quality of production or distribution, or with technical and technological progress. The exemption may not permit restrictions that are not strictly necessary for the purposes of this subsection, and may not permit competition to be eliminated in a substantial part of the market.
2. The Authority may subsequently, after giving notice, revoke the exemption referred to in subsection (1) in cases where the party concerned abuses it, or when any of the conditions on which the exemption was based no longer obtain.
3. Requests for exemption shall be submitted to the Authority, which shall avail itself of the powers of investigation referred to in article 14 and decide within a period from 120 days of the date on which the application is filed.

Article 5 Concentrations
1. A concentration shall be deemed to arise when:
a) two or more undertakings merge;
b) one or more persons controlling at least one undertaking or one or more undertakings, acquire the direct or indirect control of the whole or parts of one or more undertakings, whether through the acquisition of shares or assets, or by contract or by any other means;
c) two or more undertakings create a joint venture by setting up a new company.
2. Control of an undertaking shall not be deemed to have been acquired in the case of a bank or financial institution which acquires shares in an undertaking when constituted, or when its share capital is raised, with a view to re-selling them on the market, provided that it does not exercise any voting rights vested in those securities while it holds them; in no case the holding period shall exceed 24 months.
3. Operations, which have as their main object or effect the coordination of the actions of independent undertakings shall not constitute concentrations.

Article 6 Prohibition on concentrations restricting free competition
1. The Authority shall appraise concentrations subject to notification under article 16, to ascertain whether they create or strengthen a dominant position on the domestic market with the effect of eliminating or restricting competition appreciably and on a lasting basis. This situation shall be appraised taking into account the possibilities of substitution available to suppliers and users, the market position of the undertakings, the access conditions to supplies or markets, the structure of the relevant markets, the

competitive position of the domestic industry, barriers to the entry of competing undertakings and the evolution of supply and demand for the relevant goods or services.
2. Whenever the investigation under article 16(4) shows that the operation entails the consequences referred to in subsection (1) the Authority shall either prohibit the concentration or authorize it laying down the necessary measures to prevent such consequences.

Article 7 Control
1. For the purposes of this title, control is acquired in the cases provided by Article 2359 of the Civil Code, and by the holding of rights, contracts or other legal relations which, separately or in combination, and having regard for the considerations of fact and law involved, confer the possibility of exercising decisive influence on an undertaking, in particular by:
a) the ownership or right of use over all or part of the assets of an undertaking;
b) rights, contracts or other legal relations which confer a decisive influence over the composition, resolutions or decisions of the board of an undertaking.
2. Control is acquired by persons or undertakings or groups of persons or undertakings which:
a) are holders of the rights or beneficiaries under the contracts or are parties to the other legal relations;
b) while not being holders of the rights or beneficiaries under the contracts or parties to such legal relations, have the power to exercise the rights deriving there from.

Article 8 Public undertakings and statutory monopolies
1. The provisions of the preceding articles apply to both private and public undertakings and to those in which the State is the majority shareholder.
2. The provisions of the preceding articles do not apply to undertakings, which, by law, are entrusted with the operation of services of general economic interest or operate on the market in a monopoly situation, only in so far as this is indispensable to perform the specific tasks assigned to them.
2-*bis*. The undertakings referred to in subsection (2) shall operate through separate companies if they intend to trade on markets other than those on which they trade within the meaning of the same subsection (2).
2-*ter*. The incorporation of undertakings and the acquisition of controlling interests in undertakings trading on the different markets referred to in subsection (2-*bis*) require prior notification to be submitted to the Authority.
2-*quater*. In order to guarantee equal business opportunities, when the undertakings referred to in subsection (2) supply their subsidiaries or

controlled companies on the different markets referred to in subsection (2-*bis*) with goods or services, including information services, over which they have exclusive rights by virtue of the activities they perform within the meaning of subsection 2, they shall make these same goods and services available to their direct competitors on equivalent terms and conditions.
2-*quinquies*. In the cases referred to in subsections (2-*bis*), (2-*ter*) and (2-*quater*), the Authority shall exercise its powers under article 14. When offences are committed under articles 2 and 3, the measures and the penalties provided by article 15 shall be applied.
2-*sexies*. In the event of failure to comply with the obligation of notification referred to in subsection (2-*ter*), the Authority shall impose a fine of up to 100 million lire.
Article 9 Internal production
1. The statutory monopoly granted to the State or to a public entity or agency, as well as any statutory monopoly granted to an undertaking entrusted with the sale of goods and services to the public does not imply a prohibition on third parties from producing the same goods or services for their own internal use, or for their parent or subsidiary companies.
2. Internal production is not allowed in cases where public order, public safety and national defence are the grounds for the relevant statutory monopoly provisions, or for telecommunications services, unless a government franchise is granted.

TITLE II ESTABLISHMENT AND FUNCTIONS OF THE COMPETITION AUTHORITY

Chapter I THE ESTABLISHMENT OF THE AUTHORITY

Article 10 The Competition Authority
1. The Competition Authority, hereinafter referred to as 'the Authority' is hereby instituted, with its headquarters in Rome.
2. The Authority shall act with total autonomy and independence of judgment and assessment, and is a collegial body consisting of the President and four members proposed and appointed jointly by the Presidents of the Italian Chamber of Deputies and Senate. The President shall be a person of well-known independence, and who has already held high office with broadly-based institutional responsibilities. The four members shall be persons of well-known independence, and chosen among judges serving on the Supreme Administrative Court ('Council of State'), the Court of Auditors, the Court of Cassation, full professors of Economics or Law or respected business executives of particularly high professional repute.
3. The members of the Authority shall be appointed for a non-renewable period of seven years. While holding office they may not exercise any

professional or consultancy activities, or acquire directorships or be employees of public or private entities, or hold public office of any kind whatever. Civil servants shall be given temporary leave throughout their full term of office.

4. The Authority may correspond with any government department and with any other statutory bodies or agencies under public law, and may request information and co-operation in the performance of its duties. Being the national Competition Authority, it shall be responsible for relations with the institutions of the European Community provided by the relevant provisions of Community law.

5. Within 90 days of the entry into force of this Act, the President of the Republic shall issue a Decree, at the proposal of the Minister of Trade and Industry, in consultation with the Minister of the Treasury, following a decision by the Council of Ministers, establishing the investigation procedures for ensuring full disclosure of any documents used in the course of the Authority's investigations, and the right of reply, debate and the submission of defences

6. The Authority shall draw up rules governing its own organization and operations, regulations for staff salary scales and conditions of employment and promotion, and rules for keeping expenditure within the limits laid down in this Act, even if they constitute exceptions to the general provisions governing public accounting.

7. The Authority is responsible for expenditure relating to its own operations, within the limits provided in the national budget and entered under a single heading in the budget of the Ministry of Trade and Industry. Its annual financial management shall be based on the budget approved by the Authority by 31st December of the previous year. The content and structure of the budget, in which expenditure shall be restricted within the limits of the forecast revenue, shall conform to the rules referred to in subsection (6), which also govern the procedures for introducing amendments. The financial statements, which shall be approved by 30th April of the following year, shall be audited by the Court of Auditors. The budget and the financial statements shall be published in the Official Gazette of the Italian Republic.

8. The emoluments of the Chairman and Members of the Authority shall be laid down by Prime Ministerial Decree, as proposed by the Minister of Trade and Industry, by agreement with the Minister of the Treasury.

Article 11 Staff of the Authority

1. By Prime Ministerial Decree a specific record shall be instituted for the staff of the Authority. The number of posts may not exceed 150 Staff shall be recruited by public competitive examination, except for those grades for

which recruitment is provided by article 16 of Law no. 56 of 28th February 1987.
2. The staff salaries and conditions of employment and promotion shall be in accordance with to the criteria laid down in the collective labour contract for Bank of Italy staff, taking account of the Authority's specific functional and organizational requirements.
3. Staff members of the Authority are forbidden to take any other employment or duties, and to exercise any professional, commercial or industrial activities.
4. The Authority may recruit up to 50 members of staff under fixed-term contracts governed by private law provisions. The Authority may, if appropriate, also engage experts for consultation on specific matters and problems, whenever necessary.
5. The Secretary-General is responsible for overseeing the operations of the Authority's services and offices, and shall report to the Chairman. He is appointed by the Minister of Trade and Industry, acting on a proposal of the Chairman of the Authority.

Chapter II THE AUTHORITY'S POWERS OVER AGREEMENTS RESTRICTING COMPETITION AND ABUSE OF A DOMINANT POSITION

Article 12 Powers of investigation
1. After assessing the elements in its possession and those brought to its notice by the public authorities or by any other interested party, including bodies representing consumers, the Authority shall conduct an investigation to ascertain any infringements of the prohibitions provided by articles 2 and 3.
2. The Authority may also institute a general fact-finding investigation at its own initiative, or at the request of the Minister of Trade and Industry, or of the Minister of State Shareholdings, in areas of business in which the development of trade, the evolution of prices or other circumstances suggest that competition may be impeded, restricted or distorted.

Article 13 Notification of agreements
1. Undertakings may notify the Authority of any agreements they conclude. The Authority shall commence the investigations under article 14 within 120 days of notification, after which time no investigation may take place, except where the notification is found to be incomplete or untrue.

Article 14 Investigation
1. In the event of an alleged infringement of articles 2 or 3 the Authority shall notify the undertakings and entities concerned that an investigation is being opened. The owners or legal representatives of such undertakings or entities

may submit representations in person or through a special attorney by the deadline set at the moment of notification, and may make submissions and opinions at any stage during the course of the investigation, as well as further representations before the investigations are completed.

2. The Authority may, at any stage in the investigation, request undertakings, entities and individuals to supply any information in their possession and exhibit any documents of relevance to the investigation; it may conduct inspections of the undertaking's books and records and make copies of them, availing itself of the cooperation of other government agencies where necessary; it may produce expert reports and economic and statistical analyses, and consult experts on any matter of relevance to the investigation.

3. Any information or data regarding the undertakings under investigation by the Authority are wholly confidential and may not be divulged even to other government departments.

4. In the exercise of their functions, officials of the Authority shall be considered 'public officials'. They are sworn to secrecy.

5. The Authority may fine anyone who refuses or fails to provide the information or exhibit the documents referred to in subsection (2) without justification, in an amount up to 50 million lire, which is increased up to 100 million lire in the event that they submit untruthful information or documents, in addition to any other penalties provided by current legislation.

Article 15 Service of notice and penalties

1. If the investigation provided in article 14 reveals infringements of articles 2 or 3, the Authority shall set a deadline within which the undertakings and entities concerned are to remedy the infringements. In the most serious cases it may decide, depending on the gravity and the duration of the infringement, to impose a fine up to ten per cent of the turnover of each undertaking or entity during the prior financial year; time limits shall be laid down within which the undertaking shall pay the penalty.

2. In the case of non-compliance with the notice referred to in subsection (1), the Authority shall impose a fine of up to ten per cent of the turnover or, in cases where the penalty provided by subsection (1) has already been imposed, a fine of no less than double the penalty already imposed with a ceiling of ten per cent of the turnover as defined in subsection (1). It shall also set a time limit for the payment of the fine. In cases of repeated non-compliance, the Authority may decide to order the undertaking to suspend activities for up to 30 days.

Chapter III THE AUTHORITY'S POWERS TO PROHIBIT CONCENTRATIONS

Article 16 Notification of concentrations

1. The concentrations referred to in article 5 shall be notified in advance to the Authority if the combined aggregate domestic turnover of all the undertakings concerned exceeds 500 billion lire or if the aggregate domestic turnover of the undertaking which is to be acquired exceeds 50 billion lire. These figures shall be increased each year by an amount equivalent to the increase in GDP price deflator index.
2. In the case of banks and financial institutions the turnover used shall be equal to the value of one-tenth of their total assets, with the exclusion of memorandum accounts and, in the case of insurance companies, to the value of premiums collected.
3. Within five days of receiving notification of a concentration, the Authority shall inform the Prime Minister and the Minister of Trade and Industry.
4. If the Authority considers that a concentration may be subject to prohibition under article 6, within 30 days of receiving the notification or of being informed thereof by any other means, it shall commence the investigations pursuant to the provisions of article 14. When formal notification is received of a concentration in respect of which the Authority deems the investigation unnecessary, it shall notify the undertakings and the Minister of Trade and Industry of its conclusions on this matter, within 30 days of receiving notification.
5. When notification is given to the 'Commissione Nazionale per le Società e la Borsa' of any public takeover bid which might result in a concentration subject to notification under subsection (1) the Authority shall be notified thereof at the same time.
6. With 15 days of receiving notification of a takeover bid pursuant to subsection (5), the Authority shall give notice that the investigation is being initiated and shall inform the Commissione Nazionale per le Società e la Borsa at the same time.
7. The Authority may commence the investigation beyond the time limits provided by this article when the information notified by the undertakings is seriously inaccurate, incomplete or untrue.
8. Within 45 days of the commencing of the investigation provided in this article, the Authority shall notify the undertakings concerned, and the Minister of Trade and Industry of its conclusions. This period may be extended in the course of the investigation for a further period of not more than 30 days whenever the undertakings fail to supply the information and the data in their possession upon request.

Article 17 Temporary suspension of a concentration

1. When conducting the investigation provided in article 16, the Authority may order the undertakings concerned not to proceed with the concentration until the investigation is concluded.
2. The provisions of subsection (1) shall not suspend a takeover bid that has been notified to the Authority under article 16(5), provided that the acquirer does not exercise any voting rights conferred by the securities in question.

Article 18 Conclusion of investigations of concentrations

1. If, following the investigation provided by article 16, the Authority ascertains that a concentration falls within the scope of article 6 of this Act, it shall prohibit it.
2. When the investigation produces insufficient evidence to justify action to be taken in respect of a concentration, the Authority shall close the investigation and immediately inform the undertakings concerned and the Minister of Trade and Industry of its conclusions. This measure may also be taken at the request of the undertakings concerned, if they are able to demonstrate that any aspects of the concentration deemed likely to distort competition as originally planned have since been removed.
3. If the concentration has already taken place, the Authority may require measures to be taken in order to restore conditions of effective competition, and remove any effects that distort it.

Article 19 Fines for failure to comply with the prohibition on concentrations or the notification requirement

1. The Authority shall impose administrative fines on undertakings which implement a concentration in violation of the prohibition provided by article 18(1) or which fail to comply with the instructions issued pursuant to article 18(3), ranging from a minimum of one per cent to a maximum of ten per cent of the turnover of the business forming the object of the concentration.
2. The Authority may impose administrative fines on undertakings which fail to comply with the prior notification requirements provided by article 16(1) in the amount of one per cent of the turnover of the year prior to the year in which the undertaking is challenged, over and above any other penalties for which it may be liable under subsection (1), following the investigation provided by Chapter III, counted from the date on which the penalty referred provided by this subsection is notified.

Chapter IV SPECIAL PROVISIONS

Article 20 Banks, insurance companies and the broadcasting and publishing undertakings

1. [Repealed].
2. With respect to banks, the provisions of articles 2, 3, 4 and 6 shall be enforced by their own supervisory authority.
3. Measures by the supervisory authorities referred to in subsections (1) and (2) to enforce the provisions of articles 2, 3, 4 and 6 of this Act shall be adopted after hearing the opinion of the Competition Authority within the meaning of article 10, which shall be issued within 30 days of receiving the documentation on which the measure is based. If the opinion is not issued within 30 days, the supervisory authorities may adopt the measures for which they are empowered.
4. In the case of operations involving insurance companies, the measures shall be adopted by the Authority within the meaning of article 10 after hearing the opinion of Istituto per la Vigilanza sulle Assicurazioni Private e d'Interesse Collettivo (ISVAP), which shall be issued within 30 days of receiving the documentation on which the measure is based. If the opinion is not issued within 30 days, the Authority within the meaning of article 10 may adopt the measures for which it is empowered.
5. The statutory authority for the supervision of banks may also waive the prohibition provided by article 2 authorizing agreements to proceed for a limited period in order to guarantee the stability of the monetary system, in accordance with the criteria provided by article 4(1). Such authorization shall be adopted by agreement with the Authority within the meaning of article 10, which shall judge whether or not the agreement impedes competition.
6. The Authority referred to in article 10 may notify the supervisory authorities referred to in subsections (1) and (2) above of any cases of possible infringement of articles 2 and 3.
7. As an exception to the provisions of the preceding subsections, where the agreement, abuse of a dominant position or concentration relate to undertakings operating in sectors falling within the competence of more than one Authority, each of those authorities may adopt measures falling within its competence.
8. The supervisory authorities referred to in this article shall follow the same procedures provided for the Authority within the meaning of article 10.
9. The provisions of this Act governing concentrations do not constitute a derogation from the statutory provisions in force governing banking, insurance, broadcasting and publishing.

TITLE III THE AUTHORITY'S FACT-FINDING AND CONSULTATIVE POWERS

Article 21 Powers to notify Parliament and the Government

1. In order to contribute to more effective protection of competition and the market, the Authority shall identify cases of particular relevance in which the provisions of law or regulations or general administrative provisions are creating distortions to competition or to the sound operation of the market, which are not justified by the requirements of general interest.
2. The Authority shall notify Parliament and the Prime Minister of any distortions arising as a result of legislative measures, and the Prime Minister, other relevant ministers, and the relevant local authorities of distortions arising in any other cases.
3. At its discretion, the Authority shall issue an opinion on any measures needed to remove or prevent distortions, and it may also publish the cases notified and the opinions as appropriate according to the nature and the importance of the distortions.

Article 22 Consultation activities

1. The Authority may express opinions on draft legislation or regulations and on problems relating to competition and the market whenever it deems this appropriate or whenever requested to do so by the government departments and agencies concerned. The Prime Minister may also request the opinion of the Authority in relation to legislation or regulations whose direct effect is:
- to place quantitative restrictions on the exercise of an activity or access to a market:
- to lay down exclusive rights in certain business areas;
- to impose general pricing practices or conditions of sale.

Article 23 Annual report

1. By 30th April of each year the Authority shall submit a report to the Prime Minister on its activities during the preceding year. The Prime Minister shall submit the report to Parliament within thirty days thereafter.

Article 24 Report to the Government on certain sectors

1. After consulting the relevant government departments, within 18 months of its constitution the Authority shall submit a report to the Prime Minister on the steps that must be taken in order to adapt the legislation relating to public tenders, public franchise-holders and commercial distribution to the principles of competition.

TITLE IV PROVISIONS ON GOVERNMENT POWERS OVER CONCENTRATIONS

Article 25 Government powers over concentrations
1. The Council of Ministers shall, at the proposal of the Minister for Trade and Industry, lay down the general criteria to be used by the Authority when issuing authorization as a waiver to the prohibitions provided by article 6 of the law, when major general interests of the national economy are involved in the process of European integration, provided that competition is not eliminated from the market or restricted to an extent that is not strictly justified by the aforementioned general interests. In all these cases the Authority shall also prescribe the measures to be adopted in order to restore full competition by a specific deadline.
2. In the case of the concentrations referred to in article 16 involving entities or undertakings of countries which do not protect the independence of bodies or undertakings under provisions having an equivalent effect to those given in the Titles above, or apply discriminatory provisions or impose clauses having similar effects in relation to acquisitions by Italian undertakings or entities, the Prime Minister may, within 30 days of the notification referred to in article 16(3) and acting on a resolution of the Council of Ministers, proposed by the Minister of Trade and Industry, prohibit the concentration on the grounds that it is against the essential national economic interests.

Article 26 Publication of decisions
1. The decisions referred to in articles 15, 16, 18, 19 and 25 shall be published within 20 days in a special bulletin issued by the Prime Minister's Office. The findings of the investigations provided by in article 12(2) shall also be published in this bulletin, if the Authority deems this appropriate. [...]

TITLE VI FINAL PROVISIONS

Article 31 Penalties
1. The administrative fines for infringements of this Act are provided, where applicable, by Chapter I, Parts I and II of Law no. 689 of 24 November 1981.

Article 32 Financial cover
1. The cost of enforcing this Act, assessed at 20 billion lire for 1990, 32 billion lire for 1991, and 35 billion lire for 1992, shall be covered by a matching reduction in the allocation to heading 6856 of Ministry of the Treasury 1990 budget under the three-year budget for 1990-1992, using the specific provision "For the protection of competition and the market".

Article 33 Jurisdiction
1. Appeals against administrative measures adopted under the provisions of Titles I to IV of this Act fall within the exclusive jurisdiction of the administrative courts. They must be filed before the Latium Regional Administrative Tribunal.

2. Annulment proceedings and claims for damages, and petitions for emergency measures to be adopted in respect of infringements of the provisions of Titles I to IV, must be filed before the Court of Appeal having jurisdiction over the place.

Article 34 Entry into force
1. This Act shall come into force on the day following the date of publication in the Official Gazette of the Italian Republic. It shall be entered into the Statute Book, bearing the Seal of State, and is binding on all and shall be enforced as the law of the land.

7 Index

7.1 Bibliography

Books and essays

Auletta/Salanitro, Diritto Commerciale[10] (1996).

Bartosch, Von der Freistellung zur Legalausnahme: Der Vorschlag der EG-Kommission für eine „neue Verordnung Nr. 17“, EuZW 2001, 101.

Benedettelli, Sul rapporto fra diritto comunitario e diritto italiano della concorrenza, Il Foro Italiano 1990 IV, 235.

Bishop, Modernisation of the rules implementing Articles 81 and 82, in Ehlermann/Atanasiu, European Competition Law Annual 2000 (2001), 55.

Bogdandy, Legal equality, legal certainty and subsidiarity in transnational economic law - decentralized application of Art 81 par 3 EC and WTO law: why and why not, European integration and international co-ordination 2001, 13.

Bourgeois/Humpe, The Commission's draft "New Regulation 17", ECLR 2002, 43.

Bovis, Transforming the application of EC competition laws: the case of decentralisation, European Business Law 2001, 98.

Bronett in Groeben/Thiesing/Ehlermann, Kommentar zum EU-/EG-Vertrag[5].

Burrichter, Modernisation of EU competition law: the application of Article 81 (3) by national courts. Remarks from the point of view of a practitioner, in Ehlermann/Atanasiu, European Competition Law Annual 2000 (2001), 539.

Clarkson/Hill, Jaffey on the conflict of laws (1997).

Collins Paperback English Dictionary[4] (1999).

Corsi, Diritto dell'impresa (2001).

Deringer, Stellungnahme zum Weißbuch der Europäischen Kommission über die Modernisierung der Vorschriften zur Anwendung der Art. 85 und 86 EG-Vertrag (Art. 81 und 82 EG), EuZW 2000, 5.

Edward, The modernisation of EC antitrust policy. Issues for courts and judges, in Ehlermann/Atanasiu, European Competition Law Annual 2000 (2001), 565.

Ehlermann, The modernisation of EC Antitrust policy: a legal and cultural revolution, CMLR 2000, 37.

Ehlermann/Atanasiu, The Modernisation of EC Antitrust Law: Consequences for the future role and function of the EC Courts, ECLR 2002, 72.

Eilmannsberger, Europarecht II (2000).

Emmerich, Wettbewerbsregeln: Kartellrecht: § 1 Art 81 und 82 EGV in Dauses, Handbuch des EU-Wirtschaftsrechts 2001.

Europäische Kommission, Die Anwendung der Artikel 85 und 86 des EG-Vertrags durch die Gerichte der Mitgliedsstaaten (1997).

European Commission, Green Paper on vertical restraints, http://europa.eu.int/comm/competition/antitrust/96721en_en.pdf, 27.08.2003.

European Commission, Notice concerning agreement, decision and concerted practices in the field of co-operation between enterprises, 1968, http://europa.eu.int/smartapi/cgi/sga_doc?smartapi!celexapi!prod!CELEXnumdoc&lg=es&numdoc=31968Y0729(01)&model=guichett, 27.08.2003.

European Commission, Notice concerning agreements of minor importance (*de minimis* rule), 2001, http://europa.eu.int/eur-lex/pri/en/oj/dat/2001/c_368/c_36820011222en00130015.pdf, 27.08.2003.

European Commission, Notice from the Commission on the application of the competition rules to the postal sector and on the assessment of certain State measures relating to postal services, 1998, http://europa.eu.int/smartapi/cgi/sga_doc?smartapi!celexapi!prod!CELEXnumdoc&lg=EN&numdoc=31996H0280&model=guichett, 27.08.2003.

European Commission, Notice of 18 December 1978 concerning its assessment of certain subcontracting agreements in relation to Article 85 par 1 of the EEC Treaty,
http://europa.eu.int/smartapi/cgi/sga_doc?smartapi!celexapi!prod!CELEXnumdoc&lg=EN&numdoc=31979Y0103(01)&model=guichett, 27.08.2003.

European Commission, Notice on co-operation between national competition authorities and the Commission in handling cases falling within the scope of Articles 85 and 86 of the EC Treaty, 1997,
http://europa.eu.int/comm/competition/antitrust/legislation/coope_en.html, 27.08.2003.

European Commission, Notice on co-operation between national courts and the Commission applying Articles 85 and 86 of the EEC Treaty, 1993,
http://europa.eu.int/smartapi/cgi/sga_doc?smartapi!celexplus!prod!CELEXnumdoc&lg=EN&numdoc=31993Y0213(01), 27.08.2003.

European Commission, Notice on exclusive agency contracts made with commercial agents, 1962,
http://europa.eu.int/comm/competition/antitrust/legislation/edc_en.html, 01.09.2003.

European Commission, Notice on immunity of fines and reduction of fines in cartel cases, 2002,
http://europa.eu.int/eur-lex/pri/en/oj/dat/2002/c_045/c_04520020219en00030005.pdf, 27.08.2003.

European Commission, Notice on Import of Japanese products, 1972,
http://europa.eu.int/comm/competition/antitrust/legislation/japag_en.html, 01.09.2003.

European Commission, Notice on the definition of relevant market for the purposes of Community competition law, 1997,
http://europa.eu.int/smartapi/cgi/sga_doc?smartapi!celexapi!prod!CELEXnumdoc&lg=EN&numdoc=31997Y1209(01)&model=guichett, 27.08.2003.

European Commission, Notice on the internal rules of procedure for processing requests for access to the file in cases pursuant to Articles 85 and 86 of the EC Treaty, Articles 65 and 66 of the ECSC Treaty and Council Regulation (EEC) No 4064/89, http://europa.eu.int/servlet/portail/RenderServlet?search=RefPub&lg=en&nb_docs=25&domain=&in_force=NO&year=1997&month=&day=&coll=JOC&nu_jo=23&page=3, 01.09.2003.

European Commission, Recommendation of 3 April 1996 concerning the definition of small and medium-sized enterprises, 1996, http://europa.eu.int/smartapi/cgi/sga_doc?smartapi!celexapi!prod!CELEXnumdoc&lg=EN&numdoc=31996H0280&model=guichett, 27.08.2003.

European Commission, White Paper on reform of Regulation 17, Summary of observations, 2000, http://europa.eu.int/comm/competition/antitrust/others/wp_on_modernisation/summary_observations.pdf, 27.08.2003.

European Commission, XXVIIth Report on Competition Policy 1997, http://europa.eu.int/comm/competition/publications/broch97_en.pdf, 27.08.2003.

European Commission, XXXIIst Report on competition policy 2002, http://europa.eu.int/comm/competition/annual_reports/2002/report_short_en.pdf , 27.08.2003.

European Commission; White Paper on modernisation of the rules implementing articles 85 and 86 of the EC treaty, 1999, http://europa.eu.int/comm/competition/antitrust/wp_modern_en.pdf, 27.08.2003.

Fiale, Diritto commerciale[14] (2002).

Forrester, The modernisation of EC antitrust policy: compatibility, efficiency, legal security, in Ehlermann/Atanasiu, European Competition Law Annual 2000 (2001), 75.

Forrester, The Reform of the Implementation of Articles 81 and 82 following Publication of the Draft Regulation, Legal Issues of Economic Integration 2001, 173.

Frigani/Rossi, EU and Italian antitrust rules: concordances and discordances, Diritto del commercio italiano 2001, 811.

Geiger, Das Weißbuch der EG-Kommission zu Art. 81, 82 EG – eine Reform, besser als ihr Ruf, EuZW 2000, 165.

Gerber, Modernising European Competition Law: A developmental perspective, ECLR 2001, 122.

German Monopolies Commission, Cartel policy change in the European Union? – On the European Commission's White Paper of 28th April 1999, http://www.monopolkommission.de/sg_28/text_e.htm, 27.08.2003.

Goyder, EC Competition Law³ (1998).

Goyder, Providing support to national judges in dealing with competition cases, in Ehlermann/Atanasiu, European Competition Law Annual 2000 (2001), 571.

Gröning, National judges in a modernised Community law system. A special view to procedural aspects, in Ehlermann/Atanasiu, European Competition Law Annual 2000 (2001), 579.

Gustafsson, Legal Implications Facing the Realisation of the Commission White Paper on Modernisation of EC Antitrust Procedure and the Role of National Courts in a Post-White Paper Era, Legal Issues of Economic Integration 2000, 159.

Hack, Handlungsmöglichkeiten Einzelner bei Kartellrechtsverletzungen, ecolex 2003, 311.

Hildebrand, The European School in EC Competition Law, Journal of World Competition 2002, 3.

Hirsch/Burkert in Gleiss/Hirsch, Kommentar zum EG-Kartellrecht 1⁴ (1993).

Holmes, The EC White Paper on modernisation, Journal of World Competition 2000, 51.

Hossenfelder/Lutz, Die neue Durchführungsverordnung zu den Artikeln 81 und 82 EG-Vertrag, WuW 2003, 118.
Immenga, Eine Wende in der gemeinschaftsrechtlichen Kartellpolitik?, EuZW 1999, 609.

Immenga, Harmonisierung des Wettbewerbsrechts als Aufgabe, EuZW 1997, 449.

Klocker, Fit machen für den "Kulturwechel"!, WuW 2002, 1151.

Mangini/Olivieri, Diritto Antitrust (2000).

Marenco, Does a legal exemption system require an amendment of the treaty?, in Ehlermann/Atanasiu, European Competition Law Annual 2000 (2001), 145.

Mastroianni, Osservazioni in merito alla effettività del sistema italiano di tutela "decentrata" del diritto comunitario della concorrenza, Il diritto dell'Unione Europea 2001, 78.

Mathijsen, A guide to European Union Law[7] (1999).

Mavroidis/Neven, From the White Paper to the Proposal for a Council Regulation: How to Treat the New Kids on the Block?, Legal Issues of Economic Integration 2001, 151.

Mazzarolli/Pericu/Romano/Roversi Monaco/Scoca, Diritto amministrativo II/V[2] (1998).

Meli, Il progetto di modernizzazione del sistema di controllo delle intese anticoncorrenziali ed il ruolo del giudice ordinario, Europa e diritto pirvato 2001, 117.

Mestmäcker, Versuch einer kartellpolitischen Wende in der EU, EuZW 1999, 523.

Mestmäcker, The modernisation of EC Antitrust Policy: a constitutional challenge or administrative convenience, in Ehlermann/Atanasiu, European Competition Law Annual 2000 (2001), 223.

Monti, A European Competition policy for today and tomorrow, Journal of World Competition 2000, 1.

Negri, Ruolo più forte all'Antitrust, Il sole - 24 ore, 249 (2003), 26.
Pace, L'evoluzione della tutela amministrativa della concorrenza nel diritto antitrust comunitario e nazionale Il diritto dell'Unione Europea 1999, 356.

Pardolesi, Deroghe al divieto di intese restrittive della libertà di concorrenza, in Frignani, Diritto Antitrust Italiano (1993), 400.

Paulweber, The End of a Success Story? The European Commission's White Paper on the Modernisation of the European Competition Law: A comparative

Study about the Role of the Notification of Restrictive Practices within the European Competition and the American Antitrust Law, Journal of World Competition 2000, 3.

Petsche, Das neue EG-Kartellverfahrensrecht, ecolex 2003, 304.

Pirie, The complainant in EC competition law; Competition Law 2000, 107.

Pizzicaroli, L'applicazione decentrata della disciplina comunitaria della concorrenza da parte dell'autorità garante del mercato in Italia, Diritto Comunitario e degli scambi internazionali 2001, 601.

Rittner, Kartellpolitik und Gewaltenteilung in der EG, EuZW 2000, 129.

Salord, Concurrent application, the April 1999 White Paper and the future of national laws, ECLR 2000, 128.

Satta/Punzi, Diritto processuale civile[12] (1996).

Schaub, Die Reform der Regeln zur Durchführung der Artikel 81 und 82 EG-Vertrag, in Baudenbacher, Neueste Entwicklungen im europäischen und internationalen Kartellrecht 2002, 3.

Schaub, The reform of Regulation 17: The issues of compatibility, effective enforcement and legal certainty, in Ehlermann/Atanasiu, European Competition Law Annual 2000 (2001), 241.

Schmidt/Schmidt, Europäische Wettbewerbspolitik – Eine Einführung (1997).

Schweitzer/Hummer, Europarecht[5] (1996).

Siragusa, The modernisation of EC competition law: risks of cohabitation, private enforcement and other issues, in Ehlermann/Atanasiu, European Competition Law Annual 2000 (2001), 443.

Siragusa/Sforzolini, Il diritto della concorrenza italiano e comunitario: un nuovo rapporto, Il Foro Italiano 1992 IV, 249.

Stillfried/Stockenhuber; Der Entwurf einer neuen Verfahrensordnung zum EG-Kartellrecht, Zeitschrift für österreichisches und europäisches Wirtschaftsrecht 2001, 145.

Stockenhuber, Europäisches Kartellrecht (1999).

Stockenhuber in Grabitz/Hilf, Das Recht der europäischen Union (2001).

Tavassi, Towards the application of Article 81 (3) by national courts in Italy, Rivista italiana di diritto pubblico comunitario 2001, 123.

Tizzano, L'applicazione decentrata degli art 85 e 86 Ce in Italia, Il Foro Italiano, 1997 IV, 33.

Todino, L'autorità e l'applicazione decentrata degli articoli 85 e 86 del trattato CE, Temi e problemi 1997, http://www.agcm.it, 27.08.2003.

Todino, Modernisation from the perspective of national competition authorities: impact of the reform on decentralised application of E.C. competition law, ECLR 2000, 348.

Trabucchi, Istituzioni di diritto civile[35] (1994).

Weitbrecht, Das neue EG-Kartellverfahrensrecht EuZW 2003, 69.

Wesseling, The Commissions White Paper on Modernisation of EC Antitrust law: unspoken consequences and incomplete treatment of alternative options, ECLR 1999, 420.

Wise, Review of competition law and policy in Italy, OECD Journal of competition law and policy 2001, 66.

Wißmann, Decentralised enforcement of EC Competition Law and the new policy on cartels, Journal of World Competition 2000, 123.

Zambrano, Principi ed orientamenti dell'Autorità Garante in materia di intese nel corso del 1999, Concorrenza e mercato - rassegna degli orientamenti dell'Autorità Garante 2000, 3.

Legislation

Brussels Convention on jurisdiction and the enforcement of judgements in civil and commercial matters, http://curia.eu.int/common/recdoc/convention/en/c-textes/brux-idx.htm, 28.08.2003.

Commission Directive 96/19/EC of 13 March 1996 amending Directive 90/388/EEC with regard to the implementation of full competition in telecommunications markets,
http://europa.eu.int/smartapi/cgi/sga_doc?smartapi!celexapi!prod!CELEXnumdoc&lg=EN&numdoc=31996L0019&model=guichett , 28.08.2003.

Commission Regulation 99/63 governing procedures of hearings of individual cases by the Commission, as replaced by Commission Regulation 2842/98,
http://europa.eu.int/eur-lex/pri/en/oj/dat/1998/l_354/l_35419981230en00180021.pdf, 28.08.2003.

Commission Regulation 82/91 of 5 December 1990 on the application of Art 85 par 3 of the Treaty to certain categories of Agreements, Decisions and concerted practices concerning ground handling services,
http://europa.eu.int/smartapi/cgi/sga_doc?smartapi!celexapi!prod!CELEXnumdoc&lg=EN&numdoc=31991R0082&model=guichett , 28.08.2003.

Commission Reg 1617/93, as amended by Relation 1105/2002,
http://europa.eu.int/eur-lex/pri/en/oj/dat/2002/l_167/l_16720020626en00060007.pdf, 01.09.2003.

Commission Regulation 3385/94 of 21 December 1994 on the form, content and other details of applications and notifications provided for in Council Reg 17,
http://europa.eu.int/smartapi/cgi/sga_doc?smartapi!celexapi!prod!CELEXnumdoc&lg=EN&numdoc=31994R3385&model=guichett, 28.08.2003.

Commission Regulation 2790/1999 on the application of Art 81 par 3 (block exemption on vertical agreements and concerted practices)
http://europa.eu.int/smartapi/cgi/sga_doc?smartapi!celexplus!prod!CELEXnumdoc&lg=EN&numdoc=31999R2790, 28.08.2003.

Commission Regulation 823/2000 on the application of Art 85 par 3 of the Treaty to certain categories of agreements, decisions and concerted practices between liner shipping companies (consortia),
http://europa.eu.int/eur-lex/pri/en/oj/dat/2000/l_100/l_10020000420en00240030.pdf, 01.09.2003.

Commission Regulation 2658/2000 on the application of Art 81 par 3 (block exemption on specialisation agreements), http://europa.eu.int/smartapi/cgi/sga_doc?smartapi!celexapi!prod!CELEXnumdoc&lg=en&numdoc=32000R2658&model=guichett , 28.08.2003.

Commission Regulation 2659/2000 on the application of Art 81 par 3 (block exemption on research and development agreements), http://europa.eu.int/smartapi/cgi/sga_doc?smartapi!celexapi!prod!CELEXnumdoc&lg=en&numdoc=32000R2659&model=guichett , 28.08.2003.

Commission Reg 1400/2002 of 31 July 2002 on the application of Art 81 par 3 of the Treaty to categories of vertical agreements and concerted practices in the motor vehicle sector, http://europa.eu.int/smartapi/cgi/sga_doc?smartapi!celexapi!prod!CELEXnumdoc&lg=en&numdoc=32002R1400&model=guichett , 28.08.2003.

Council Directive 91/440/EEC of 29 July 1991 on the development of the Community's railways 440/91, http://europa.eu.int/smartapi/cgi/sga_doc?smartapi!celexapi!prod!CELEXnumdoc&lg=EN&numdoc=31991L0440&model=guichett, 28.08.2003.

Council Directive 92/44/EEC of 5 June 1992 on the application of open network provision to leased lines, http://europa.eu.int/smartapi/cgi/sga_doc?smartapi!celexapi!prod!CELEXnumdoc&lg=EN&numdoc=31992L0044&model=guichett , 28.08.2003.

Council Reg 17/62/EEC implementing Art 85 and Art 86 of the Treaty, http://europa.eu.int/smartapi/cgi/sga_doc?smartapi!celexapi!prod!CELEXnumdoc&lg=en&numdoc=31962R0017&model=guichett , 28.08.2003.

Council Regulation 26/62, competition rules - agricultural sector, http://europa.eu.int/smartapi/cgi/sga_doc?smartapi!celexapi!prod!CELEXnumdoc&lg=en&numdoc=31962R0026&model=guichett , 28.08.2003.

Council Reg 1017/68 of the Council of 19 July 1968 applying rules of competition to transport by rail, road and inland waterway, http://europa.eu.int/smartapi/cgi/sga_doc?smartapi!celexapi!prod!CELEXnumdoc&lg=EN&numdoc=31968R1017&model=guichett , 28.08.2003.

Council Regulation 4056/86, laying down detailed rules for the application of the Community competition rules to maritime transport, http://europa.eu.int/comm/competition/antitrust/legislation/405686_en.html, 28.08.2003.

Council Regulation 3975/87, as amended by Reg 1284/91 and Regulation 2410/92, http://europa.eu.int/comm/competition/antitrust/legislation/397587_en.html, 28.08.2003.

Council Regulation 3976/87, as amended by Regulation 2344/90, and by Regulation 2411/92, http://europa.eu.int/comm/competition/antitrust/legislation/397687_en.html , 28.08.2003.

Council Regulation 4064/89 on control of mergers, http://europa.eu.int/comm/competition/mergers/legislation/regulation/consolidated/en.pdf , 28.08.2003.

Council Reg 1534/91, Council Reg 1534/91 of 31 May 1991 on the application of Art 85 par 3 of the Treaty to certain categories of agreements, decisions and concerted practices in the insurance sector, http://europa.eu.int/smartapi/cgi/sga_doc?smartapi!celexapi!prod!CELEXnumdoc&lg=EN&numdoc=31991R1534&model=guichett , 28.08.2003.

Council Reg 1215/99/EC amending Reg 19/65/EEC on the application of Art 85 par 3, http://europa.eu.int/smartapi/cgi/sga_doc?smartapi!celexapi!prod!CELEXnumdoc&lg=en&numdoc=31999R1215&model=guichett , 28.08.2003.

Council Reg 1/2003 of 16 December 2002 on the implementation laid down in Art 81 and Art 82 of the Treaty, http://europa.eu.int/eur-lex/pri/en/oj/dat/2003/l_001/l_00120030104en00010025.pdf, 28.08.2003.

Directive 95/62/EC of the European Parliament and of the Council of 13 December 1995 on the application of open network provision (ONP) to voice telephony, http://europa.eu.int/smartapi/cgi/sga_doc?smartapi!celexapi!prod!CELEXnumdoc&lg=EN&numdoc=31995L0062&model=guichett, 28.08.2003.

Directive 97/33/EC of the European Parliament and of the Council of 30 June 1997 on interconnection in Telecommunications with regard to

ensuring universal service and interoperability through application of the principles of Open Network Provision (ONP),
http://europa.eu.int/smartapi/cgi/sga_doc?smartapi!celexapi!prod!CELEXnumdoc&lg=EN&numdoc=31997L0033&model=guichett, 28.08.2003.

ECSC-Treaty, Art 65 and Art 66,
http://europa.eu.int/comm/competition/antitrust/legislation/art65_en.html, 28.08.2003
http://europa.eu.int/comm/competition/antitrust/legislation/art66_en.html, 28.08.2003.

EGV consolidated version
http://europa.eu.int/eur-lex/en/treaties/dat/EC_consol.pdf , 28.08.2003.

European Commission, Proposal for a Council Regulation on the implementation of the rules on competition laid down in Articles 81 and 82 of the Treaty and amending Regulations (EEC) No 1017/68, (EEC) No 2988/74, (EEC) 4056/86 and (EEC) No 3975/87, 2000,
http://europa.eu.int/comm/competition/antitrust/others/modernisation/comm_2000_582/en.pdf, 27.08.2003.

Law 52 of 6 February 1996, Art 54 - Cooperation with the European Commission in the matter of competition
http://www.agcm.it/eng/index.htm, 28.08.2003.

Law 287 of 10 October 1990 (Competition and Fair Trading Act) http://www.agcm.it/eng/index.htm, 28.08.2003.

Second Council Directive 89/646/EEC of 15 December 1989 on the coordination of laws, regulations and administrative provisions relating to the taking up and pursuit of the business of credit institutions and amending Directive 77/780/EEC,
http://europa.eu.int/smartapi/cgi/sga_doc?smartapi!celexapi!prod!CELEXnumdoc&lg=EN&numdoc=31989L0646&model=guichett, 28.08.2003.

Vienna Convention on the Law of Treaties,
http://www.un.org/law/ilc/texts/treaties.htm, 27.08.2003.

Case law of the Court of First Instance

CFI case T-24/90 (Automec II),
http://europa.eu.int/smartapi/cgi/sga_doc?smartapi!celexplus!prod!CELEXnumdoc&lg=en&numdoc=61990A0024, 29.08.2003.

CFI case T-83/91 (Tetrapak),
http://europa.eu.int/smartapi/cgi/sga_doc?smartapi!celexplus!prod!CELEXnumdoc&lg=en&numdoc=61991A0083, 21.10.2003.

CFI case T-114/92 (Industrie Musicales),
http://europa.eu.int/smartapi/cgi/sga_doc?smartapi!celexplus!prod!CELEXnumdoc&lg=en&numdoc=61992A0114, 29.08.2003.

CFI case T-450/93 (Lisrestal),
http://europa.eu.int/smartapi/cgi/sga_doc?smartapi!celexplus!prod!CELEXnumdoc&lg=en&numdoc=61993A0450, 29.08.2003.

CFI case T-528/93 (Metropole),
http://europa.eu.int/smartapi/cgi/sga_doc?smartapi!celexplus!prod!CELEXnumdoc&lg=en&numdoc=61993A0528,30.08.2003.

CFI case T-575/93 (Koelman),
http://europa.eu.int/smartapi/cgi/sga_doc?smartapi!celexplus!prod!CELEXnumdoc&lg=en&numdoc=61993A0575, 29.08.2003.

CFI case T-309/94 (KNP),
http://europa.eu.int/smartapi/cgi/sga_doc?smartapi!celexplus!prod!CELEXnumdoc&lg=en&numdoc=61994A0309, 29.08.2003.

CFI case T-327/94 (SCA Holding),
http://europa.eu.int/smartapi/cgi/sga_doc?smartapi!celexplus!prod!CELEXnumdoc&lg=en&numdoc=61994A0327, 29.08.2003.

CFI case T-347/94 (Mayr Melnhof),
http://europa.eu.int/smartapi/cgi/sga_doc?smartapi!celexplus!prod!CELEXnumdoc&lg=en&numdoc=61994A0347, 29.08.2003.

CFI case T-380/94 (AIUFASS),
http://europa.eu.int/smartapi/cgi/sga_doc?smartapi!celexplus!prod!CELEXnumdoc&lg=en&numdoc=61994A0380, 29.08.2003.

CFI case T-387/94 (Asia Motor France),
http://europa.eu.int/smartapi/cgi/sga_doc?smartapi!celexplus!prod!CELEXnumdoc&lg=en&numdoc=61994A0387, 29.08.2003.

CFI case T-25/96 (Arbeitsgemeinschaft deutsche Luftfahrt),
http://europa.eu.int/smartapi/cgi/sga_doc?smartapi!celexplus!prod!CELEXnumdoc&lg=en&numdoc=61996B0025, 29.08.2003.

Case Law of the European Court of Justice

ECJ case 13/61 (Bosch),
http://europa.eu.int/smartapi/cgi/sga_doc?smartapi!celexplus!prod!CELEXnumdoc&lg=en&numdoc=61961J0013, 29.08.2003.

ECJ case 26/62 (Van Gend & Loos),
http://europa.eu.int/smartapi/cgi/sga_doc?smartapi!celexplus!prod!CELEXnumdoc&lg=en&numdoc=61962J0026, 29.08.2003.

ECJ case 56/64 (Consten and Grundig),
http://europa.eu.int/smartapi/cgi/sga_doc?smartapi!celexplus!prod!CELEXnumdoc&lg=en&numdoc=6196400056, 29.08.2003.

ECJ case 56/65 (Société Technique Minieré),
http://europa.eu.int/smartapi/cgi/sga_doc?smartapi!celexplus!prod!CELEXnumdoc&lg=en&numdoc=61965J0056, 29.08.2003.

ECJ case 14/68 (Walt Wilhelm),
http://europa.eu.int/smartapi/cgi/sga_doc?smartapi!celexplus!prod!CELEXnumdoc&lg=en&numdoc=61968J0014, 29.08.2003.

ECJ case 43/69 (Bilger),
http://europa.eu.int/smartapi/cgi/sga_doc?smartapi!celexplus!prod!CELEXnumdoc&lg=en&numdoc=61969J0043, 29.08.2003.

ECJ case 48/69 (ICI),
http://europa.eu.int/smartapi/cgi/sga_doc?smartapi!celexplus!prod!CELEXnumdoc&lg=en&numdoc=61969J0048, 29.08.2003.

ECJ case 5/69 (Volke),
http://europa.eu.int/smartapi/cgi/sga_doc?smartapi!celexplus!prod!CELEXnumdoc&lg=en&numdoc=61969J0005, 29.08.2003.

ECJ case 48/72 (Braisserie de Haecht),
http://europa.eu.int/smartapi/cgi/sga_doc?smartapi!celexplus!prod!CELEXn
umdoc&lg=en&numdoc=61972J0048, 29.08.2003.

ECJ case 6/72 (Europemballage and Continental Can),
http://europa.eu.int/smartapi/cgi/sga_doc?smartapi!celexplus!prod!CELEXn
umdoc&lg=en&numdoc=61972J0006, 29.08.2003.

ECJ case 8/72 (Cementhandelaren),
http://europa.eu.int/smartapi/cgi/sga_doc?smartapi!celexplus!prod!CELEXn
umdoc&lg=en&numdoc=61972J0008, 29.08.2003.

ECJ case 40/73 (Suiker Unie),
http://europa.eu.int/smartapi/cgi/sga_doc?smartapi!celexplus!prod!CELEXn
umdoc&lg=en&numdoc=61973J0040, 29.08.2003.

ECJ case 6/73 (Commercial Solvents),
http://europa.eu.int/smartapi/cgi/sga_doc?smartapi!celexplus!prod!CELEXn
umdoc&lg=en&numdoc=61973J0006, 29.08.2003.

ECJ case 127/73 (BRT),
http://europa.eu.int/smartapi/cgi/sga_doc?smartapi!celexplus!prod!CELEXn
umdoc&lg=en&numdoc=61973J0127(00), 29.08.2003.

ECJ case 17/74 (Transocean Marine),
http://europa.eu.int/smartapi/cgi/sga_doc?smartapi!celexplus!prod!CELEXn
umdoc&lg=en&numdoc=61974J0017, 29.08.2003.

ECJ case 26/76 (Metro),
http://europa.eu.int/smartapi/cgi/sga_doc?smartapi!celexplus!prod!CELEXn
umdoc&lg=en&numdoc=61976J0026, 29.08.2003.

ECJ case 27/76 (United Brands),
http://europa.eu.int/smartapi/cgi/sga_doc?smartapi!celexplus!prod!CELEXn
umdoc&lg=en&numdoc=6197600027, 29.08.2003.

ECJ case 85/76 (Hoffmann-La Roche),
http://europa.eu.int/smartapi/cgi/sga_doc?smartapi!celexplus!prod!CELEXn
umdoc&lg=en&numdoc=61976J0085, 29.08.2003.

ECJ case 19/77 (Miller),
http://europa.eu.int/smartapi/cgi/sga_doc?smartapi!celexplus!prod!CELEXnumdoc&lg=en&numdoc=61977J0019, 29.08.2003.

ECJ case 59/77 (Bloos),
http://europa.eu.int/smartapi/cgi/sga_doc?smartapi!celexplus!prod!CELEXnumdoc&lg=en&numdoc=61977J0059, 29.08.2003.

ECJ case 209/78 (Van Landewijk),
http://europa.eu.int/smartapi/cgi/sga_doc?smartapi!celexplus!prod!CELEXnumdoc&lg=en&numdoc=61978J0209, 29.08.2003.

ECJ case 258/78 (Nungesser and Eisele),
http://europa.eu.int/smartapi/cgi/sga_doc?smartapi!celexplus!prod!CELEXnumdoc&lg=en&numdoc=61978J0258, 29.08.2003.

ECJ case 30/78 (Distillers Company),
http://europa.eu.int/smartapi/cgi/sga_doc?smartapi!celexplus!prod!CELEXnumdoc&lg=en&numdoc=61978J0030, 29.08.2003.

ECJ case 136/79 (National Panasonic),
http://europa.eu.int/smartapi/cgi/sga_doc?smartapi!celexplus!prod!CELEXnumdoc&lg=en&numdoc=61979J0136, 29.08.2003.

ECJ case 155/79 (AM & S),
http://europa.eu.int/smartapi/cgi/sga_doc?smartapi!celexplus!prod!CELEXnumdoc&lg=en&numdoc=61979J0155, 29.08.2003.

ECJ case 37/79 (Marity),
http://europa.eu.int/smartapi/cgi/sga_doc?smartapi!celexplus!prod!CELEXnumdoc&lg=en&numdoc=61979J0037, 29.08.2003.

ECJ case 792/79 (Camera Care),
http://europa.eu.int/smartapi/cgi/sga_doc?smartapi!celexplus!prod!CELEXnumdoc&lg=en&numdoc=6197900792, 29.08.2003.

ECJ case 99/79 (Lancome),
http://europa.eu.int/smartapi/cgi/sga_doc?smartapi!celexplus!prod!CELEXnumdoc&lg=en&numdoc=61979J0099, 29.08.2003.

ECJ case 100/80 (Musique Diffusion France),
http://europa.eu.int/smartapi/cgi/sga_doc?smartapi!celexplus!prod!CELEXnumdoc&lg=en&numdoc=61980J0100, 29.08.2003.

ECJ case 126/80 (Salonia),
http://europa.eu.int/smartapi/cgi/sga_doc?smartapi!celexplus!prod!CELEXnumdoc&lg=en&numdoc=61980J0126, 29.08.2003.

ECJ case 158/80 (Rewe),
http://europa.eu.int/smartapi/cgi/sga_doc?smartapi!celexplus!prod!CELEXnumdoc&lg=en&numdoc=61980J0158, 29.08.2003.

ECJ case 31/80 (L'Oreal),
http://europa.eu.int/smartapi/cgi/sga_doc?smartapi!celexplus!prod!CELEXnumdoc&lg=en&numdoc=61980J0031, 29.08.2003.

ECJ case 61/80 (Cooperative Stremsel),
http://europa.eu.int/smartapi/cgi/sga_doc?smartapi!celexplus!prod!CELEXnumdoc&lg=en&numdoc=61980J0061, 29.08.2003.

ECJ case 15/81 (Schul),
http://europa.eu.int/smartapi/cgi/sga_doc?smartapi!celexplus!prod!CELEXnumdoc&lg=en&numdoc=61981J0015, 29.08.2003.

ECJ case 322/81 (Michelin),
http://europa.eu.int/smartapi/cgi/sga_doc?smartapi!celexplus!prod!CELEXnumdoc&lg=en&numdoc=61981J0322, 29.08.2003.

ECJ case 107/82 (AEG),
http://europa.eu.int/smartapi/cgi/sga_doc?smartapi!celexplus!prod!CELEXnumdoc&lg=en&numdoc=6198200107(01), 29.08.2003.

ECJ case 199/82 (San Giorgio),
http://europa.eu.int/smartapi/cgi/sga_doc?smartapi!celexplus!prod!CELEXnumdoc&lg=en&numdoc=61982J0199, 01.09.2003.

ECJ case 228/82 (Ford),
http://europa.eu.int/smartapi/cgi/sga_doc?smartapi!celexplus!prod!CELEXnumdoc&lg=en&numdoc=61982J0228,30.08.2003.

ECJ case 319/82 (Société de Vente), http://europa.eu.int/smartapi/cgi/sga_doc?smartapi!celexplus!prod!CELEXnumdoc&lg=en&numdoc=61982J0319,30.08.2003.

ECJ case 7/82 (GVL), http://europa.eu.int/smartapi/cgi/sga_doc?smartapi!celexplus!prod!CELEXnumdoc&lg=en&numdoc=61982J0007,30.08.2003.

ECJ case 123/83 (BNIC), http://europa.eu.int/smartapi/cgi/sga_doc?smartapi!celexplus!prod!CELEXnumdoc&lg=en&numdoc=61983J0123,30.08.2003.

ECJ case 161/84 (Pronuptia), http://europa.eu.int/smartapi/cgi/sga_doc?smartapi!celexplus!prod!CELEXnumdoc&lg=en&numdoc=61984J0161,30.08.2003.

ECJ case 209/84 (Ministere Public), http://europa.eu.int/smartapi/cgi/sga_doc?smartapi!celexplus!prod!CELEXnumdoc&lg=en&numdoc=61984J0209,30.08.2003.

ECJ case 311/84 (CBEN), http://europa.eu.int/smartapi/cgi/sga_doc?smartapi!celexplus!prod!CELEXnumdoc&lg=en&numdoc=61984J0311,30.08.2003.

ECJ case 42/84 (Remia), http://europa.eu.int/smartapi/cgi/sga_doc?smartapi!celexplus!prod!CELEXnumdoc&lg=en&numdoc=61984J0042,30.08.2003.

ECJ case 53/85 (Akzo), http://europa.eu.int/smartapi/cgi/sga_doc?smartapi!celexplus!prod!CELEXnumdoc&lg=en&numdoc=61985J0053,30.08.2003.

ECJ case 277/87 (Sandoz), http://europa.eu.int/smartapi/cgi/sga_doc?smartapi!celexplus!prod!CELEXnumdoc&lg=en&numdoc=61987J0277,30.08.2003.

ECJ case 46/87 (Hoechst), http://europa.eu.int/smartapi/cgi/sga_doc?smartapi!celexplus!prod!CELEXnumdoc&lg=en&numdoc=61987J0046,30.08.2003.

ECJ case 234/89 (Delimitis), http://europa.eu.int/smartapi/cgi/sga_doc?smartapi!celexplus!prod!CELEXnumdoc&lg=en&numdoc=61989J0234,30.08.2003.

ECJ case C-48/90 (Nederlandse and Koninkljike), http://europa.eu.int/smartapi/cgi/sga_doc?smartapi!celexplus!prod!CELEXnumdoc&lg=en&numdoc=61990J0048,30.08.2003.

ECJ case C-159/91 (Poucet and Pistre), http://europa.eu.int/smartapi/cgi/sga_doc?smartapi!celexplus!prod!CELEXnumdoc&lg=en&numdoc=61991J0159,30.08.2003.

ECJ case C-320/91 (Corbeau), http://europa.eu.int/smartapi/cgi/sga_doc?smartapi!celexplus!prod!CELEXnumdoc&lg=en&numdoc=61991J0320,30.08.2003.

ECJ case C-67/91 (Asociación Espanõla de Bance Privada), http://europa.eu.int/smartapi/cgi/sga_doc?smartapi!celexplus!prod!CELEXnumdoc&lg=en&numdoc=61991J0067,30.08.2003.

ECJ case C-266/93 (Bundeskartellamt), http://europa.eu.int/smartapi/cgi/sga_doc?smartapi!celexplus!prod!CELEXnumdoc&lg=en&numdoc=61993J0266,30.08.2003.

ECJ case C-465/93 (Atlanta Fruchthandelsgesellschaft), http://europa.eu.int/smartapi/cgi/sga_doc?smartapi!celexplus!prod!CELEXnumdoc&lg=en&numdoc=61993J0465,30.08.2003.

ECJ case C-244/94 (Societé d'Assurance), http://europa.eu.int/smartapi/cgi/sga_doc?smartapi!celexplus!prod!CELEXnumdoc&lg=en&numdoc=61994J0244,30.08.2003.

ECJ case 343/95 (Diego Cali), http://europa.eu.int/smartapi/cgi/sga_doc?smartapi!celexplus!prod!CELEXnumdoc&lg=en&numdoc=61995J0343,30.08.2003.

ECJ case C-91/95 (Tremblay), http://europa.eu.int/smartapi/cgi/sga_doc?smartapi!celexplus!prod!CELEXnumdoc&lg=en&numdoc=61995J0091,30.08.2003.

ECJ case C-39/96 (KVBB), http://europa.eu.int/smartapi/cgi/sga_doc?smartapi!celexplus!prod!CELEXnumdoc&lg=en&numdoc=61996J0039,30.08.2003.

ECJ case C-55/96 (Job Centre), http://europa.eu.int/smartapi/cgi/sga_doc?smartapi!celexplus!prod!CELEXnumdoc&lg=en&numdoc=61996J0055,30.08.2003.

ECJ-case C-344/98 (Masterfoods), http://europa.eu.int/smartapi/cgi/sga_doc?smartapi!celexplus!prod!CELEXnumdoc&lg=en&numdoc=61998J0344, 01.09.2003.

Decisions of the European Commission

Aerlingus/British Midland, 1992, http://europa.eu.int/smartapi/cgi/sga_doc?smartapi!celexapi!prod!CELEXnumdoc&lg=EN&numdoc=31992D0213&model=guichett ,31.08.2003.

Atka A/S/BP Kemi, 1979, http://europa.eu.int/smartapi/cgi/sga_doc?smartapi!celexapi!prod!CELEXnumdoc&lg=EN&numdoc=31979D0934&model=guichett ,31.08.2003.

Belgian Banks, 1987, http://europa.eu.int/smartapi/cgi/sga_doc?smartapi!celexapi!prod!CELEXnumdoc&lg=EN&numdoc=31987D0013&model=guichett ,31.08.2003.

Bomee Stichting, 1975, http://europa.eu.int/smartapi/cgi/sga_doc?smartapi!celexapi!prod!CELEXnumdoc&lg=EN&numdoc=31975D0781&model=guichett ,31.08.2003.

Carlsberg, 1984, http://europa.eu.int/smartapi/cgi/sga_doc?smartapi!celexapi!prod!CELEXnumdoc&lg=EN&numdoc=31984D0381&model=guichett ,31.08.2003.

Dutch Bank, 1989, http://europa.eu.int/smartapi/cgi/sga_doc?smartapi!celexapi!prod!CELEXnumdoc&lg=EN&numdoc=31989D0512&model=guichett ,31.08.2003.

Eurotunnel, 1994, http://europa.eu.int/smartapi/cgi/sga_doc?smartapi!celexapi!prod!CELEXnumdoc&lg=EN&numdoc=31994D0894&model=guichett ,31.08.2003.

France-Japanese Ballbearings, 1974,
http://europa.eu.int/smartapi/cgi/sga_doc?smartapi!celexapi!prod!CELEXnumdoc&lg=EN&numdoc=31974D0634&model=guichett ,31.08.2003.

Irish Sugar, 1997,
http://europa.eu.int/smartapi/cgi/sga_doc?smartapi!celexapi!prod!CELEXnumdoc&lg=EN&numdoc=31997D0624&model=guichett ,31.08.2003.

Landing Fees at Zaventem, 1995,
http://europa.eu.int/smartapi/cgi/sga_doc?smartapi!celexapi!prod!CELEXnumdoc&lg=EN&numdoc=31995D0364&model=guichett ,31.08.2003.

IMA-Statuut, 1980,
http://europa.eu.int/smartapi/cgi/sga_doc?smartapi!celexapi!prod!CELEXnumdoc&lg=EN&numdoc=31980D1071&model=guichett ,31.08.2003.

Nuovo Cegam, 1984,
http://europa.eu.int/smartapi/cgi/sga_doc?smartapi!celexapi!prod!CELEXnumdoc&lg=EN&numdoc=31984D0191&model=guichett ,31.08.2003.

Price Waterhouse Cooper & Lybrand, 1999,
http://europa.eu.int/smartapi/cgi/sga_doc?smartapi!celexapi!prod!CELEXnumdoc&lg=EN&numdoc=31999D0152&model=guichett ,31.08.2003.

Reuter/BASF, 1976,
http://europa.eu.int/smartapi/cgi/sga_doc?smartapi!celexapi!prod!CELEXnumdoc&lg=EN&numdoc=31976D0743&model=guichett ,31.08.2003.

Sea Containers/Stena, 1994,
http://europa.eu.int/smartapi/cgi/sga_doc?smartapi!celexapi!prod!CELEXnumdoc&lg=EN&numdoc=31994D0019&model=guichett ,31.08.2003.

Welded Steel Mesh Cartel, 1989,
http://europa.eu.int/smartapi/cgi/sga_doc?smartapi!celexapi!prod!CELEXnumdoc&lg=EN&numdoc=31989D0515&model=guichett ,31.08.2003.

VNP/Cobelpa, 1977,
http://europa.eu.int/smartapi/cgi/sga_doc?smartapi!celexapi!prod!CELEXnumdoc&lg=EN&numdoc=31977D0592&model=guichett ,31.08.2003.

WEA-Filipachi, 1972, http://europa.eu.int/smartapi/cgi/sga_doc?smartapi!celexapi!prod!CELEXnumdoc&lg=fr&numdoc=31972D0480&model=guichett ,31.08.2003.

Italian Case Law

Italian Competition Authority, case A274 (Stream/Telepiù), http://www.agcm.it, 01.09.2003.

Italian Competition Authority, case I318 (Consorzio industrie fiammiferi), http://www.agcm.it, 01.09.2003.

Italian Competition Authority, case A263 (Unapace/Enel), http://www.agcm.it, 01.09.2003.

Italian Competition Authority, case I318 (Consorzio industrie fiammiferi), http://www.agcm.it, 01.09.2003.

Italian Competition Authority, case A274 (Stream/Telepiù), http://www.agcm.it, 01.09.2003.

Italian Competition Authority, case A247 (Aeroporti di Roma), http://www.agcm.it, 01.09.2003.

Italian Competition Authority, case A291 (Assoviaggi/Alitalia), http://www.agcm.it, 01.09.2003.

Italian Competition Authority, case A329 (Blugas/SNAM), http://www.agcm.it, 01.09.2003.

Italian Competition Authority, case A299 (International Mail Express Italy/Poste Italiane), http://www.agcm.it, 01.09.2003.

Italian Competition Authority, case A333 (ENEL Trade clienti idonei), http://www.agcm.it, 01.09.2003.

TAR Lazio, Codacons/Autoritá garante della concorrenza e del mercato, 2001 http://www.giust.it/tar1/tarlazio1_2001-7286.htm, 27.08.2003.

7.2 Abbreviations

Art	Article
CC	codice civile
CFI	Court of First Instance
CMLR	Competition Market Law Review
CPC	codice procedura civile
Dir	directive
EC	European Community
ECJ	European Court of Justice
ECLR	European Competition Law Review
ECSC	European Coal and Steal Community
ECT	European Community Treaty
EFTA	European Free Trade Association
eg	for example
ESA	European Space Agency
EU	European Union
EURATOM	European Atomic Energy Community
EuZW	Europäische Zeitschrift für Wirtschaftsrecht
ie	that is to say
NCA	national competition authority
OEEC	Organisation for European Economic Co-operation
par	paragraph
Reg	regulation
SME	small and medium enterprises
subpar	subparagraph
TAR	Latium Regional Administrative Court